Dr. Anderson's hope-filled stories help eliminate any doubt of heaven. *Appointments with Heaven* will comfort all who long to know that death is a transition—not the final word.

✦ **MARY C. NEAL, MD**
New York Times *bestselling author of* To Heaven and Back

In an age when so much energy, time, and money are spent to help us forget about our mortality, Dr. Reggie reminds us not just of its inevitability but even more of its right and beautiful place in our journey. *Appointments with Heaven* is a deeply honest and moving story, told by a true "eyewitness." You will be encouraged and challenged by this remarkable journey to the very door of heaven.

✦ **GEOFF MOORE**
Contemporary Christian recording artist

Appointments with Heaven is so much more than a marvelous memoir. It's a heart-wrenching look at doubt, death, and grief. It's a mind-stretching account of supernatural encounters. And it's a soul-stirring story of just how close God really is. Read it, believe it, and you will never again fear your appointment with heaven.

✦ **LYNN EIB**
Author of When God & Cancer Meet

This was a great read. Intriguing, encouraging, inspirational. . . . I couldn't put it down!

✦ **MARK SCOTT**
Retired president, LifeWay Christian Stores

Appointments with Heaven is not only Reggie's powerful personal story; it is also a call to each of us to live with our eyes and hearts open because heaven is closer than we think. *Appointments with Heaven* is a welcome reminder that we are never separated from the presence of God.

✦ **MARK MILLER**
Lead singer of country music group Sawyer Brown; producer of contemporary Christian artist Casting Crowns

Appointments with Heaven is a moving and inspirational experience that describes real-life encounters with God and illuminates how his light shines brightest when our lives are at their darkest.

✦ **FRANK MILLER**
  Business manager for Sawyer Brown; Casting Crowns; and Colton Dixon

Appointments with Heaven

✦ ✦ ✦

Appointments with HEAVEN

*The true story of a country doctor's
healing encounters with the hereafter*

✦ ✦ ✦

DR. REGGIE ANDERSON
with JENNIFER SCHUCHMANN

**TYNDALE™
MOMENTUM**

*An Imprint of
Tyndale House Publishers, Inc.*

Visit Tyndale online at www.tyndale.com.

Visit Tyndale Momentum online at www.tyndalemomentum.com.

Visit www.appointmentswithheaven.com.

TYNDALE is a registered trademark of Tyndale House Publishers, Inc. *Tyndale Momentum* and the Tyndale Momentum logo are trademarks of Tyndale House Publishers, Inc. Tyndale Momentum is an imprint of Tyndale House Publishers, Inc.

Appointments with Heaven: The True Story of a Country Doctor's Healing Encounters with the Hereafter

Designed by Dean H. Renninger

Published in association with the literary agency of Creative Trust, Inc., 5141 Virginia Way, Suite 320, Brentwood, TN 37027.

Unless otherwise indicated, all Scripture quotations are taken from the *Holy Bible*, New Living Translation, copyright © 1996, 2004, 2007 by Tyndale House Foundation. Used by permission of Tyndale House Publishers, Inc., Carol Stream, Illinois 60188. All rights reserved.

Scripture quotations marked KJV are taken from the *Holy Bible*, King James Version.

ISBN 978-1-4143-8045-2 Softcover

Printed in the United States of America

19	18	17	16	15	14	13
7	6	5	4	3	2	1

To Karen,
my North Star, my tether!
Soli Deo Gloria!

✦ ✦ ✦

Contents

Foreword

✦ ✦ ✦

We have known Reggie Anderson for twenty-plus years. The Anderson and Chapman families have shared many ups and downs, creating a bond that few families will ever know.

Our children grew up together, attended the same school, played on the same teams, and did a lot of life together. So much so that in 2009, our son Caleb and their daughter Julia got married, thus continuing our journey. Now if only those kids would surprise us with a grandbaby!

We've experienced much laughter, tears, good times, and hard times. On a beautiful sunny day in spring 2008, our youngest daughter made her journey home to heaven because of an accident at our house. It was truly the day the world went wrong, and our lives came crashing in on us. Life as we knew it changed forever. Two of the first phone calls we made were to Karen and Reggie Anderson. They came to the hospital immediately and have been by our sides on this incredibly difficult journey ever since. They held us, housed us, and offered us the cup of compassion over and over in those first days, weeks, and months that followed. They were the hands and feet of Christ as we began all over again with our lives.

In the months that followed losing Maria, we began the process of grieving, healing, and coming to terms with what had happened. During that time we noticed Reggie writing a lot into what we assumed was a journal. We discovered at some point that he was actually beginning to write down the stories of loss in his own personal life, as well as in his professional life as a medical doctor. Maria's death had stirred in him the impulse to write his own story.

As time went by, we would SEE that recording these memories was helping Reggie heal and reconcile the hard parts of his life. He began to identify these stories as divine appointments, and the more he wrote, the more he understood that God had been creating a much bigger picture than he ever imagined. Reggie also realized that he had never been alone and that the God of the universe had been orchestrating an elaborate story of redemption and purpose, which has now culminated in this deep, rich book.

God clearly speaks to Reggie in the form of miraculous happenings. Reggie recognizes those miracles for what they are: divine and deliberate pursuits by God to let Reggie know that he is intimately cared for. This country doctor from Tennessee is loved by God and has been blessed with an amazing gift. As Reggie embraces this, he wants to be faithful to tell others of the amazing lengths to which God goes so we can truly SEE him.

In *Appointments with Heaven*, Reggie has woven a beautiful tapestry, intertwining his own journey with the stories of other people he has come to know, whether through family, friends, or doctoring. In a poignant way, Reggie communicates his transformation from a grieving, scared young boy running from God into an amazingly intuitive doctor who now runs toward God in times of darkness and tragedy. From encountering Christ on a camping trip to meeting his wife, Karen, Reggie truly hears from God in unique ways.

Reggie has offered a precious treasure to you, the reader. First, his story unveils something you and I need to hear, know, and experience in our hearts . . . the truth that God pursues us in extreme and magnificent ways! Second, it provides a glimpse of God's eternal purposes. Reggie's appointments with heaven, woven through life stories, reveal that God has a plan for each one of us—a plan that includes pain, surprises, and joy—and that there is a reason for everything under the sun, if we choose to SEE it.

And now may you, the reader, treasure this book for what it is . . . an appointment with heaven that will make you smile and cry as you soak it in.

Choosing to SEE God in all of life,
Mary Beth and Steven Curtis Chapman

PS As an addendum to this foreword, I (Mary Beth) would like to remind you that behind every good man, there is an even greater woman . . . LOL. But in the case of Dr. Reggie Anderson, it's true. Karen is a woman who lives out the fruit of the Spirit. I have witnessed her giving of herself to her husband, children, and friends in amazing and unselfish ways. She has taught me to seek and pursue peace, and she is full of wisdom. Without Karen, there is no Reggie, and everyone who knows them knows this to be true. I am indebted to her for the encouragement she has been to me and to my children. . . . I love you, sweet friend.

Part 1:

IF THERE'S A GOD, WHERE WAS HE?

Chapter 1
THE PATIENT

✦

SEPTEMBER 2011
ASHLAND CITY HOSPITAL, ASHLAND CITY, TENNESSEE

He was an eighty-two-year-old, proud Alabama boy, lying in the intensive care unit, and while I didn't yet know his time of death, I already knew the cause.

For more than a year, he had been struggling with myelodysplastic syndrome—his bone marrow had stopped producing the blood cells needed to fight off infection. He was immunocompromised and had developed a severe staph infection that was almost impossible to treat. His body had become septic, and the inflammation was devastating his organs. I knew his days were numbered, but I couldn't stand the thought of his passing.

I had known him all my life. He was a teacher and a farmer—intelligent and determined, proud and stubborn. He was also a man of great faith. He didn't see any reason to prolong his life on earth past the purpose God had for him. Like many of my elderly patients, he believed that he had an appointment with heaven and that Jesus was waiting for him on the other side.

As a doctor, I've seen what happens to the patient whose loved ones hang on too long. They desperately cling to their family member, demanding that doctors use extraordinary means to keep that person here when, really, the dying believer just wants to

3

slip gently to the other side. Sometimes doctors can postpone a patient's death for weeks or months, but it often involves drastic measures with the person being kept alive by machines and feeding tubes. The patient's quality of life isn't what relatives expect when they initially make the decision, and it's rarely what a patient desires.

Whenever God called him home, he was ready.

I didn't want this patient kept alive by machines, and he didn't want it either. But I had good reasons to lengthen his life. He had a close, extended family, some of whom lived out of town and wanted a chance to say good-bye. With intensive medical intervention, I could postpone his death long enough to allow them the opportunity to see him one last time. His family wasn't ready to let him go, and I understood that in the most intimate way possible. I wasn't ready for him to be gone either.

I thought of other deaths I had witnessed—including an unforgettable experience that happened while I was a medical resident.

✦ ✦ ✦

Throughout medical school I had taken care of dying patients, but this was the first time that I, as the senior resident, would be the one in charge when a patient died. I didn't know what to expect.

"Dr. Anderson," the elderly woman began, her voice starting to fade. "Will you hold my hand? I'm going to see Jesus, and I need an escort."

That night, I experienced the veil parting—the veil that separates this life from the next. As I held the dying woman's hands, I felt the warmth of her soul pass by my cheek when it left her body, swept up by an inexplicably cool breeze in an otherwise stagnant room. I smelled the familiar fragrance of lilac and citrus, and I knew the veil was parting to allow her soul to pass through.

Since that first patient, I've walked with countless others to the doorstep of heaven and watched them enter paradise. On many occasions, as I held hands with the dying, God allowed me to peer into heaven's entryway where I watched each patient slip into the next world.

I've sensed Jesus on the other side, standing in heaven's foyer, welcoming the dead who are made whole again. I've glimpsed surreal colors and sights and heard sounds more intense than anything I've ever experienced in this ordinary world. I've inhaled the scents of lilac, citrus, freshly carved cedar, and baking bread—more fragrant than I ever thought possible.

Sometimes I've even witnessed patients leave this world and come back. As they've shared their stories with me, I've often remembered the time early in my life when God allowed me to step into heaven's foyer, even though I no longer believed he was real.

The one thing these experiences have in common is the intensity of the sights, sounds, fragrances, and feelings that I sensed. Heaven is more real than anything we experience here, and the sense of peace, joy, and overwhelming love is beyond description.

✦ ✦ ✦

Memories of other dying patients, as well as my personal glimpses into heaven, drifted through my mind as I sat at my patient's bedside in the ICU that day. I had every confidence that what awaited him would be more joyous than anything he'd ever experienced. But, selfishly, I wasn't ready to see him disappear through the opening. As the attending physician, the family looked to me for guidance. I could recommend a blood transfusion that would prolong his life for a few more days; with several transfusions, maybe I could extend it a week or more.

Or I could let him go.

Either way, I knew that he and his family would listen to me and do what I suggested.

I had a difficult decision to make, and my medical decisions were complicated by what my patients and I had experienced on heaven's side of the veil. But my struggle was even greater because of who I was.

I wasn't just the patient's physician—I was also his son.

Chapter 2
THE FIRST DREAM

✦

JUNE 1962
PLANTERSVILLE, ALABAMA

Dad and Mom came from a long line of teachers, preachers, and farmers. For generations, the farmers had taught us how to work hard; the preachers had taught us that without God, hard work was meaningless; and the teachers had taught us that everything in life was a lesson.

My parents were high school educators. They were equally intentional about teaching my siblings and me at home, and they didn't need schoolbooks or technology to do it. In the early sixties, the only technology we had was a radio and a black-and-white Zenith TV—we couldn't have afforded more, even if it had been available. Our textbook was the land we lived on and the community we lived in.

We grew up in the country in Plantersville, Alabama. The nearest stoplight was twenty miles away in Selma. Dad taught agriculture at the local high school, and Mom had taken time off from teaching home economics to raise us. Cathy, my oldest sibling, was the only one in school at the time, yet our parents tried to instill in us the same lessons they taught their teenage students in class. At home, Mom taught Cathy the art of homemaking, and Dad taught me and my younger brother, Tim, about farming and raising animals. From the time I was old enough to sit up by myself in the car, Dad took me with him when he visited his students' farms to check out their class projects—typically, animals they were raising for an upcoming fair. After the visit, we bumped home on those old country roads, and Dad would tell me what the student was doing right and what he or she could do better.

"One day, you'll have a calf of your own," he'd say, as he emphasized the importance of the right feed for the animal or the proper way to groom it. Dad knew that the responsibility of caring for an animal taught a boy lessons he couldn't learn from a textbook.

Each year, Dad bought one or two calves for us, and we would raise them for meat. At four years old, I would mix the milk and hold the bottle for the animals to suckle until they were old enough to eat grain and hay. Once, a baby deer got caught in my grandfather's chicken coop, and we included him in our little animal menagerie and raised him by hand. I loved the animals we raised, but I also understood they would one day be our dinner. While I didn't relish the thought of eating the animals I cared for, I was grateful for the meat, whether it came from a deer, a cow, or a squirrel.

As I busied myself with my chores, feeding and grooming the animals or working in the garden, I dreamed of being a vet and taking care of sick and injured animals. But with only poor preachers, teachers, and farmers as role models, veterinary medicine was about as realistic a career choice as my other fantasy—being a cowboy.

✦   ✦   ✦

After finishing our chores, we often watched TV as a family. We had three channels, and we each had a favorite program. Dad liked the evening news, while Cathy, Tim, and I preferred *The Popeye Show*. Together, we'd laugh at the antics of our beloved sailor as he tried to get out of an impossible predicament and save Olive Oyl, using only his brain, brawn, and a can of spinach. Cousin Cliff, the kindhearted magician dressed in a yachting cap and nautical coat, hosted the show, and between cartoons he would delight his young fans with puppets and magic tricks.

One of my earliest memories was of a hot June day in 1962, when I was four and a half. We were watching *Popeye*, and when the cartoon ended, Cousin Cliff made an extraordinary announcement. He and Popeye were having a contest.

"How would you like to win this beautiful Shetland pony?" Cousin Cliff asked.

On-screen, a grainy film showed him parading a pony around the stable. A child dressed in riding gear and a cowboy hat sat on the pony's back holding the reins. Cousin Cliff continued, "He comes complete with bridle and saddle all ready for ya to ride, and he is first prize in a contest that Popeye and I are having on our show."

It's hard to imagine anything more exciting to three kids from Plantersville than the thought of having such a beautiful animal— one we could take turns riding. We admired his long silky mane as we imagined ourselves on his back holding the reins.

"Just send a postcard to Popeye at WAPI in Birmingham. You don't have to write anything, no box tops to send in, and there is nothing to buy," Cousin Cliff said.

"Mom, can we enter the contest?" I asked.

"Everyone who watches channel 13," Cliff reminded us, "is eligible to win the pony."

Cathy joined my plea, "Can we *please* send in a postcard for the pony?"

Mom agreed, turning it into a lesson on reading, writing, and how the postal system worked. She let us each choose a postcard and showed us how to address it and how to write our names and address—though she had to do most of the writing for Tim and me. She gave us each a stamp to lick and showed us where to place it.

"I'll take you to the post office in the morning to mail them," she promised.

To a four-year-old boy and his seven-year-old sister—and even to our two-year-old brother—winning a pony would be like striking gold.

Cathy was already talking about brushing the pony's coat and putting ribbons in his mane. "I want to get a matching cowgirl dress, so I can wear it when I ride him," she said.

My thoughts were more practical.

"I'll ride him to rope the cattle when it's feeding time," I said, remembering the cowboy movies I'd seen on TV. At four and a half, my dreams weren't based in reality. I hadn't considered that we never had to rope the calves at feeding time. They just followed Dad to the trough when he brought out the feed bucket.

The next morning as Mom drove us to the post office, we were still thinking about all that we could do with the pony.

"I can ride him when I play cowboys and Indians," I said from the backseat of the car.

"When I win the pony, I am going to ride him to school!" Cathy said.

Her comment concerned me. I turned my attention to Mom in the front seat. "Don't send in Tim's and Cathy's cards," I said.

"Why not?" she asked.

"I had a dream last night, and God told me I was going to win the pony, so you only need to send in *my* postcard."

Cathy looked at me like I was crazy, so I didn't go into details. But the night before, I'd had a dream in which I was riding the pony bareback in a red clover field. The sky was clear, and there was a coolness in the air. A voice with authority, though not alarming, spoke to me. "You will win this pony, but you must share this gift with everyone who wants to ride this special horse." The voice was calm and reassuring, and I knew at once it was God. And then he paraphrased something I had heard in church: "To whom much is given, much is expected."

I didn't share those details with Cathy and Mom. Instead, I continued with what I thought was logical reasoning. "Cathy and Tim won't win, so just don't mail theirs or they'll be disappointed," I said.

Obviously, I had a lot to learn about sibling relationships.

"That's not fair; I want to send my card too!" Cathy protested.

"I wanna da pony!" Tim cried, not understanding what was happening.

By now, Mom had parked the car and turned off the ignition. She turned to look at me in the backseat. She paused before she spoke and looked me in the eye. I could see she was choosing her words carefully. "Reggie, there are thousands of children who have sent in cards. I don't want you to be disappointed if you don't win."

"I won't," I said in complete confidence, "because I'm *going* to win the pony. God told me so in my dream."

She sighed.

"If God chooses someone else, I want you to know that he is still very real, and I don't want you to get mad at him if you don't win."

"I understand, Mama, but I'm going to win," I said as I tugged on the car door handle.

The four of us walked into the post office, and Mom explained to the postman, Mr. Fisher, that we had postcards to mail to Popeye. He wasn't surprised; that day, there had already been a steady stream of excited children with postcards.

"I'm going to win that pony," I said with confidence to Mr. Fisher as I handed him my card.

"Well, son, don't get your hopes up too high," he said in a kind voice. "A lot of other boys and girls have already mailed their cards too."

I wanted to tell Mr. Fisher that the high hopes I had weren't just wishful thinking—they were assurances. And they didn't come from me—they came from God. But I didn't yet have the language skills to express all that I was thinking. Besides, it was becoming obvious that people were finding it hard to believe me.

"Yes, sir," I said politely.

✦ ✦ ✦

Mom says I accepted faith in God easier than my brother and sister did. If that's true, I don't remember why or how. Growing up in the country, I can't remember a time when I didn't believe in God. My faith was as real to me as the red clay beneath my calloused bare feet, and God was as gentle as the cotton that blew from the fields. Like kudzu, it rooted and grew in every direction without anyone tending to it. I knew God was as ever-present as the century-old oak trees that grew on our acreage. His goodness, grace, and mercy were as alive and abundant to me as the doves, squirrels, and pine trees I saw every day.

Of course, growing up in the South, we also had formal religion. My parents were stereotypical Baptists—at church every time the doors were open. While I always attended with them, I didn't always agree with what I heard. I preferred to think God used honey, not vinegar, to attract his followers, and when the revival preachers talked about hell, I shut down a bit.

Mom taught Sunday school and Dad was a deacon, so I was always in and around church. But unlike my parents, I never really embraced the idea that God was *in* church. God was *everywhere*. I heard sounds of him in the lake when I was fishing and saw him when I lay on my back in the fields watching the cumulus clouds drifting by on a sea of blue sky. For me, getting close to God wasn't about sitting silently in church; it was about becoming quiet in the presence of his creation and listening for his still, small voice. God was as visible and present as the landscape, especially the foothills of the Appalachian Mountains. The outdoors had become my cathedral, and from the land, God had abundantly blessed us with food, clothing, and a home.

There wasn't anything else I needed—or wanted.

✦ ✦ ✦

Our family was working in the garden near the house and Tim was napping when, through an open window, we heard the phone ring. Mom ran inside to answer it. Soon she called to us from the door, "Stop what you're doing and come in!"

I dropped the hoe and gingerly stepped between the shoots that were just breaking ground.

"Hurry!" she said.

Dad, Cathy, and I quickened our pace, and when we got inside, Mom was in the living room fiddling with the TV. I could hear the static as I entered through the back door.

"It's still on CBS; someone run outside and change the antenna!" she hollered while she continued to adjust the dial.

"What's going on?" I heard my dad ask as he ran back out to where the antenna was located. Two of the three stations came from Birmingham, and the third was from Montgomery. Someone had to go outside to physically move the antenna in the direction of the signal, and then we'd yell through the window to get it right if we wanted to watch a station coming from the other direction. "Does it work?" he yelled.

"A little more to the left," Mom said.

He adjusted it again.

"No, that's too far," Mom said, quickly followed by, "Right there!"

The static had quieted, and now I could hear the familiar voice of Cousin Cliff.

"What's going on?" Dad said as he flew in the back door and joined us in the living room.

"Shhh!" Mom said, pointing at the TV.

"Earlier today, we drew for the first prize in our contest," said Cousin Cliff. "Congratulations to the winner of Tex the pony, Reginald Anderson from Plantersville!"

Cathy and my parents looked stunned.

Cousin Cliff continued, "We'll be calling you next week, Reginald, and Tex can't wait for you to ride him!"

That's when they all turned to look at me. They were waiting for a response, or an outburst of emotion, but I wasn't sure what to do or say. I was thankful, but I wasn't surprised.

"Reggie, you won the pony!" Cathy said, throwing her arms around me.

"I know," I said quietly. "I told you."

"But how did you know?" Mom asked.

"God told me in my dream," I reminded her.

A week later, Tex the pony arrived amid great Plantersville fanfare. Cousin Cliff slid out of the car in his sailor cap and helped unload the black-and-white Shetland. Holding the reins, he walked Tex up the front yard to where we stood as a family. After Cousin Cliff saddled Tex, I climbed up, and then Cousin Cliff helped Cathy straddle the pony behind me. I held the reins, and Cathy held a Popeye doll that Cousin Cliff had given her. Dad and Mom stood behind us holding Tim, who wasn't sure what to make of it all.

For reasons I couldn't understand, I was suddenly a local celebrity. A crowd gathered, and a photographer snapped pictures while another man from WAPI filmed us. Cathy and I took turns riding the pony around the yard, and a week later, we saw ourselves in the same scene—only this time on our TV. Cathy and I looked happy. Mom and Dad had puzzled looks on their faces.

There were approximately five hundred people living in Plantersville at the time, and over the next few weeks, we became friends with many of them. I think they all heard about the local boy who won the pony, and they would stop by so their kids could take a ride on Tex. They were surprised at the good fortune that had fallen on me. I knew it had happened just like it was supposed to.

The way God said it would.

Once my parents got over their astonishment, I think they were pleased with all the lessons that came with Tex. I learned to share Tex, not only with my siblings but with the community. I learned to feed and groom him, as well as to clean out his stall.

There were also subtler and even more important lessons gained. I learned that God talks to me—to all of us—but hearing him requires faith. I learned to trust him and my experiences with him, even when others were skeptical. And I learned that God was active in my life, that he was good, and that he had plans for me.

But some of those lessons would soon be forgotten, and I would have to learn them all over again in the most painful way imaginable.

Chapter 3
THE DAY SANTA DIED

✦

Christ was always a part of Christmas in Plantersville. Whether we were at home, at church, or even at school, the story of the Virgin Birth was told through the words of the book of Matthew. In those days, "winter holidays" were unheard of; we had "Christmas break," and everyone in town went to one of the three Christian churches on the tree-lined town square. Each year, our tree was decorated in the same silver icicles and familiar twinkling lights. Though the manger scene underneath its branches was rearranged daily, the baby Jesus was always front and center.

The days leading up to my eighth Christmas didn't feel any different from the days that led up to my first seven. We'd cut down a tree and placed it in the same corner of the house. The smell of fresh-cut pine and the sticky, fallen needles gave us permission to start dreaming of the toys Santa would soon bring. Christmas was predictable in its traditions. So was Santa.

But this Christmas would be different. During my third-grade gift exchange, the model car I'd brought from home wasn't the biggest or fanciest gift, but it was received with a big smile and an enthusiastic "Thank you!" However, when it was my turn to open a present,

I was disappointed to see that mine came from Arthur. Everyone knew Arthur's family struggled to put food on the table. His clothes were patched, and his shoes were worn. While I was saddened that I wouldn't be getting a new toy, I vowed not to let it show. I knew that whatever Arthur gave me was more than his family could afford.

Arthur must have felt as awkward as I did when I lifted the lid and saw the Life Savers. My gift wasn't even a toy; it was candy! My classmates held their breaths as they waited to see how I'd react. "My favorite!" I said, popping one into my mouth. Everyone smiled; Arthur's grin was the biggest of all.

I was genuinely thankful for Arthur's gift. I felt sorry for him; it had to be hard to be poor.

✦ ✦ ✦

This year I would not be sitting on Santa's lap at Woolworth's Five and Dime. At eight, I was too old for that. Instead, my brother, Tim, and I decided a letter would accomplish the same purpose. We gathered at the kitchen table, pencils and paper in hand, to salivate over the catalogs of possibilities. In our letters, not only did we tell Santa in great detail what we wanted, but we also informed him that it had been a good year—we'd mostly obeyed our parents, and we hadn't fought too much.

We also reminded him of how hard we'd worked.

At this time, Dad was the only one with a paying job. Mom took care of us, tended the garden, and canned fruits and vegetables so we would have food through the winter. Money was especially tight that year. My parents had scraped together everything they could to buy an old schoolhouse that was being demolished. The plan was to use the scrap brick and wood to build a new home for our growing family. But their meager savings weren't enough. Without borrowing money, they couldn't afford the ramshackle building, and without the salvaged materials, they'd never be able to afford to build a new house. So though they loathed doing it, they'd borrowed from the bank.

Since there wasn't money available to hire help, it was up to my brother and me to salvage the building materials. Tim and I pitched in, cleaning old bricks, pulling nails from scrap wood, and sorting usable lumber from boards that were warped beyond use. Then, in their spare time (which wasn't much), my dad and grandfather used the reclaimed materials to build our new home. Tim and I helped when we could. Surely, this would earn us extra favor from Santa.

On Christmas Day, I was the first one up. But tradition and respect said I shouldn't approach the tree with the waiting pile of presents unless my siblings were with me. I woke Tim and Cathy, which wasn't hard. They were as excited as I was to find out how much loot we'd each scored from the man with the white beard.

The three of us raced to the living room where the tree stood. But we came to an abrupt stop when we saw the unexpected. The pile of presents under the tree wasn't a pile at all. In fact, there were only two gifts: one with Cathy's name on it and one with Tim's name.

"Where are all the presents?" Tim asked, disappointed at the meager offerings under the tree.

"Oh, these are for me!" Cathy squealed as she spotted a couple of dime-store dolls propped against the right side of the tree.

Tim's question hung in the air, but he moved on. "Army men!" he shouted, spotting the green figurines on the left.

On the tree, I saw a large envelope with my name on it. But that was it. There were no more presents in sight. *Had Santa hidden them? Was there a clue inside the envelope?*

Cathy cooed over her dolls, and in Tim's voice, I heard a general yelling for a soldier to "get in line." I pulled the letter out of the envelope, my hands shaking in anticipation, or maybe just fear. The letter was written on the same kind of paper I'd written my letter to Santa, but this time it was from him to me.

"Dear Reggie," the letter began. Oddly, it was penned in my mother's familiar scrawl. "The BB gun you got for your birthday was also for Christmas. Sorry that Santa can't bring you anything else this year. Next year will be better. Remember, your parents love you very much. Santa."

Shocked, I did what any eight-year-old would do. I burst into tears and sobbed uncontrollably.

Of course, I remembered the gun. I'd asked for it so I could help shoot squirrels to feed the family. As farmers, we grew our food— and as hunters, we shot it. I needed that gun to do my part. Looking again at the tearstained letter, I remembered Dad saying a gun was an expensive gift, but somehow they had been able to afford it. But now, on Christmas Day, as my brother and sister held their new toys and stared at me, I had to try to understand how Santa, with all his resources, couldn't afford anything for me. I threw myself on the sofa and sobbed louder.

My parents woke at the sound and rushed to the living room. I stopped crying long enough to catch my breath. As I did, I saw them look at each other, and then they began whispering.

"I didn't think he would be so hurt," Mom said. "I never got Christmas presents when I was growing up."

"I didn't see this coming either," my father said.

At that, I wailed louder. They didn't understand. I wasn't hurt just by my lack of presents; I was hurt that my older sister and younger brother *both got presents*. Why would Santa get something for them, but not for me? Even Arthur could afford Life Savers. Couldn't Santa have gotten me *something*?

I buried my head in the pillow and continued to cry. Mom sat next to me on the couch and rubbed my back. When I was all cried out, I rolled onto my side and looked up at her. "Why?" I asked. "Why was I the only one who didn't get a present?"

Mom suddenly got up and went into another room with my father, where again I could hear them whispering. After they finished talking, my dad picked up the phone. Wiping my tears away with the back of my hand, I was suddenly filled with hope. "Is he calling Santa?" I asked.

"No, he's calling Tom Tomlinson," Mom said.

Initially, I was disappointed. I didn't see how this would help anything. Mr. Tomlinson was the owner of the local hardware store. *What can he do?*

Then I heard my dad talking. He was trying to persuade him to open up on Christmas Day. "It will only take a few minutes," Dad said. "Santa forgot my boy, and I have to do something about it. We want to come in and pick out a new bike."

Apparently, that caught Mr. Tomlinson's attention. And mine as well. *A new bike?* Could it be true? Was I going to pick out a new bike for Christmas?

Dad was able to persuade Mr. Tomlinson that he was the kind of customer worth opening the store for on Christmas Day. Dad hung up the phone, grabbed his keys, and said, "C'mon, son, we're headed to the hardware store." This was beyond anything I had expected. Santa may have forgotten me, but Dad and Mom were about to make it up to me in the biggest way possible—a new bike! In the front seat of the car, I was giddy with anticipation. I whistled and swung my legs back and forth. It had never taken so long to get to town as it did that Christmas Day.

I noticed the whole town was deserted as we parked. I didn't even think the hardware store was open until I saw a light go on. Mr. Tomlinson met us at the door and led us to the shiny, new bicycles in the back. "Here they are," Mr. Tomlinson said, with a flourish of his hand.

I looked up expectantly at my dad. "Go ahead. See which one you like," he said, gesturing toward the row of metal frames and black tires. I walked around the display several times before eyeing a twenty-six-inch, red Schwinn racer. It had white lettering, handlebar brakes, and pedals that spun when I flipped them with my feet. This bike would be my pride and joy forever.

Dad looked at the price tag and then looked up at Mr. Tomlinson. While I imagined myself riding up ramps and racing down hills, I saw Dad and Mr. Tomlinson checking out the price tags on the nearby Huffys. "Do you want to look at one of these?" Dad asked.

I didn't. I wanted the red Schwinn.

"Okay, we'll take it then," Dad said, nodding to Mr. Tomlinson.

"Thank you!" I gushed, wrapping my arms around my father in a bear hug. My father's face lit up like the Christmas tree waiting for us at home.

While Mr. Tomlinson and my dad walked to the front, they discussed the price. I picked up the bike and carefully maneuvered it through the aisles toward the front door. As I reached the cash register, I heard Dad say, "I think it's a fair price; the problem is I don't have that much money. Can I give you a dollar today, and then a dollar a week until it is paid off?"

I couldn't hear Mr. Tomlinson's reply, but he clearly wasn't happy.

"Please, it's for my son, and it's Christmas," my father said.

"I know it's Christmas! I came in just to open the store for you, and now you're telling me you don't have the money to pay for it?"

"Please, I'm begging you!" my father said in a whisper that was meant to keep me from hearing him. "I promise I'll come in every Friday and pay you what I can." His voice sounded desperate. I knew Dad wasn't asking for a handout, only for credit—but to him, it was the same thing. I'd never seen my father act that way. He never begged for anything. He was a proud man who never asked anyone for help.

Then it all clicked.

Santa hadn't forgotten me.

The good-hearted man in the red suit that I had believed in for so many years would never have allowed my father to grovel for something he himself could so easily have given me. Unless Santa really didn't have the powers I believed he had. Or he wasn't real. That's when I knew. There was no Santa. He didn't exist.

The men finished talking, and I looked up as the door opened and the bell tinkled. "Thank you. You don't know how much this means to me," my father said, shaking Mr. Tomlinson's hand. He held the door open while I pushed the bike through. We walked toward the car, and I gazed down the road so I wouldn't have to look Dad in the eye. We loaded the bicycle into the trunk. "She sure is a beauty," Dad said. But to me, the bike had lost its luster.

Shamed by what I had seen and how I had acted, I would have gladly given the bike back in exchange for my father's lost pride. But I knew I couldn't undo what had already been done. Dad had groveled to get me a bike. Dad knew it. Mr. Tomlinson knew it. And by New Year's Eve, the whole town would know it. So now it was up to me to pretend that I didn't know it—that was the only way to make his sacrifice worth it.

The whole way home I tried to keep up the charade of happiness.

"Do you love your new bike?"

"It's the best bike in the whole world!"

"You'll probably have that bike for years!"

"Probably for the rest of my life," I said, with all the enthusiasm I could muster. "Thank you for buying it for me."

When we got home, Dad helped me get it out of the car.

"Can I go for a ride right now?" I asked.

"Sure. But don't be gone too long. Your mother will have Christmas dinner on the table soon." Dad's smile lit up his face, and I climbed on the bike and pedaled as fast as I could down the street.

He mistook my eagerness to get away as love for my new bike. The truth was, I just couldn't bear to see him tell Mom how much the bike cost, or what he had to give up to get it for me.

As I sailed down our country road, past the swollen creek, I couldn't get the scene I'd witnessed at the hardware store out of my mind. As soon as I was out of his sight, I veered off the pavement. I pedaled past the mulberry trees and headed into the woods. There I jumped off my brand-new bike and pushed it across the field. Once I was hidden, I let the bike flop down to the ground, and then I collapsed next to it. There among the dried leaves and brown vines, I cried hot tears of shame and swore I would never let something like that happen again.

✦ ✦ ✦

When Christmas break ended, I returned to school and begged the janitor for a job. For twenty-five cents a day, I helped the custodian empty trash cans, wipe off blackboards, and pick up litter.

Santa died for me that Christmas. From then on, I knew there would be no more free gifts in life. If I wanted something, I was going to have to earn it.

Chapter 4
COUNTRY BRED

✦

When I was young, I knew it mattered which side of the tracks you were born on, although I didn't understand why. Though we were poor, we lived on Mulberry Street, on the right side of the tracks. Our house sat in the shadow of "The House," a grand, old antebellum mansion built by King Cotton and owned by the Martin family who reigned there.

Mac Martin, their oldest son, and I became friends, and I was welcomed into the historic house where the family treated me as one of their own. Yet I knew financial differences existed between us. One day, the doors of the prestigious Auburn University would swing wide open for Mac. If I worked hard, the doors of the University of Alabama would crack open for me, and I could force my way through them.

But for another friend of mine, the doors would *never* open.

Sam also lived on Mulberry Street. Financially, my family was much closer to Sam's family than to the Martins, but Sam lived on the other side of the tracks. Despite the crossties that divided us, we shared a love of squirrel hunting. Taking his dog and my .22 rifle, we'd forge a trail into the woods, and with those excursions came a bond of friendship, just like with Mac. But the adults around us saw it differently, and I saw the effects of their prejudice. Sam, for example, couldn't come to Mac's house with me. I was too young to know that the reason was because of the color of his skin. To me, Sam being black didn't matter any more than Mac or me being white.

But it mattered to a whole lot of people. And in March of 1965, the National Guard moved into our small town and asked us to stay inside our houses. They'd been sent to keep the peace as civil rights marchers descended on Selma, less than twenty miles away. From then on, speeches seemed to linger in the air, and what I heard depended on whose door I opened.

When I opened a door on one side of the tracks, even two years after he first gave the speech, I would hear hope and optimism for the future as someone recounted the highlights of Martin Luther King's "I Have a Dream," speech. But a door to a house across the tracks would open to the rhetoric of the Old South and states' rights, as Alabama's governor George Wallace found a voice and fervently tried to hold on to the past. Years would pass before these thresholds to the future could be freely crossed and the barriers broken down.

Growing up in the shadows of Selma and having friends like Mac and Sam would teach me to hold open the door for all who came after me.

✦ ✦ ✦

My mother's family was from Georgia, where we saw a different line of demarcation. The "gnat line" was a geographic demarcation that separated north Georgia, which was free of gnats, from south Georgia, which was full of gnats. If a traveler headed south in Georgia, they would know when they had crossed that line because screens suddenly appeared on every front porch, window, and door.

Mom's family lived south of the gnat line in a little, old farming community called Desser, which seldom appeared on any map and was located just a few miles from both the Alabama and Florida state lines. We had relatives spread up to twenty miles away from Desser all the way to Donalsonville, which boasted the region's only stoplight. The roots of the area were so tangled, they reminded me of something my Grandmother Anderson always used to say: "Marry someone from out of state."

Though she had no training in genetics and didn't have more than an eighth-grade education, Grandmother was wise beyond her years, and she had the good sense to warn all her grandchildren of what she knew. In Desser, the locals were pretty sure that every white person was related to nearly every other white person, and every black person was related to nearly every other black person in some way too. I'm pretty sure there were also a few white people who were kin to a few black people, but in those days, no one really talked about that.

My grandfather owned a store, which stood on one corner of the main street running through Desser, and the church was on another. The seventy-five-member church, which swelled to a hundred during revival week, had a graveyard that held generations of my family, dating back to the seventeen hundreds.

Whenever we were in town, we stayed with Aunt Sophie and Uncle Luther—their house was bigger than my grandparents' home. They had two kids, Susie and Johnny. Susie and I were the same age, but I preferred to hang out with Johnny, who was seven years older. He taught me how to fish and hunt and how to drive a tractor. I thought Johnny hung the moon, and I wanted to do everything he did.

✦ ✦ ✦

With only one son and a couple of farmhands, Uncle Luther needed help on the farm, and during the summer I was glad to do it. Especially when I learned that I'd get paid. Uncle Luther was primarily a peanut farmer. He had hundreds of acres of peanuts, but peanuts weren't harvested and sold until late August or early September, so by June and July, Luther's family was literally living on what was left of last year's peanuts. To make ends meet, Uncle Luther planted watermelon, a cash crop that could be harvested and sold during the summer.

I was only eight when I started working the fields. On my first day, I woke while it was still dark to the smell of farm-fresh bacon and buttered biscuits. I dressed quickly and met the rest of the men downstairs in the kitchen where the sounds of the women cracking eggs, then sizzling them in the grease-cured iron skillet awakened my senses and made my stomach howl.

It was still dark after breakfast, and we left the house with only tractor lights to guide our movements. We drove to the watermelon fields, arriving just as daylight peeked over the horizon. The field hands, Leroy and Big John, were already there waiting. These men became my mentors on how to spot a good melon. They taught me the difference between a melon that needed more time in the sun and one that was ripe and ready for market—its sweet red meat bursting with flavor and begging to be eaten.

I knew Leroy and Big John had to use the back door to my grandfather's store, but I never attributed it to the color of their skin. When we worked in the fields, we may have started out the day as two different colors, but by the end of the day we were all the same color: dirt.

Uncle Luther and Leroy were the most experienced cutters. They could look at a watermelon and tell if it was ripe or not; if they were unsure, they would lay hands on it, and immediately they'd know if it should stay in the field longer. Using a knife, they quickly slashed the vines on the ready watermelons and rolled the melons' fat, yellow bellies skyward, so those who followed would know which ones were ready to be loaded on the trailer. The line in the field formed behind their expert hands. Following them would be seasonal workers, who picked up the watermelons and tossed them down the line to more workers until they reached the trailer on which they'd be loaded.

At eight, I was too small to throw the watermelons, so I drove the tractor as the men cut and tossed the ripe fruit into the trailer. But within a year, I had gotten big enough to pick up and lob a thirty-pound melon about ten feet, which meant I was promoted. Once on the line, I tossed melons to Big John, who hurled them thirty or forty feet to one of the farmhands, who eventually passed them to my cousin Johnny to stack on the trailer. After both trailers were full, we pulled them under a shade tree where we loaded the melons onto the truck.

By early morning, the summer heat was sweltering, and the lunch break couldn't come soon enough. Once the trucks were loaded, we'd celebrate the morning's accomplishments with a Southern farm lunch, which was nothing short of a feast and second only to Sunday church dinners.

After lunch, Johnny and the men would leave for Atlanta with a truck full of five or six hundred melons to sell at the Atlanta State Farmers Market. As soon as a truck was emptied at the market, the driver would be sent back to pick more melons and to fill the truck again. The only break from the routine was on Sunday when we attended church. After we'd observe the Sabbath, we'd start all over again.

At the end of each summer, my Uncle Luther would tally the receipts, deducting the money spent for gas and other expenses, and then he would generally give me about five hundred dollars. To a kid who was making twenty-five cents a day helping the janitor, this was a ton of money. By the time I left for college, I had three or four thousand dollars in the bank.

✦ ✦ ✦

The summer after I turned ten was a big summer for all of us. Johnny got his driver's license, and Uncle Luther decided to expand his ten acres of watermelons to twenty. That meant he could set up two stalls at the market, potentially doubling his income. Not to mention doubling his risk. To make it work, he bought a second truck for Johnny to drive, so he and his son could take two trucks at a time to Atlanta. But that required twice as much time in the fields picking watermelons.

After consulting with my parents, Uncle Luther decided I was old enough to man the stalls while the men went back to southwest Georgia and reloaded the trailers. He trusted me to stay by myself at the market for twenty-four to forty-eight hours. Times were different then, but it was still a lot of trust to put in a ten-year-old boy. My job was to sell as many melons as I could, as fast as I could, to the buyers who came to the market, while Johnny and Luther burned up the roads in between, bringing fresh watermelons.

While we worked in the fields gathering watermelons for the market, Uncle Luther prepared me to take over the stalls. He explained how the melons were grown and what to tell buyers looking for the best fruit for their stores and restaurants.

"You tell 'em southwest Georgia grows the best watermelons in the world!" he said. "And remind 'em that these are family grown melons and that they're grown with love." He explained how they were planted and nurtured through the spring, until it was time for the first cutting. He showed me how to tell buyers when a melon was ripe and how to stack them so the ripest ones were always on top.

After lunch that day, we loaded up two trucks: Luther's old pickup and Johnny's brand-new, two-and-a-half-ton, five-speed Ford. Both had the farm's name, "Odom and Son Farms," freshly painted on the doors.

"Can I ride with you, Johnny?" I asked, and he agreed. I preferred to ride with Johnny, not only because his truck was new and he had an eight-track tape installed so we could listen to Charley Pride, Elvis, and Tammy Wynette, but because he didn't smoke unfiltered Camels like my uncle did.

We drove the trucks to my granddaddy's store, where we met up with Jimmy and Jerry Alday and their trailers of watermelons. Their farm was just down the road from ours, and they operated the stall next to Luther's at the market. I'd met them before, and I knew we were kin—distant cousins of some kind—but that was true of almost everyone in the Donalsonville area. So with four loaded trucks, we set out on the back roads, caravan style.

On our way to catch I-75 north to Atlanta, we were traveling a stretch of road from Americus to Vienna that had a steep dropoff on both sides. When I looked out the window, I noticed there wasn't much of a shoulder on the road, and when I say not much, I mean *none*. If Johnny overcorrected while driving or hit something and lost control, we'd be buried under six hundred melons at the bottom of the drop-off.

I started thinking about the sermon the preacher had preached the day before. "Trust and obey. Fear not, if Jesus is in your heart." I tried to remember what else he'd said. Something about "the way is straight and narrow, and few will make it" and "hell is full of the foolish." I started to think about how foolish I was to be riding this dangerous road with a novice truck driver, and I began to pray the sinner's prayer as best I could. Johnny must have been worried about the drop-off too. He stepped on the brakes and tried to slow down.

"I hope the new brakes hold up under this load," he said, glancing in my direction with a worried look on his face.

From the mirror on my side, I could see that we were leaving a cloud of smoke in our wake.

Uncle Luther, following behind us, was used to smoke in the cab of his truck, but when it smelled like burning rubber rather than Camel cigarettes, he opened the squawk box on the CB. "Breaker, breaker, Johnny, slow down! Your tires are burning!"

We were headed down the steepest part of the hill, when suddenly a shotgun-like noise went off in my ear. The CB crackled again.

"Stop! You blew a tire!"

God was definitely with us that day as Johnny ground all ten gears down, gently riding the brakes until we were at a standstill at the bottom of the hill. I'm not sure what the weight rating on that tire jack was, but we tested its limits that evening when we had to change the inside tire on a fully loaded truck of watermelons. A fifteen-minute job turned into a two-hour ordeal, even with the help of the Alday brothers.

✦　✦　✦

At ten, I was oblivious to the divides that separated blacks from whites, rich from poor, and no gnats from lots of gnats. There was another distinction that others saw that I didn't—the barrier between this world and the next. Even if someone had told me it was there, I wouldn't have believed them.

I didn't see heaven and earth as separate. To me, there was no barrier between the place where I lived and the place where God resided. As farmers and churchgoers, we knew that the Lord we worshiped on Sunday was the same God who gave us rain and sun in just the right amounts, at the right time, to grow the crops that sustained us. The way I saw it, the veil flowed freely between the two realms. As farmers, we tilled the soil, planted the seeds, and prayed for rain. If it came, it came, and it was God's will. If it didn't, that was God's will too.

As long as a church worshiped God, whether it was Baptist or Methodist, I didn't think there was a difference. In fact, the only difference I saw between our church in Plantersville and the one in Desser was that the Desser church had more interesting revival preachers.

The summer I was twelve, I took a break from manning the farmers market to hear a revival preacher who visited Desser. As a family, we went to church every night during the weeklong revival. Something the preacher said made me realize I needed to tend to my soul the same way a farmer nurtured his growing plants. If I wanted to produce fruit, I had to put down my own roots of faith. I decided to get baptized.

Though I knew God had created me and I had never felt separated from him, this was my moment of *telling* that to everyone I knew. So one night during the revival, Susie and I, like all our cousins before us, walked the redemptive aisle to acknowledge our sins and claim Jesus as our Savior. The preacher dunked us, and we were baptized by submersion.

I had never felt cleaner.

My parents had never felt prouder.

But just four years later, everything about God that had mattered to me that night would cease to exist.

Chapter 5

WATERMELON KIN

✦

Though I was out of school for the summer and a long way from home, lessons of a different sort continued for me at the Atlanta State Farmers Market. Not only did I learn how to run a business, but I also learned how to be a man.

My summer instructors were Jerry and Jimmy Alday, my mother's third or fourth cousins—no one really knew for sure. Our stalls shared a long shed divided by concrete pillars, and their stalls were located next to mine.

Like most of the farm families from our area, the oldest Alday brother worked on the farm and transported produce to market with their dad, Ned, while the youngest brothers stayed at the market in Atlanta. Jimmy was the youngest brother in his family and closest to my age. Though nine years separated us, Jimmy and I bonded at the farmers market, simply by our family position.

Jerry was the middle brother. He was ten years older than Jimmy and nineteen years older than me. He had dark hair and sideburns that grew longer with each passing year. The first summer I spent at the market, he was still in his twenties and unmarried. But shortly after turning thirty, he married a local girl from Donalsonville named Mary. If Jimmy was the older brother I never had, Jerry was like a second father. During the summers at the market, we lived together 24/7, and I grew to love these men as much as my own family.

✦ ✦ ✦

The Atlanta State Farmers Market first opened in 1959 and was supposedly the largest open-air farmers market in the southeastern United States. With more than 150 acres of stalls, every kind of seasonal produce imaginable was for sale. From tomatoes in the summer to pumpkins in the fall to Christmas trees in December—if it grew in regional soil, you could buy it there.

Inside the market, the first few sheds were dedicated to Georgia farmers—that's where our stalls were located. During the night, farmers would bring in trucks and trailers full of produce and unload them in their stalls.

Though both families sold watermelons, there wasn't competition between us. We'd help each other get the melons unloaded and stacked in the stalls ready for the predawn customers. If I sold a big order of watermelons, they would help me load them onto the customer's truck, and I'd do the same for them.

The busiest time of the day was between three and five o'clock in the morning when the wholesalers came in. We were their first stop because they always wanted to buy from local farmers. Watermelons typically sold for $2.50 to $3.00 a melon, depending on the crop that season.

"If they buy over a hundred melons, you can drop the price," Uncle Luther taught me.

I could charge them anywhere from $1.50 to $2.00 a melon, but it was my responsibility to maximize the price without losing the sale. Wholesalers and distributors showed up at the market with piles of cash, and of course, their job was to get the best produce at the lowest price. I learned math and negotiating skills on the job, so I could hold my own against their seasoned haggling. The market was a major distribution point for fresh produce, not only for the Southeast but for the entire United States, and forming good relationships with wholesalers and distributors who'd come back week after week was an important part of a successful business.

Once the price was agreed on, the buyer would hand me a wad

of cash, which I would stuff in my overall pockets for safekeeping until my uncle Luther arrived. One particularly successful week, the summer I was twelve, I remember emptying bills from every pocket and handing over more than two thousand dollars in cash.

Nearly every buyer needed help getting his load onto his truck. "I've got a heart condition," the buyer would say, clutching his chest as soon as the sale was done. "You're going to have to load this for me." If Jerry and Jimmy were too busy with their own customers to help me, I would get on the intercom and call for help. For five cents a watermelon, there was always someone willing to help load.

After eight or nine o'clock in the morning, things would start to slow down, but sales would continue throughout the day. Restaurateurs would shop for the freshest ingredients, and families would shop for the best deals.

The cafeteria and the nearest shower were at the truck stop a half mile away. But even the most dirt-covered farmers didn't want to shower in those unsanitary conditions unless they had to.

To get there, you had to walk the half mile uphill, through unlit areas, behind the sheds, and past the trash bins where spoiled produce—the smelly underbelly of the market—was tossed. Jerry and Johnny told me that this is where men who had been drinking too much often slept. Since this was a cash business, it wasn't safe for me to go there alone. On those rare occasions I went to the cafeteria for a break from the monotony and a hot meal, Jimmy or Jerry walked with me.

✦ ✦ ✦

Though the summers passed quickly, the days at the market were long, and we were always looking for ways to amuse ourselves.

"Betcha I can do more chin-ups than you," Jimmy taunted me one hot afternoon.

"No way!" I said, grabbing the bar over my head and pulling myself up.

"One, two, threeee . . . four!" Jimmy said, exaggerating my

attempts to pull up one last time. I let go and dropped to the market floor.

Jimmy grabbed the bar with both hands and pulled himself up ten times before I begged him to stop. It wasn't a surprise; Jimmy was older, bigger, and stronger. From that day on, we had lots of other contests—push-ups, jumping jacks, or wrestling matches. Jimmy always won. But it didn't stop me from competing or from believing that one day I would beat him.

If Jimmy and I were horsing around too much, Jerry would step in as the father figure.

"That's enough!" he'd say after the wrestling got to be too much. Or, when we "accidentally" dropped a watermelon just so we could eat the heart out of it, he'd give us a hard look and say, "That was a two-dollar watermelon you broke!"

When unloading the trucks, the three of us would have a contest to see which guy dropped the most melons—the loser would have to buy the others ice cream. Jimmy and Jerry gave me the advantage. They put me first in line so I only had to throw instead of catch. Next, they counted the total of their drops against mine. Somehow, they always ended up dropping more melons than I did. "I think he's throwing them short," Jerry said to Jimmy with a wink after he dropped an already damaged melon.

"Somebody must be hungry for ice cream!" Jimmy teased.

I treasured those moments. They made me feel loved and accepted—like I was their third brother.

I worked at the market from the time I was ten until I was sixteen. The first year or two, I stayed by myself at the market for twenty-four to forty-eight hours at a time, but as I got older, I was there by myself the entire week. Uncle Luther and Johnny would show up on Monday or Tuesday, and together we'd unload fifteen hundred watermelons into our ten-by-twenty-foot stalls. They'd collect the week's receipts, get a little sleep, and head out for south Georgia to harvest more fruit, hoping that by the time they returned, the stalls would be at least partially empty.

✦ ✦ ✦

The Alday brothers were hardworking, God-fearing young men. In south Georgia there was a church every five miles or so, and you went to the closest one. The Alday family had helped build the church they attended, and they were the cornerstone of their community. Jimmy and Jerry were some of the best Christian folks I knew. They never tolerated any cursing or any kind of disrespect—especially toward women. I learned how to respect a woman by watching how they treated the females in their family.

God was very much a part of their lives, in both the big and the little things. They were always quick to credit God if something good happened. Whether it was a bumper crop of watermelons, feeling better after a summer cold, or just a vanilla ice cream cone, they would stop and thank God for their blessings, realizing that it all came from him. Every day for five summers, they tutored me in how to be thankful and how to trust God. They wanted me to grow up to be more than a good man; they wanted me to be a godly man.

Though I had always gone to church, the whole concept of sin confused me. Sure, I heard preachers talk about it. I knew we weren't supposed to go to the movies on Sunday, for example, but since no one took me, I didn't really have the opportunity to sin. Once when I was twelve, I played penny poker with a cousin. I knew it was wrong, but I did it anyway. I lost thirty-seven cents. It was the first and only time I ever gambled in my life. Even then, I knew God forgave us for our sins, so I didn't carry around any guilt. I simply confessed my sin, forgave myself as God forgave me, and moved on in much the same way my parents did when they forgave me for doing something wrong.

I had lived a pretty sheltered life. My faith was innocent. It wasn't built on struggle or hardship, and it had never been tested. My life was charmed, and I was happy. I believed God was all-powerful and ever-present. The role models in my life all demonstrated grace and kindness, which further reinforced my beliefs that God was good.

+ + +

The market had its own morality, and Jimmy and Johnny taught me the rules. When they saw a farmer getting drunk or flirting with female customers, Jimmy would say, "That's dangerous, and it's not good for you."

"Those men are headed to hell," Jerry would remind me as the drunks stumbled through the market cursing, shouting, and starting fights. The Aldays weren't mocking or making fun of those men—they were the first to help someone who needed help, even if that person were drunk—and they weren't trying to sound judgmental. They were just trying to instruct a younger brother on the way he should go, and rather than use their own lives as good examples, they used the bad behavior of others as object lessons to teach me right from wrong.

Almost anything could be bought and sold at the market, and it was available around the clock, but especially at night. Jimmy and Jerry warned me to steer clear of the "ladies of the evening." (Their good manners prevented them from referring to them as anything else.) "If you have a customer at two o'clock in the morning, it's fine as long as it's not a female customer. Do not deal with those people," Jerry had told me my first summer at the market.

A few years later, I learned why. Nearly every night we would watch cars with ladies of the evening arrive and park in the dark. Wearing flashy clothes and gaudy makeup, they would walk the dark alleys of the market, making deals with farm boys who paid them for favors. "The ways of the world bring sin and destruction," Jerry said one night as we watched several farmers we knew slip off into the dark. "That's sinful behavior, and God doesn't tolerate it."

The Aldays shunned this activity. "Just like the market is open 24/7, faithfulness to God is required 24/7," Jimmy said. "Don't ever let me catch you doing something like that."

They wouldn't. I wanted to be as good as they were. And I knew Uncle Luther placed a lot of trust in me. With that trust came a tremendous amount of responsibility for a young boy, but I thrived under the pressure and the freedom of those long, hot summer days at the market. That time in Atlanta helped shape me in ways no other experience could have, and the Alday brothers were a huge part of it. For me, those summers at the market were like Disneyland—the happiest place on earth.

Chapter 6
THE DEVILS WENT DOWN TO GEORGIA

✦

By May 1973, the civil rights marches in Selma had been settled. "Peace" and "love" were the new slogans of the day, and denim was the fabric of choice. At my high school, we wore it plain, faded, and sometimes beaded. But on that warm, spring day when the door to my freshman history class swung open, it wasn't denim that I saw—it was my father's suit. I knew something big was about to happen.

Dad was not only the agriculture teacher at my small high school, he was also the assistant principal in charge of discipline—and unless you were raising a calf for the fair, you didn't want to have a reason to see him. While Dad's presence was commonplace in the hallway, I rarely saw him in my classroom, and I'd *never* seen him interrupt a class. As he whispered to Mr. Peters, my history teacher, I said a quick prayer for the friend who had gotten into so much trouble that he needed to be pulled out of history.

"Reginald, Mr. Anderson would like to see you in the hallway," Mr. Peters said.

Confused, I looked up at Dad. Seeing his face, I could tell that something was horribly wrong. He motioned for me to come out in the hall.

I stood up, my legs shaking, and walked across the classroom. I had no idea what was up. I followed him into the hallway and closed the door behind me. With the lockers to his back, Dad put his hands on my shoulders and looked me in the eyes. His gaze was so intense and so sad that I couldn't bear to look at him. Instead, I focused on a gum wrapper on the floor.

"Son, I just got a call from your aunt. Something terrible has happened near Donalsonville." He paused to calm the tremble in his ordinarily strong voice. "There was a shooting. Jerry and Jimmy were murdered. I'm so sorry; I know how much they meant to you."

I looked up and saw him blink back tears.

"No! There must be a mistake!" I said. *How could this happen to the Alday brothers?* "They can't be dead! Everyone loves Jerry and Jimmy. It's impossible!"

"It's not a mistake. The police found their bodies at about two o'clock this morning. They've been out at their mobile home investigating ever since then."

"Are you sure?" I asked. I tried to make sense of what he was saying.

"Yes. Reggie, I know this will be hard to hear, but not only were Jimmy and Jerry murdered, but so were Chester, Ned, and Aubrey. It was a massacre out there."

A massacre? In Donalsonville? It was too horrible to believe. My mind couldn't take it all in. Chester was Jimmy and Jerry's brother. He brought melons to market with their father, Ned. Aubrey was Ned's brother, and he'd occasionally join them, so I knew them all.

My father continued, "There is speculation that some strangers had driven through the area. The police are looking for their car, but there aren't any more details right now. Your aunt Sophie said she'll call us at home tonight. I'm sure they'll know more by then."

In that single moment, my world flipped upside down. I was too stunned to react. I should have cried or screamed, but instead, in a state of shock, I just turned and started walking toward my history class. Dad slipped his arm around my shoulder.

"I'm sorry I had to tell you this way," he said, "but I know how close you were to those boys, and I figured you'd want to know." I nodded.

We reached the door, and Dad paused before opening it. "One more thing. Say a prayer for Jerry's wife, Mary. She's still missing, and they can't find her."

I looked up at him, and he opened the door for me to reenter. I rejoined my class—and found everyone staring at me.

"Are you okay?" Mr. Peters asked.

I nodded. Class had stopped, and everyone was waiting for some kind of explanation.

How do I explain this?

"Something bad happened to my family in Georgia," I mumbled, and I took my seat.

Immediately concerned, Mr. Peters looked at my father who was still standing in the doorway. "Does he need to leave?"

"He's all right," Dad said. "He'll be fine."

Then he left, closing the door behind him.

✦ ✦ ✦

Dad was wrong. I wasn't *all right,* and I'd never again be *fine.* Two people I loved, and the people they loved most, were dead or missing. As Mr. Peters resumed his lecture, I stoically stared straight ahead, willing my body not to betray the feelings churning inside.

I slogged through my next two classes with fear, hurt, and anger building like storm clouds in my mind.

What would someone want with the Aldays? If they wanted money, there were richer people in town. *And why did they have to kill them?* Jimmy and Jerry would have given them anything they wanted. I'd seen them do it countless times at the farmers market. They'd give a watermelon to a poor family who looked like they couldn't afford one, they bought me ice cream when I didn't deserve it, and they paid for people's lunch at the cafeteria if they were short of money.

Three years earlier, when Jerry and Mary had gotten married, they'd bought a mobile home and parked it on family land in a remote part of the county. Their home was on an isolated dead-end road, surrounded by acres of farmland near Lake Seminole.

Of all the places on the planet that seemed safe, I would have said Donalsonville was one of the safest. But the five deaths in that mobile home meant that nobody was secure.

Are the men who did this still in the area? Who else is at risk? My chest tightened as I thought of Uncle Luther, Aunt Sophie, Johnny, and Susie in their big house where we'd all spent so many summers and holidays. Not far from them lived my grandparents and other aunts, uncles, and cousins. I thought of the field hands, Leroy and Big John, and their families; the people who worked in my grandfather's store and served me Cokes and MoonPies; and all the people at church where we ate Sunday dinner. I shuddered at the thought that some of them could be next.

As I prayed for their safety, I thought about Mary. *Where is she? Is she hiding somewhere in fear, afraid to come out? Did she get hurt while trying to escape? Did they take her with them?*

Suddenly the heat I felt from my hatred of the killers began to thaw the shock that had kept me frozen. Fear and anger fueled the growing tempest inside me. I did my best to hold it together until the final bell, but as soon as I heard it, I sprinted from my last class to my hideout deep in the woods, behind our house.

The storm that had been brewing inside hit full blast. Sweat and tears blinded my eyes as I ran, and I gasped for air. Once I was deep enough in the woods so no one could hear or see me, I let out one long scream and then exploded. Kicking at the trees and screaming, I beat my thundering fists on the bark. I lost control and let it happen.

"Why?" I screamed at God. "Why did you do this?" Over and over I screamed, "Why did you let this happen, God? *They loved you!*"

✦   ✦   ✦

That night, Uncle Luther and Aunt Sophie called. Dad and Mom spent most of the time on the phone with them, but I got to speak with them briefly when I answered their call. Even over the phone, they sounded shell-shocked. Jerry and Aubrey had been found in the south bedroom; Ned and Chester had been taken to the north bedroom. Jimmy was found facedown on the sofa in the living room. The Alday men had all been shot execution style. Blood had pooled or splattered throughout their home, even in the kitchen. No one knew how it happened or why. It was the most grisly crime scene the sheriff in Seminole County had ever witnessed and probably the most horrific in the state's history.

I continued to hear snippets of details as my parents spoke on the phone, but one stood out: Mary's car was gone, and she still hadn't been found.

I didn't want to hear any more of it. I went into my room and got ready for bed. Usually, the last thing I did before I got under the covers was to turn out the light, but that night I left it on. Lying in bed looking out the window, I felt helpless and despondent. There was nothing I could do to fix this; I could barely comprehend what had happened.

I tried to pray, but even my prayers were filled with questions and accusations. *Why did you let this happen? They trusted you. How could you do this? Those madmen are still out there. Who's next? How can I trust you to protect me, or anyone else, when you didn't protect them?*

Worn out by the emotions of the day, I felt myself growing sleepy. But I had one more important prayer; it was really more of a plea. Jerry and Mary had been married three years, and they had been trying to have kids. Though they hadn't announced it yet, there were rumors that Mary had finally gotten pregnant. I fell asleep that night doing the only thing I could for the family I loved so much and who had loved me so well. I begged God to protect Mary the same way Jerry and Jimmy had protected me.

Dear God, please, please protect Mary. Keep her from harm, and let her and her baby be found safe and unhurt. Amen.

✦ ✦ ✦

The next day, I learned Mary had already been found in the woods. She had one bullet in her back and another through her skull.

The story came out in pieces, but over time, we learned she'd been violated in the worst way imaginable—raped twice under her kitchen table and again in the woods before the monsters shot her and discarded her body. I had to fight a wave of nausea when I heard the news. Jimmy and Jerry had a deep respect for the women in their family. Only evil incarnate could have committed such incomprehensible and heinous acts.

Investigators followed the criminals' trail, and within a week, the animals were caught in West Virginia. The sickening details of their crimes were revealed through newspaper reports and, eventually, court transcripts.

Carl Isaacs, the ringleader, had escaped from a Maryland penal institution with his half brother, Wayne Coleman, and Wayne's friend, George Dungee. On their way to Florida, the three also picked up Carl's younger brother, Billy Isaacs, who was fifteen years old at the time. While driving through Seminole County, the three brothers and their friend were low on gas. Thinking they saw a gas pump behind Jerry and Mary's trailer, they pulled in. Though there wasn't a pump, they decided to burglarize the empty home.

Unaware of what was happening inside his mobile home, Jerry pulled up with his father, Ned. Carl met them at the door and ordered them inside where they were told to empty their pockets. They were then sent to separate bedrooms where they were shot in the back of the head. Minutes later, Jimmy drove up on a tractor and knocked at the back door. Wayne forced Jimmy into the living room and onto the sofa, where Carl shot him from behind. Carl then headed outside to move the tractor that was now blocking their car.

Oblivious of the evil lurking in her home, Mary drove up next, and as she entered the trailer, the men accosted her, tied her up, and left her in the kitchen. Once again, Carl went out to move the tractor, but that's when Chester and Aubrey drove up in their truck. The criminals met the farmers at the door and forced the innocent men into separate bedrooms where their relatives were already dead, lying in their own pooling blood. They shot each man while Mary, still tied up in the kitchen, listened and screamed. Then Carl sent George and Billy outside, while he and Wayne took turns raping Mary in the kitchen before ordering her to get dressed and leave with them.

In addition to their car, they also took Mary's. Realizing they didn't need two cars, they dumped the car with the out-of-state plates in the woods. And since Mary could now identify them, they dumped her, too, but only after raping her again before shooting her. They left her lying in the woods, naked and facedown in a mound of fire ants.

✦ ✦ ✦

The funeral was held on May 17, but because school was about to end, we weren't able to attend. More than five thousand people attended the service, which had to be held in an open field to accommodate the crowd.

The six coffins were buried behind the church the Aldays had helped build.

✦ ✦ ✦

Even from the backseat of my parents' car, I could tell things had changed in Seminole County as we arrived that summer. Rain was falling, and what had once been a bright and cheery landscape of blue skies and golden sunlight was now shrouded in a gray pall. Clouds hid the sun, and shadows covered the locals' hearts. A heaviness hung in the air, and the whole county seemed to smell of sulfur. To me, everything seemed smoky and dirty—maybe because people stayed inside and smoked more.

Everyone was shaken up. Edgy. Nervous. Neighbors who once trusted one another were now suspicious. I used to walk freely in and out of my cousins' homes; their doors were always wide open. Now, I had to knock because the doors stayed locked and shades remained drawn. At night, it was harder to see the stars, because lights stayed on—the locals were afraid of the dark.

Even at church, things seemed different. The preacher continued to talk about how God was still in charge and could bring comfort to our trials, but few seemed to pay attention. The men picked at their nails or stared vacantly; the women wrung their hands and pulled tissues from their sleeves to dab their eyes. Everyone was crying—out of fear, anger, and love for the lost. They were also more withdrawn; they had discovered how painful it was to lose someone you cared about. It was as if they felt it was better to stop caring than to risk experiencing that heartache again.

Every King James Bible in Seminole County seemed to be open to Psalm 23. I was familiar with that passage and the comfort it brought to many. Several times I picked it up and read it myself.

"The LORD is my shepherd; I shall not want. He maketh me to lie down in green pastures: he leadeth me beside the still waters."

But there are no more green pastures, and the waters are turbulent.

"Yea, though I walk through the valley of the shadow of death, I will fear no evil: for thou art with me; thy rod and thy staff they comfort me."

I've been through the valley of death, but your rod and staff weren't there to protect those I loved, or even to comfort me. God obviously didn't care about me or about the Aldays, but I continued to read.

"Thou preparest a table before me in the presence of mine enemies."

Surely, God didn't allow Mary's enemies to prepare the kitchen table for her.

I closed the book. I couldn't stomach any more of it.

The captured criminals had been brought back to Donalsonville to be charged. I couldn't wait to leave. As soon as the watermelons were ripe enough to harvest, I headed to Atlanta, north of all the evil that lingered over Seminole County.

✦　✦　✦

Jimmy and Jerry's stalls were rented out to other southern Georgia farmers. I knew them, but it wasn't the same. There were no push-up or chin-up contests. No one dropped watermelons just to eat them. After unloading the first trailer full of melons and watching Johnny and Uncle Luther drive off, I bought my first ice cream cone. But one lick was enough to know that it didn't taste the same. I threw it behind the shed and never bought another one.

Back in Seminole County, locals were so outraged that there was talk of a lynching. But Bud Alday, Ned's youngest brother, spoke out against it. Eventually, the prisoners were moved to the state penitentiary in Atlanta for their own safety.

Evil had followed me north.

Nothing seemed right. I spent a lot of time reading books that summer. I often felt sick. The stench from the rotting produce was overwhelming and made it hard to breathe.

The regular customers knew what had happened, so each time they came by, they spoke condolences and prayers. Though the lights were always on at the market, that summer they seemed to dim. The mood was more subdued than I ever remembered it. The painted ladies of the evening, with their red lips, seemed more sad than sinful.

I spent that summer at the market alone with my memories and frightened by my new ability to imagine evil. Sin had new depths, and depravity had new meaning. I had no protection from the darkness that lurked nearby.

My big brothers and earthly protectors were gone.

My heavenly Protector couldn't be trusted.

God seemed useless to me now.

✦　✦　✦

Maybe Bud Alday would have made a different decision about the lynching if he had known then how slow justice would move. Carl Isaacs would be on death row for thirty years before he was executed, Wayne Coleman and George Dungee would serve life in prison, and Billy Isaacs would be released in 1994 for cooperating with the authorities. But it took at least two trials and countless appeals before any of that happened. Many folks felt that justice was never really served.

In the end, the murders that came to be known as the Alday Massacre left everyone in Seminole County feeling violated.

✦ ✦ ✦

As my family left Donalsonville late that August and headed back to Plantersville to get ready for school, I sat with my head in my hands, staring out the car window. I still had more questions than answers—especially about God. What had been his role in all this?

When we passed a church with a graveyard behind it, I turned to watch it out the back window. It grew smaller and smaller, and I thought of another church with a graveyard in back. Though I never wanted to see it, I knew six coffins were buried in the dirt behind the church that the Alday family had built. As I watched the church we passed continue to shrink in the distance, I figured it out.

God doesn't exist.

It was suddenly so obvious to me. He didn't care because he wasn't there!

The epiphany didn't surprise me; it only surprised me that it had taken me so long to figure it out. I had figured out that Santa wasn't real when I was eight.

When we crossed over the county line, I took one last look out the back window.

The church was gone.

And so was God.

He had died and was buried with the bloodstained bodies of my cousins.

Chapter 7
ACADEMIC IDOLS

✦

I always assumed I would grow up to be a farmer. Farming is what men in my family did. God told Adam to till the soil, and that same career advice had been in my family ever since. It was man's first and oldest line of work, and for most of my life, it had been my *only* choice. It had been ingrained in me that farming was a sacred profession where hard work and faith united in a fruitful marriage. But now that I had left God behind, farming had lost its appeal.

The summer after the Alday family massacre was a turning point for me. I started lying to my parents, telling them I was going to church with my girlfriend when the truth was I wasn't going at all. That's also when I decided I was going to college—not to get an education but to get off the farm. Though I had been saving money for college since I was eight, I'd always assumed I would be like my dad—an educated farmer who returned to the family land. But now, I wanted to get away from the family that was so rooted in faith.

I couldn't wait to go away to school and get a job that was indoors. I didn't want to spend the rest of my life thinking about the elements and who controlled them. I wanted a job that had air-conditioning in the summer and heat in the winter. If God hadn't intervened when we needed him most, why should I spend the rest of my life working for him?

Instead, I would be a scientist; I would deal in the world of facts and evidence, not faith.

Books had always been an escape for me, but now they became an escape *hatch*. They were my emergency evacuation plan whenever I needed to evade a difficult situation. Picking up a book would take me to a new place where my mind was fully occupied and free from the pain of the world I lived in. Whether it was a novel or a textbook for school, I chose books that were based on science and rejected those based on religion. Opening the cover and turning the gently worn pages guaranteed that all I had to think about were the black-and-white ideas in front of me.

Reading not only sequestered me from my family and talk of God, but it also isolated me from my emotions. If there was anything on television or the radio that even hinted at God or faith, I turned it off and went to my bedroom. My parents saw the changes in me. Mom responded by praying longer and more frequently, but neither of my parents asked me about it, which was good, because I didn't want to talk about it.

✦ ✦ ✦

With my new focus on academics, life once again became smooth sailing. School and knowledge were easy gods to worship. They didn't take much time, and they constantly showered accolades on me in the form of good grades. I was a model student in high school, and by my junior year, I had taken all the science classes my school offered. I transferred to a high school in Selma that offered advanced courses in chemistry and physics.

At my new school, I met Mike O'Brien. He shared my height and hair color, but the similarities stopped there. I came from a long line of good ol' Southern Baptist boys from 'Bama. Mike's family was Irish Catholic from up north.

Despite our differences, we became fast friends when we learned we both planned to attend the University of Alabama in Tuscaloosa the following year.

"I'm going to apply for an Air Force scholarship," Mike said.

Mike's dad had been a pilot in the US Air Force. Though I had never flown in an airplane, I was intrigued with the idea, so when Mike suggested that I also apply, it didn't take me long to agree. Being a fighter pilot was better than not having a career plan, and a scholarship would be really helpful in paying for college.

A few weeks after turning in our applications, Mike and I were notified that we had both received full-ride scholarships. Unfortunately for Mike, he'd have to settle for being an engineer. He hadn't passed the eyesight test, and he wasn't eligible for one of the fifty pilot scholarships granted that year. But I'd passed my physical with flying colors and was on my way to becoming a pilot.

In exchange for studying science and my future service, the Air Force agreed to pay for my tuition and books and to give me a stipend of one hundred dollars a month for two years. At that point, they'd reevaluate to make sure I was on target before they renewed my scholarship for the next two years. I was beyond excited!

The next fall, at age eighteen, Mike and I headed off to the University of Alabama, where we would be roommates. I felt invincible. My life had a plan, and my education was paid for. Unemotional, unattached, and determined to make my own way in the world, I had everything I needed to be successful—a strong academic record, college savings, and an Air Force scholarship. I couldn't wait to fly into my future.

✦ ✦ ✦

"How many hours do you want to take?" the clerk asked.

I shuffled through my enrollment papers, looking for the answer. I had no idea. "Um, I'm not sure. How many should I take?"

Her look told me all I needed to know: I was wasting her time.

"Um, let me find out, and I'll come back," I said, looking at the long line of impatient freshmen waiting to register.

I slipped outside, found a pay phone, and called home. "Dad, how many classes am I supposed to take?"

"At Auburn, I took twenty to twenty-two hours," he said.

"Thanks!" I said and rushed to the back of the long line.

By the time I made it back to the clerk, I was prepared. The Air Force required us to major in a hard science—physics, chemistry, or engineering. I decided to start with a chemistry class because that had been my favorite in high school. Plus, Mike was taking it, so I would know someone in my class. I also signed up for a few English classes. I loved the written word and thought that studying it would be a nice break from my science classes.

For the first few weeks, I enjoyed my classes and thought I was doing well. Then came the first chemistry exam. Mike and I studied together, but the test was challenging. I found myself changing answers several times. When I turned it in, I wasn't sure if my paper had more pencil marks or erasures on it. The tests came back a few days later and confirmed my worst suspicions. I got a fifty-eight. It was my first college test, and I was already failing. I knew I had to do something quickly if I wanted to keep my scholarship. I made an appointment to visit with the professor later that afternoon. When I showed up, he seemed glad to see me.

"I think I'm in the wrong class," I told him. "I need you to sign this form, so I can drop it."

"What makes you say that?" he asked.

"My test score was a fifty-eight."

"You got the second highest score on the test. The average was forty!"

Surprised by his response, we chatted a few minutes longer. The class was designed to weed out students who weren't really interested in chemistry as a major. If I stuck with it, he assured me I'd do well.

When I got back to the dorm and found Mike, I learned he'd been equally concerned; he'd gotten a fifty-two. I told him the good news, and we decided to celebrate with drinks.

We went to a local bar called Down the Hatch, where all our drinks lived up to the establishment's name—they went down the hatch. While we were there, our chemistry professor walked in and asked if he could join us. From then on, we'd regularly see him at the bars and have a drink or two together. One night, he asked me if I would like to be his research assistant. I agreed. Though it didn't pay anything, the benefits made up for it. We'd do a little research, and then we'd hit the bars for drinks.

Chemistry was a combination of physics and math, wrapped up in a nice little scientific bow, and the more I learned about it, the clearer it became. It wasn't long before I declared chemistry as my major and English as my minor. In my second year of college, I took organic chemistry and really enjoyed it. The professor saw my passion for the subject, so he asked me to help him design and create a molecule based on his doctoral thesis. It was all very abstract—like learning a new language—but I was happy to embrace the new worlds that were opening to me.

✦ ✦ ✦

I felt as though I had a more educated view of the world at school than I'd had growing up in Plantersville. My work in chemistry and the other science classes, like biology and physics, only enhanced this feeling. As I studied the origins of life, I began rejecting the things my parents had taught me. *They're just not enlightened*, I told myself. Chemistry and science accounted for everything that religion explained, only the sciences had documented proof.

My beliefs were further reinforced as I began to identify with my dad's brother, Clyde. Uncle Clyde had a master's degree in mathematics and was a vice president at IBM during the sixties. He had made a great deal of money, always had new cars, and belonged to the local country club. But he was the social outsider in the family because he was an intellectual and an agnostic who didn't share our religious beliefs. He had put his faith not in God but in science and mathematics. At family gatherings, he was the one who always won the argument—now I knew why. My studies had confirmed that *Uncle Clyde* was the one who had it right. If I needed further proof, all I had to do was look at the material success that Clyde had—and that my other family members lacked.

I began to think of my family as misguided and possibly ignorant. It wasn't their fault that they didn't know the truth; they had never studied science. They were country bumpkins who had faith in God because they didn't know any better. I didn't want to be like them. I wanted to be successful like Uncle Clyde; and for me, success would start with my first ascent into the blue skies behind the controls of a fighter jet.

✦　✦　✦

But gravity brought me crashing back down to earth. Two years into college I was required to reapply for my scholarship. It was a mere formality. I had met all the requirements, and I was doing well in school. There was no reason for it not to be renewed. However, when I went to take the physical, I got stopped at the last station.

"Can you read that line again?" the doctor asked.

I did, but he didn't seem satisfied.

"One more time, please," he said, this time covering my other eye.

I had a class to get to, and I was getting impatient. I read it again, this time with irritation in my voice.

The doctor removed the instrument that covered my eye and set it on the tray. "I'm sorry. You didn't pass the physical. Your eyesight isn't good enough to be a pilot."

"That's not possible!" I said. "Two years ago, my eyesight was fine!"

He shrugged. "Things change. I'm sorry. I'm afraid it means you are no longer eligible for an Air Force pilot scholarship. We can fit you with glasses, and you can be a navigator. There may be other career opportunities available to you in the Air Force, but you can't be a pilot."

"Why would I want to be in the Air Force and not be a pilot? That's stupid!" I said. I was hurt. My life for the past two and a half years had been planned around flying through the clouds. Now after one eye test, I was grounded.

"Should we fit you for glasses?" the doctor asked.

"No, thank you," I said. "I don't want to be a navigator."

I returned to campus completely devastated. *What am I supposed to do now?* I knew I was doing well enough academically and would have choices, but I was clueless as to what they were. Even if I had a plan, how would I pay for it without the scholarship? I was as lost as ever. I needed wisdom, so I did the only thing I knew to do in those desperate circumstances.

I set up an appointment with my academic advisor.

✦ ✦ ✦

My advisor was a sociology professor who had been exiled from Iran. Over the past two years, we'd discovered that we had a lot in common. Because of his departure from his home country and resettlement in America, he had lost many loved ones, and those losses had affected his life in profound ways.

In his office, I sat down across the desk from him as we talked, he in his Arabic accent and me in my slow Southern drawl. I told him what had happened at my physical and how my scholarship had been taken away.

"So, my friend, now that you can't fly, what are you going to do next year when you graduate?" he asked.

"I'm in my second year. Next year will only be my third year," I reminded him.

"Yes, I know. Next year, you will graduate."

I was confused. "I thought this was a four-year school."

"It is. But you, my friend, have taken more than twenty hours each semester, so you will graduate *next* year."

That's when I remembered that early phone call to my dad. When Dad was at Auburn, they were on the quarter system, and twenty hours would have been the equivalent of fifteen hours on the semester system. When I registered for classes, I was too green to realize that my university was on the semester system. Two years later, I had taken enough classes each semester to graduate a whole year early!

"Why didn't you tell me this before?" I asked, knowing he'd signed off on my schedule each semester.

"Well, because your grades were good and you worked hard, I thought it agreed with you. So what do you want to do?" he asked.

"That's the problem. I don't know," I said quietly.

"What about being an engineer?" he asked with a gentle smile.

Engineers didn't have a lot of interaction with other people. I liked hanging out in bars with my friends and professors, so I wanted a career where I could be involved with the public. "Nah," I said. "I'm kind of a people person."

"Maybe you would like dental school. Good job, good pay, good family life."

Growing up in the country, we didn't have access to dentists or doctors. I had never known a dentist, so I had no idea what that life would entail. But recently the dental and medical schools had been on campus recruiting students to take the entrance exams for their programs. Time was short, and it was the best idea I had, so later that day, I signed up for the Dental Admission Test (DAT).

I had settled on a new plan. I would be a dentist.

✦   ✦   ✦

A few weeks later, I was back in my advisor's office with the DAT results. The first half of the exam was academic, testing my knowledge of chemistry, physics, and biology. My scores on that half were extremely high. But the second half of the exam was based on visual perception. Because I was poor, I had not gone to the eye doctor to get eyeglasses or have my vision problems corrected.

I had failed the second half of the test. Dentistry was no longer an option.

I squirmed in the chair as my advisor looked over my results, and I waited for his verdict. "You did very well on the first half of the test," he said. "But I can see you had problems with the visual portion. Take the MCAT," he said, referring to the entrance exam required for medical school. "It doesn't have any of that visual stuff on it."

Just what the world needs, I thought. *A blind doctor from Plantersville, home of kudzu and family farms.* But what choice did I have?

I took the MCAT, and this time I hit the half-court shot at the buzzer—the scores were better than expected. I celebrated with dinner at my advisor's house.

I was going to medical school. The only problem was, how would I pay for it?

Chapter 8
THE LADY OF THE LAB

✦

The chemists I hung out with in college were all agnostics or athe-
ists who never even mentioned God. My friends from my English
lit classes talked about God only in a sort of Beowulf tone, not in
any kind of personal or intimate way. One of the smartest people I
knew was my philosophy professor. He was an atheist and almost
anti-God. When the subject of religion or God came up, he would
simply respond, "If you're smart enough, you can figure it out."

And I had.

God didn't exist.

I thrived on getting people to agree with me, and I had successfully surrounded myself with people who thought like I did, further
proving that I was right. I was sure I knew all the answers—and
God wasn't in them.

I had become an intellectual snob.

But academia was not a very comforting religion. If I knew the
answers, I was rewarded with a pat on the back. If I didn't, no one
cared. I felt no emotional satisfaction at the end of the day for a
job well done.

I could find no larger purpose in life either.

✦ ✦ ✦

From 1976 through 1977, my first two undergraduate years in
Tuscaloosa, I roomed with my friend from high school, Mike

O'Brien. We had a mutual friend who was also named Mike, and he became my roommate during my third year in college. Mike Ledet was a Cajun from Louisiana, and he taught me how to drink whiskey from a bottle. Both O'Brien and Ledet were Catholic and often attended mass on Saturday nights.

"Come with us," Ledet said one night.

"I'm not interested," I said. "I don't really believe in God."

"Do you believe in beer?" Ledet asked.

"You know I do!"

After that first chemistry test celebration, I had often frequented the local bars, carousing and behaving badly. Why not? There was nothing in my belief system that prevented me from acting that way. The only thing that slowed me down was my lack of beer money.

"Just come with us," O'Brien said. "You can sleep during mass if you want, but afterward the priest has a keg!"

Suddenly, I could see the appeal of Catholicism. If this was what good Catholic boys did, I wanted to learn more. So I started attending the liturgy on Saturday nights. But I didn't *sleep*. I actually paid attention to the service and to the teachings.

After mass we would drink beer, go to the movies, play cards, and roll dice with the priest. It was the antithesis of everything I had experienced growing up in the Baptist church and not at all what I was used to. It was refreshing to experience a religious system that didn't take the fun out of life.

✦   ✦   ✦

For most students who enrolled in medical school, being a doctor was their Plan A, and they had spent years saving for it. For me, it was Plan C. The idea came up so suddenly that I didn't even have the resources to apply to medical school. I had to be strategic with my applications to ensure I got in somewhere, so I limited my choices to the two in-state schools. I already had two strikes against me. I was young (graduating college after three years instead of four), and there were more qualified candidates from my school—some of whom hadn't been accepted anywhere. So I was ecstatic when the medical school at the University of Alabama called at the last minute and said, "We had a slot open up, and we'd like you to join us next week."

Medical school was expensive, and I didn't have the money to pay for it. During the summers, I had sold books door-to-door and done well, but it wasn't nearly the amount of money I would need for four years of medical school. I researched my options and eventually signed up with the National Health Service Corps. In exchange for my agreeing to work as a primary care physician in an underserved community once I graduated, they would provide me with scholarships and loans to help pay my way through medical school.

It might not have been my Plan A, but it was a good Plan C.

✦ ✦ ✦

Birmingham was hot on my first day at the University of Alabama Medical School in July of 1979, and the pungent and slightly sweet scent of formaldehyde hit our nostrils as soon as we entered the lab. One hundred sixty live bodies and thirty dead ones were spread throughout the room. The live ones were nervous because they had never been so close to dead ones.

Most of us had never seen so many bodies or touched a cadaver, let alone dissected one. As we moved closer to the cadavers, the scent was overpowering, irritating our eyes and nostrils. Just when we thought we couldn't take it anymore, two professors entered the room. The one in charge had long hair, graying at the temples, and a matching gray beard. He wore wire-rimmed glasses and reminded me of an aging hippie. But he spoke in hushed tones with all the reverence of a priest at a wake.

"Welcome to Gross Anatomy. I am Dr. Jerry Brown, and together with Dr. Hand, we will teach you many things in this class. However, the most important lesson you will learn is how to honor and respect those who have donated their bodies so you can grow up and become doctors."

His authoritative air unnerved us as he reminded us that families had sacrificed so we could learn medicine. "The least you can do is honor their sacrifice by treating their bodies with dignity. No foul play will be tolerated," he said, trying to make eye contact with all one hundred sixty of us.

"Two years ago, a couple of med students decided to take their cadaver for a drive. They're no longer in medical school," he said, pausing to let his words sink in.

We stood at attention while he continued with the rules and regulations of the lab. It reminded me of a revival preacher I once heard presenting a sermon on the Ten Commandments. "You can do this, but you can't do that. You can be here, but don't be here alone. You can touch this, but never touch that!"

Once the rules were thoroughly explained, Dr. Brown, assisted by Dr. Hand, peeled back the cloths from the body in the front of the room. With the solemnness of a religious ceremony, he pulled back a section of the pleated coverings to reveal just a portion of the body that lay on the dissection table—the altar of his anatomy class. The only exposed area of the cadaver was the part he was referencing, so he was constantly rearranging the body cloths as he moved from head to toe.

He first instructed us in the correct way to hold a scalpel. We couldn't even do that right at first. But with practice, we learned. Over the next few months, we worked our way up from making an initial incision to dissecting muscles, arteries, nerves, veins, and the intersection of muscles into bone. As instructed, we would carefully drape and undrape the body, revealing only what was necessary to do our work.

"This is not only a matter of respect to the ladies and gentlemen who sacrificed their bodies for your education, but it is a practical matter," Dr. Brown often reminded us. "The formaldehyde-soaked cloths keep the bodies from drying out."

The rituals of the lab were more liturgical than most churches I had attended. Each day, from the front of the room, Dr. Brown would use hushed tones and an air of awe to demonstrate the day's assignment, simultaneously making all of us first-year students marvel at the sheer amount of information that he knew—and we didn't. We were mere mortals while he was a kind of god, and we knew it.

In six years, this was the closest I'd come to reverence.

✦　✦　✦

During our lessons in the lab, we worked in groups of five or six, always with the same cadaver. My group referred to our cadaver as "The Lady of the Lab." The name reminded me of the respect that Jimmy and Jerry had always shown women by calling them "ladies." They even referred to prostitutes as *ladies* of the evening.

The Lady of the Lab taught me much about the inner workings of anatomy, but for every question she answered, new ones emerged. The day we finished working on the torso and started working on the head and neck was an important one for me. Prior to that, the Lady of the Lab seemed physically similar to other animals. From an anatomical perspective, she could just as easily have been a monkey or another primate. But once we moved to the head, I could see that the human anatomy was different from anything else on the planet. The day we dissected an eye was like a religious experience for me. I was awestruck by the complexity involved in being able to see and process images in the human mind. *Where did this come from?* I asked myself more than once.

Looking at the inner workings of the human body, I found that the Lady of the Lab proved to be evidence of something greater than a set of systems. She was more than a dead body or a medical school cadaver, and she wasn't a random accident of time and space.

She was a work of art.

And art required an artist.

It was obvious to me that there was something different about humans. We are so much more complex than any other animal. How could this marvelous lady come into being by accident? How could anyone say that *I* randomly came to be? I was intrigued, fascinated, and confused all at the same time. But mostly, I was curious.

I was also being humbled by my own ignorance.

As students, we were asked to retain enormous amounts of information. I went from reading books of less than three hundred pages to tomes of more than a thousand pages, with the expectation that I would recall every detail in all of them. And it wasn't just me. The best student in my first-year classes didn't know it all; he had a grade point average of only ninety.

Within medicine, the rules changed with new research. What was good for you last year was found to cause cancer the next year. The sheer volume of information in the medical world intimidated me. If med school taught me anything, it taught me that it was impossible for one person to know everything.

The more I became aware of how much I didn't know, the more my ignorance started to chip away at the arrogance I had displayed in college. If there was so much to learn about medicine—my chosen field of study—there had to be an infinite number of things I didn't know about other parts of our existence. If the world I could see and study was this difficult to understand, how much more the one I couldn't?

My philosophy professor in college had said, "If you're smart enough, you'll figure it out." I was pretty sure none of us were that smart. I was beginning to understand that the universe was so complex that there was no way *anyone* could know everything.

Opening the cadaver's head opened mine, too. She was a body of evidence that something greater than chance was at work. The Lady of the Lab made it obvious that whether or not we *evolved*, we were also *created*.

Could I have made a mistake by denying the existence of a creator?

I was too embarrassed to ask these kinds of questions of my peers or my professors; I had to find out on my own.

✦ ✦ ✦

The faith of my childhood was as familiar and ordinary to me as my own skin. But that skin had been charred by my cousins' deaths. When the blackened pieces sloughed off, the only thing left was raw, oozing wounds.

In one of my medical school classes, I learned that burn victims are treated with a saline solution that is similar in its chemical makeup to tears. Apparently, tears not only heal emotionally but physically. I thought about all the tears I'd seen in Seminole County and how, perhaps, there had been a healing purpose in them. I had cried initially, but after I left Donalsonville, I had refused to shed more tears.

What would have happened if I had let the tears continue?

I knew it would take more than a few tears for things to be right between God and me, *if* there was a God. Like a burn victim who receives a skin graft, I would have to have something entirely new— a faith graft—to restore my relationship with God. *But how would that happen? Would I even want it to?*

When I discovered that a couple of my medical school friends were Catholic, I started attending mass with them. If the answers to life's questions weren't in my Baptist roots or in my science notebooks, perhaps the Catholic Church held the answers. Maybe the Catholic Church could be my faith donor.

I started to badger my friends with questions. Tired of my insatiable curiosity, one day after mass my friends took me to the priest's office.

"I'm Father Frank," the young priest said, introducing himself to me.

He invited me in, and I pulled up a chair. During our conversation, he told me a little about his background. He wasn't Catholic by birth; in fact, he'd been an intellectual who had come to know God on his own without the influence of his family. I wanted to know more, and we set up another time to talk.

At another meeting I said, "I've denied the existence of a creator for years, but now I'm seeing evidence of one. I think there's something here that science can't explain. The evidence suggests it. It might not be anything, but I think there has to be more than what we see. I'm wondering if I've made a mistake in denying God's existence." He was intrigued with my story and encouraged my questions. He suggested several books on faith and science, but he also invited me to a catechism class he was teaching. I accepted his invitation and began attending regularly.

I was open to learning more.

Chapter 9

BEAUTIFUL BLONDE DATE
FROM OUT OF STATE

✦

After I signed the lease, the landlord handed me a bucket of paint. "Here. You'll need this."

"Why?" I asked.

"To hold the walls together," he said, pushing my check deeper into his pocket. Apparently, the first chore in my new apartment would be to paint the walls.

My apartment was in one of two old buildings connected by a courtyard. Both buildings had been built in the 1930s and had wood floors, arched doors, and steam heat. One building was a halfway house; the one I lived in was rented to students. A few of my friends from medical school also lived there, along with other graduate students. I shouldn't have expected much; the common lament among those who lived in the complex was that we were all broke. Rent was only $100 a month, including utilities.

But there were some nice features—like the courtyard between the buildings. It was well maintained by residents of the halfway house, and fragrant flower beds lined the walkways. A community grill stood in the center of the commons. In the evenings, someone would fire it up, and that became an invitation for the rest of us to bring hot dogs, hamburgers, steaks, or whatever we could afford to a sort of BYOD—bring your own dinner—in the courtyard. Occasionally, as I had time or needed a break from studying, I would participate.

One night a friend of mine, a graduate student in nutrition, invited some of her friends to join her for dinner. As I walked by, I could see them talking and laughing while they grilled their hot dogs. I had planned to go back to my apartment, but when I saw the blonde, I did a double take. She was the most gorgeous woman I'd ever seen. I turned around and joined them.

My friend introduced us. "Reggie, this is Karen. She's getting her master's in nutrition."

I took one look at Karen's winsome blue eyes and probably said something really clever like, "How are you?" or "Nice to meet you." Somehow, we made it past the awkward introduction and started talking. I asked her about her classes and learned that she had received her undergraduate degree at Southwest Missouri State.

"Why there?" I asked.

"I'm originally from St. Louis—"

I didn't hear the rest of her explanation. All I could think was *Wow, a blonde, blue-eyed babe from out of state!*

For as long as I could remember, my grandmother had told all her grandkids not to marry someone unless he or she was from out of state. She saw the children of cousins who had intermarried and how they'd had health problems. "We don't allow our cows to breed local bulls; why would we allow our children to do it?" she'd say.

Growing up and going to school in Alabama, I hadn't found a lot of out-of-state options, so I'd always dated whomever I wanted, regardless of their origin. However, the longer Karen and I talked, the more smitten I became. She was unlike any other woman I had ever met. Not only was she beautiful, but she was a fascinating conversationalist. She was the kind of girl I dreamed about—and being from St. Louis, the kind Grandma would approve of.

"We have a Gross Anatomy test on Friday afternoon, and some of my classmates and I are going to Flanagan's for a party afterward. Would you like to go with me?"

Her smile was the only answer I needed, but she also gave me a hesitant, "Okay."

My heart skipped a beat.

✦ ✦ ✦

I was in a good mood on Friday when I arrived at Karen's place. I had passed my Gross Anatomy test, and now I was excited to show her off to my friends—I was sure to have the most beautiful date at the party.

Flanagan's was a combination restaurant and bar. It also had a dance floor with a disco ball. "Do you like to dance?" I asked Karen as I helped her into the car.

"I love to dance!"

And she did.

We spent the night dancing a lot and drinking a little. I pulled out my best John Travolta moves, and she let me twirl her around on the floor. As we talked, I realized how different she was from many of the Southern women I had dated. Most of them wanted to get an MRS degree that had a matching DR to go with it. But Karen wasn't like that.

"I don't really like to date doctors," she said, "because most of them are rude."

It was my reminder to be on my best behavior.

I noticed that some of my classmates at Flanagan's were drinking a lot. But since Karen had only one drink all night, I held off, too, wanting to make a good first impression. It was a smart decision. By the end of the night, several of my friends required designated drivers.

I drove Karen home, helped her out of the car, and walked her to the apartment door. I was proud of myself for being such a gentleman. I knew how to treat a lady on a first date, and I'd had enough first dates to know that the ladies appreciated my good manners. As we neared Karen's apartment door, I hoped she'd show me *her* appreciation with a good-night kiss.

But Karen was hard to read, so I took a safer approach. "I had a great time. What would you like to do next weekend?"

"I understand from our conversation tonight that you're not a believer."

I must have looked puzzled, because she continued to explain.

"You don't believe in God, and I'm a Christian," she said.

I was confused. *What does that have to do with anything?* We had talked about God and religion a bit. *Had I said something?* I recalled telling her that I was an agnostic. It was a relatively new term for me. For more than six years, I'd been an atheist, but the questions that had recently been raised by the Lady of the Lab, plus the sheer quantity of information in the universe, left me doubting whether one could ever know whether or not God existed. *Had that offended her in some way?*

"Was it something I said?" If so, I hoped I could clear it up for her.

She sighed.

"I know you're going to be a doctor one day, and you're a very nice man. But I really don't see our lives traveling the same path spiritually. So I don't see us having a relationship beyond tonight."

She turned toward the door and started fishing in her purse for her keys. I had to do something quick to salvage this, or I would lose her forever. I thought about telling her the truth.

You're right. I'm not a Christian. I think there may be a God out there, but it's just an intellectual debate for me right now. Though it was all true, I knew I couldn't say that. Nor could I tell her that I used to believe and how I'd experienced God in the land and in the lake. Or how he'd once whispered in my dreams that he would give me a pony, which he did. Because if I told her that, I'd also have to tell her that he was heartless. If God existed, he not only gave little boys ponies, but he also allowed unspeakable things to happen to their cousins. And that wasn't first-date material.

Karen found her keys to the apartment and put the key in the lock. It was my last chance to say something, so I blurted out the first thing that crossed my mind: "Well, my parents are Christians!"

As soon as the words left my mouth, I knew they were stupid.

So did she.

She looked at me and rolled her eyes. "Exactly what I said. You don't understand. Thank you for the evening. Good night."

With that, she was gone.

I walked back to my car, and I kicked myself for saying something so dumb and for letting her get away. She was such a lovely lady.

Wow, Mom would have really liked her.

✦ ✦ ✦

As the questions continued to surface in my life, I felt a sense of inner conflict.

Everything I'd ever wanted and wished for was coming true. Though medical school hadn't been my first career choice, I had embraced it and was earning good grades in all my classes. I could date any girl I wanted—except for Karen—and I had lots of friends among both my peers and my professors. My future annual income would likely be higher than anything my own father had ever dreamed about. I was the definition of success.

Yet, I often felt empty, purposeless.

I couldn't get Karen out of my mind, not because I wanted to date her—I knew that was over—but because she was the first person to challenge me spiritually since the Alday Massacre. Karen's cold words that night forced me to ask, *Where am I going with all this? What is my endgame?*

Karen was also the first girl I'd met who cared more about my present soul than my future pocketbook. Her conversation with me that night forced me to care too. Either Karen was right or I was right, but we couldn't *both* be right.

Life went on, but the questions lingered.

✦ ✦ ✦

Other than passing her on campus, I hadn't seen Karen in more than a month. One day in early June, I was sitting outside my apartment when she pulled up and began unloading boxes from her car. "Do you need help?" I asked.

She did.

As she piled my arms full of boxes, she explained that she was moving into the apartment of a mutual friend—subleasing it for the summer—so she could save money. She asked if I could help her with her furniture on Saturday, and I agreed. I called my friend John and said, "Remember that girl who doesn't like me? Well, she's moving into my complex, and she needs our help moving her things."

A few days later, John and I helped Karen move her furniture up several flights of stairs. While we worked, Karen and I had time to talk. She told me she was helping Briarwood Presbyterian Church develop an on-campus ministry, and she was also leading a Bible study with girls from Samford University. "We're trying to prepare our hearts to conform to Jesus."

"Oh, that's interesting," I said. I wasn't all that curious about the girls' Bible study, but I was very interested in Karen. After everything was moved into her apartment and John had gone home, I offered to take her out to dinner to celebrate her new place.

"I don't think so, but thanks," she said all too quickly.

I wasn't done trying. A few nights later, I knocked on her door and asked if she wanted to hang out.

"The girls are coming over for my Bible study tonight," she said.

I tried again a few nights later.

"I have a lot of studying to do," she said.

"That's okay, we can study together," I offered. But she turned me down again.

The next day I saw her parking her car, or maybe I waited for her outside until I saw her parking her car. She had her books and a couple of bags of groceries. "Do you need help?" I asked, grabbing a bag.

"That would be great." I walked with her to her apartment, and I could tell she seemed tense.

"Is everything okay?" I asked.

"I've just got a lot to do. Not only do I have tests coming up, but I need to memorize parts of the book of Philippians before my Bible study on Wednesday."

"I'm really good at memorization; we have to do a lot of it in medical school. Would you like me to help? I could quiz you."

She studied my too-eager face for a minute. I could see she looked tired, but she still looked gorgeous to me. Finally, she sighed and said, "Fine. Come back at seven."

I practically skipped back to my apartment; I was so excited. I had worn her down! I showed up promptly at seven, and she handed me a Bible. For the next ninety minutes, this agnostic read Scripture to her or listened to her quoting it back to me. It wasn't lost on me that Philippians is one of the most grace-filled books of the Bible. It also wasn't lost on me that Karen was beautiful, inside and out.

✦　✦　✦

For the next several weeks, every couple of days or so I would go over to Karen's apartment to help her study. Occasionally, I would ask her questions about what she believed and why. During this time, I was also attending catechism classes with Father Frank, so I was learning two different approaches to faith: one from a Presbyterian Bible study leader and the other from a Catholic priest. But I still hadn't found a way to reconcile why God had destroyed my cousins' lives in such a heinous way when they had been such good people who had loved him so much.

Karen listened as I ranted, raved, and railed against the foundations of her faith. She patiently answered my questions, and she promised to pray for me. But it didn't change our relationship at all.

One night I saw her in the parking lot saying good-bye to the girls from her Bible study. I set down the books I was carrying to shake hands with each girl as she introduced me. I was on my way back to my apartment when I remembered the books and turned back to get them. As I approached, I heard her saying to the girls, "Please pray for Reggie. He's an atheist and kind of a *stalker*."

I stopped in the shadows. I couldn't believe she'd called me that. I understood being called a stalker, but I was certainly no atheist. I was an *agnostic*!

I didn't let her lack of understanding stop me, and I continued to try to spend time with her. One night after I had asked her some hard questions, she turned the tables and asked me a few questions about my background. I told her that I had been raised in a family of believers and that I had once been a believer too. I even told her about Tex the pony and how God told me that he would be mine.

Then she nonchalantly asked me a question. "Reggie, why are you so mad at God?"

She asked it the same way someone else would have asked about the heat bearing down on Alabama that June. Her question caught me off guard, and I blurted out the first thing that came to mind, "Because he failed me."

Then I spilled out my whole story. I told her about my summers with Jimmy and Jerry and how they were my moral compass while I grew up and learned to be a man. I told her about how good they were, how they respected women, and how they loved the Lord. Then I told her about the massacre and what happened to them, their brother, their father, their uncle, and Mary.

"I can't believe in a God who would allow this to happen. These were good Christian people who loved him, and he didn't protect them."

"I'm so sorry," she said softly. "I'm praying for you, and the girls are praying for you too."

On the way back to my apartment that night, I thought about her question. She was right; I was mad at God. He was supposed to be our heavenly Father and protect and take care of us. I knew from catechism classes and other conversations that people who hadn't grown up with a loving father sometimes struggled to understand a loving God. That wasn't my problem. In fact, my problem was exactly the opposite.

I remembered the Christmas I was so disappointed that I didn't have a present. My earthly father did everything he could to make it right for me. I had watched him go against his natural inclination financially, just to repair a hole in my heart. He had compromised his own values and made great sacrifices so his son wouldn't cry on Christmas.

If God, my supposed *heavenly* Father, were truly omniscient, omnipresent, and omnipotent—as I had been taught growing up— why couldn't he do at least as much as my *earthly* father?

In my mind, I had every right to be mad at him.

✦ ✦ ✦

As in all other areas of my life, catechism classes with Father Frank brought more questions than answers. Every time Father Frank would present a statement of faith by the Catholic Church, I would question it. Apparently, I was becoming a disruption. Father Frank asked me to meet him for lunch to talk about it.

He peppered his food, and then I peppered him with more questions. Finally he said, "Have you considered going to Catholic seminary? The questions you ask are so deep, they really need to be answered in a seminary."

It was another intriguing question. Perhaps if I went to seminary, I would be able to find answers there. But at this point in my life, I had obligations to medical school and to pay back the loans that had financed it. The clincher was when he said, "You should consider becoming a priest."

"I think I'll just stick with the doctor thing," I said. I knew I would never be able to take a vow of celibacy. "But thanks. And I'll try to stop asking so many questions."

A few weeks and a few more catechism classes later, I finished the class. "You passed," Father Frank joked. Then in all seriousness, he said, "I've planned your confirmation for the last Sunday in July, in case you'd like to invite anyone."

Between Father Frank and Karen, I was getting fed theologically. The problem was that I was getting so much nutrition that I didn't know how to take it all in and digest it. I had gotten the education I needed to convert to Catholicism, but at the same time, I didn't really know what I believed. I'm sure Father Frank wanted me to be confirmed for the same reason he wanted me to go to seminary—he felt it would draw me closer to God. And I understood that. I had every reason to be confirmed into the Catholic Church, and only one reason not to: I still didn't believe in a God who could be known.

+ + +

I decided to take a break during the Fourth of July weekend and go camping. Birmingham is unbearably hot in July, and classes would shut down over the holiday. Driving north into the mountains of Tennessee seemed like a good idea, so I chose a place in the mountains near Sparta, Tennessee. Camping by myself was one way for me to get away from it all, get back to nature, and spend time thinking.

A few nights before I was supposed to leave, Karen gave me a gift. I was stunned that she had thought about me enough to give me the time of day, let alone get me a gift. The only time we talked was when I helped her study. My hands shook as I unwrapped the package. It was a book, *Mere Christianity* by C. S. Lewis.

"I don't want you to hate God," she said. "When you deny him, you're just denying the truth because of the pain you've been through. C. S. Lewis struggled with the same pain and many of the same questions you struggle with. I hope reading this will help you to not hate God." Then she encouraged me to pray, "God, if you're real, make yourself known to me."

I thought it was an unusual prayer, but I promised I would try it.

The book sat on my coffee table for several days while I considered what to do with it. As I was packing for my trip, I saw it again and thought maybe I should read it while I was gone. I picked it up, and at the last minute, I also grabbed the green leather Bible off the shelf. Recognizing how far I'd strayed from my childhood faith, Mom had sent me the Bible while I was in college. But I'd never read it. Now I tossed both books into my pack and closed it.

The next day, I headed off for the wilderness, completely clueless as to how my life would be changed when I came back.

Chapter 10
THE DREAM THAT CHANGED MY LIFE

✦

I arrived at the trailhead late on July 3 and spent the night in my car. Around mid-morning on July 4, I left the parking area and began the more than six-hour hike through the plateau to Virgin Falls. Along the way, I passed several waterfalls, caves, and other unique geological formations. An underground stream from a cave forms Virgin Falls. From its opening, the waterfall drops over a one-hundred-ten-foot cliff before it pools and disappears into another cave at the bottom of the sink. Not far from the falls, I located the perfect camping spot, where I could still hear the roar in the distance.

I stopped to breathe it all in, and immediately I felt my stress melting away. The view was amazing. The mist from the waterfall produced some of the most beautiful mountain laurels and ferns I had ever seen. The spray made everything seem so green and fresh. The smell was intoxicating. I couldn't have asked for better weather. It was all blue skies and wilderness. Everything felt pristine, untouched by humans—there wasn't another soul in sight.

I had plenty of time to get my campsite and tent set up before the sun went down. Late in the afternoon, I started a fire; logs crackled, sparks flew, and flames danced. It was my private Fourth of July fireworks. I lay on my back and looked up at the hickory and oak tree canopy that protected me, and I remembered how many times in my youth I had lain in this same position, looking up at the sky. I thought about how my life had changed since I was a boy on the farm in Plantersville. My dreams of flying were dashed because of my eyesight. The dental school idea was another failure. At least I had been doing well in medical school—the epitome of intellectualism—so I should have been enjoying my success. Instead, all I could do was wrestle with my questions about God and long for answers that seemed to be hidden from me.

I sat up, reached into my backpack, and grabbed the book Karen had given me. She'd said that C. S. Lewis had been an intellectual and shared some of my life questions. I wasn't sure how the Narnia guy could know so much, but I was willing to learn. I opened the cover and began reading.

Time passed quickly, and the sun had set long before I closed the back cover. I had been reading the book by firelight and had read it all the way through without stopping.

Finally! Someone had articulated the unresolved questions I had with Christianity. I felt a kinship with C. S. Lewis. He had also believed in the promises of science and the prophets of logic and knowledge; yet he had returned to love and defend the God I had grown up with. *How?* I tried to understand how he had reached that conclusion. *Could I come to that same understanding?*

I reconsidered some of the questions that had nagged me. *Where was God when the Aldays were murdered? Why couldn't he protect them?* Then I asked myself if it was possible that God was even *more* present in tragedy than he was in our ordinary circumstances? If so, why didn't we see or hear him? Could it be that when we most needed him, we were also most likely to turn from him? Could our tears and screams blind us to his presence and deafen our ears to his voice?

This was a new thought for me.

By now, it was pitch-dark. Even though it was late, I wasn't sleepy. I grabbed my flashlight and the only other reading material I had with me—that green leather Bible my mom had sent me. I pulled back the cover, putting the first crease in the smooth spine. The leather actually creaked.

I remembered Karen saying that the Gospel of John was a good place to start, and Lewis had mentioned John in his book. I found it in the index, turned to the page, and began reading.

I expected my reading to bring forth new questions—like everything else in my life did—but this *Living Bible* spoke in such a real and practical way that I was able to read it without stopping. I seemed to have a heightened clarity of what I was reading, and I was able to picture what the writer was saying. I'd never experienced that when I'd read the Bible before.

I wasn't tired, but as soon as I finished the last page of John's Gospel, my eyes closed. Without warning, I fell into a deep sleep. But this slumber was different from any sleep I'd ever experienced. My mind was tumbling, free-falling, like the waterfall nearby. An overwhelming peace filled me, and I felt that everything was right with the world.

✦ ✦ ✦

When my mind stopped tumbling, I opened my eyes to the most fantastical countryside imaginable: everything was vivid and radiant. All of my senses were finely tuned, like I had awakened in some enhanced version of reality. In front of me, a picturesque meadow was filled with vibrantly colored wildflowers. Pops of yellow, orange, red, blue, and indigo swayed with the breeze like living rainbows. The green was the lushest green I'd ever laid eyes on; the hue so saturated, it seemed like a new color to me. The splendor before me was stunning!

I wanted to breathe in the view.

As I did, I inhaled the most fragrant scent, so light and pleasing—like a mixture of citrus and lilac. I held my breath, allowing it to cleanse my insides and open my mind. I heard a trickling noise behind me and turned to see a running stream. Crystal clear blue water flowed over shiny rocks lining the bed and made a tranquil babbling sound. I moved toward the stream, and I felt an icy but refreshing spray, almost like the feeling I got as a boy when I opened the freezer door on a hot Alabama day. The flowing water was a glassy sapphire blue, but surprisingly light and clear when I scooped it into my cupped hands.

Everything felt so real, more intense and tangible than my ordinary life. My senses seemed to awaken and open like a flower to the sun. I could see, hear, touch, smell, and feel things as never before. I didn't feel like I was in a dream; I felt like this was the real life I'd always been searching for. This was *more real* than my life.

I spied a large rock nearby beyond the brook and perched on it to gaze at the magnificence displayed. Everything was so peaceful and serene, and I marveled at it all.

The closest I'd ever come to experiencing anything like this would have been during a warm day in Georgia, when I was young and didn't have a care in the world. But even those rich childhood memories were dim imitations of the brilliant light that now burst from the scene before me.

I didn't have time to think about how I'd gotten there because I heard an unmistakable voice calling me from the distance. It was the voice of someone whom I had once loved and who still loved me. It didn't make an audible sound; instead, it resonated *inside me* and echoed outside, as if I'd heard it with my heart, or maybe my soul. It was easily the most compelling, yet comforting, voice I'd ever heard.

I spun to my right to glance at the person who had spoken to my heart, and I saw a great crowd of people moving toward me. As I scanned the crowd, a cool breeze engulfed me. That's when I recognized them.

Jimmy, Jerry, Mary, Ned, Chester, and Aubrey!

I couldn't believe what I was seeing, but there was no mistaking them. They looked ecstatic. I'd never seen *anyone* as happy as they were. They didn't speak with words, but they seemed to know how much I had struggled with their deaths, and how that trauma had put up a barrier between God and me. In the most kind and loving way possible, they communicated that they weren't the obstacles to my faith. They were there to lift the burden I had been carrying around for so long.

I scanned their faces and could see only joy. Somehow, they made it clear that what had happened to them happened for a reason. They wanted me to know that I wouldn't fully understand until I joined them, but in the meantime, I shouldn't hold it against God. It took less than a millisecond for me to understand: this is where they *belonged*. They had no regrets about their departure from a fallen world. This wasn't their new, spiritual home; this was their *true*, corporeal home.

Seeing and "hearing" from them released me from dark thoughts of their deaths. The weight that had pinned me down for so long had been removed. They were so real, so present, and so very joyful. I had never seen such bliss radiate from a person's face, but the essence of who they were was still apparent. Jimmy and Jerry even seemed to tease each other the way brothers do—in the same way the three of us had done at the farmers market. I wanted to run to them, to join them, and to live in this paradise with them.

I wanted this to be my home too.

Then I saw him.

He inhabited more of a presence in the midst of the crowd than a human form, yet he definitely had human qualities. I couldn't identify his race; he seemed to be a composite of all races, or possibly of a race I'd never seen before. Likewise, he appeared ageless—of every age and none, at the same time. He was unlike anyone I had ever seen before. Even his long hair defied description. It was at once silver, golden, and onyx-colored as it moved in the light. There was almost a glow from behind him, creating the effect of a halo.

Who was this? He was not a man like any other man I had ever known. Everything and everyone around us stopped as he spoke.

"Reggie, why are you running from me? Your friends are here with me in paradise; you can stop running."

That's when I knew. It was *Jesus*.

He communicated with such authority; he spoke Words with

a capital *W*. Yet I couldn't see his mouth moving—I somehow intuited his words. As he spoke, I noticed that the light behind him glowed brighter. His eyes shone like the cool waters of the stream between us. His smile was so reassuring, like the one a loving mother gives to her baby. And inside me, I could feel the warmth of his love wrapping itself around my heart and my soul.

All this happened in an instant. I could only glimpse him in my peripheral vision for the briefest moment; and then his brilliance was too much, and I had to look away.

"I am the one who came for you," he said.

Immediately, I knew what he meant. For more than seven years, I had been wandering aimlessly in a spiritual wilderness. He had come to rescue me from the hate and anger that had trapped me in that wasteland and to bring me back to the faith of my youth. He had come to restore me to him. But I kept my eyes deflected in shame. I felt much the same way I did that Christmas so long ago when my father had humbled himself to give me the gift of a new bicycle.

"Your friends and family are here, and they have been made whole," he said.

I looked again at the crowd and could see he was right. No gunshot wounds showed on the Aldays. There weren't even any scars. In fact, the scars they had while they were alive were no longer visible. Ned had been old and bent from arthritis, yet now he stood tall, strong, and erect. He was healthy and vigorous. Though his appearance had changed drastically, I still recognized him.

They'd all changed. Made whole. Perfect. Childhood scars and teenage blemishes were now replaced with smooth, glowing skin.

Jesus spoke again. "I have a plan for you, but you need to stop running."

I was in awe of him and knew that whatever he said, whatever he asked, I would obey him completely. But my instant devotion was challenged by his next words. "You're going to marry Karen, and together you will have four children. You will be a doctor and practice medicine in rural Tennessee."

Could this be true?

Without a doubt, I knew that he who spoke was the God of the universe. But I also knew that Karen, who barely spoke to me (unless we were studying), was convinced that I was a stalker who was going to hell. She wouldn't date me or even spend any time with me. *Why would she ever consider marrying me?*

He seemed to read my mind.

His final words to me were, "All I have told you will come to pass. All you have to do is trust in me and in my words."

✦ ✦ ✦

I felt a cool breeze flow through my hair, and I woke up. Dawn was breaking over the crest of the mountain, and I could still see the canopy of trees above me. I'd never made it inside the tent; I'd fallen asleep next to the campfire that was now smoldering. Never had I felt so profoundly connected and yet disconnected at the same time.

I tried to remember all that I had seen. I had been on the most incredible journey, one I knew I didn't deserve. When you are in the presence of someone you don't deserve to be in the presence of, your flaws have a way of suddenly being magnified. Everything about me now seemed dirty—not from a day of hiking in the Tennessee wilderness but from years spent in anger, hatred, and sin toward God.

I didn't deserve the experience I'd just had, and I knew I never would. There were other people who had been faithful to him their whole lives, people who served him, people like Karen and those at her church, who deserved to have an audience with him. I had been an angry sinner, leading others in a war cry against him. *Why did he reveal himself to me?*

I felt the weight of my own sin as I never had before, and I knew I needed to do something to cleanse myself of my past. The last time I had felt spotless was the night I walked the aisle at the Baptist church in Desser, Georgia, and was immersed by the preacher in the baptismal. That night, I'd felt so clean.

I longed to feel that way again.

Then I had an idea. I picked up my pack and hiked to the pool below Virgin Falls. There I stripped off my shirt, slipped off my boots, and lowered myself into the cold, dark waters. Standing under the waterfall, with the waters cascading over my head, I remembered what God had meant to me when I was young. I wanted him to mean that much to me again. I turned my face up toward the light of the sun and gasped for air as the water poured over my mouth and nose, and I let the tears flow.

I cried for what I had done and for the great love I'd been shown. I didn't understand why Jesus came to me, but I was so thankful he had. It had been so long since I had cried, I didn't know how to sort the joyful tears from the tears of remorse, but I knew they were all healing tears. They were the salve my soul needed, healing the hatred that had burned its way through my heart. As the water poured over my head, it was more cleansing than the baptismal experience I'd had at twelve. I felt like a new man.

I was truly changed.

Jesus was real.

God was real.

And God was good!

✦ ✦ ✦

As I dried off in the sun while walking back through the mountain laurels to my campsite, my questions and doubts about God were gone. I had met him, and he was more real than I ever could have imagined. But he was also unlike what I had imagined him to be. In the months prior to my dream, I'd spent a lot of time in a Catholic Church where there was no shortage of artwork depicting Jesus. Usually, he was on a cross or praying in a garden. He often looked like a typical Middle Eastern Jewish carpenter with brown hair and brown eyes.

But in the brief glimpse I'd had of Jesus, he didn't look like any of those images. He was strong and pure. He appeared unblemished, almost new, like you would expect Adam to look, as if he were a second Adam. I knew what I'd seen didn't match up to what I or anyone else would expect, and I didn't know why. However, I knew Jesus could manifest himself however he chose. I also knew that, just like I'd heard his words in my heart and not in my ears, my eyes and brain had been working overtime to make sense of what I saw.

But it didn't matter why Jesus had appeared to me in the form he had. The important thing was that I had seen him.

I had glimpsed heaven.

The veil had parted, allowing me to peer into the other side, and what I saw was a world far more colorful and vibrant than the one we live in. It was a world of peace and love, a place where anxiety, fear, and worry lines simply vanished. I knew the permanence of that place far outweighed the temporary life we have here.

Although I was humbled by the undeserved gift of being able to visit, I longed for the day I could go back. But I also knew it wasn't yet my appointed time. I had been tasked with things to do here. It's difficult to articulate all that I felt—an experience like that is beyond words, as it should be. I had seen and heard more in the depths of my soul than I could ever articulate with my tongue.

But this I can say for sure: God is real, and he is good. I had been in his presence, in his home in heaven, and he had spoken into the deepest part of my being.

My only response was to want more of him.

✦ ✦ ✦

The experience had completely transformed *me*, but could it also transform my future? Would I really marry Karen? Not only did it sound too good to be true, but it also seemed impossible. She had called me a stalker and told me I was going to hell.

I remembered Jesus' words: *All I have told you will come to pass. All you have to do is trust in me and in my words.*

As soon as I got back to civilization, I stopped in town, bought a postcard, and addressed it to Karen.

Karen,

I had a dream last night, and Jesus came to me in the dream.
I have become a Christian. He told me we were going to get
married.
   I will see you when I get back to Birmingham.

Reggie

It was my first act of trust. (I left the part about the four kids
out of my note though. I didn't want to scare her.) I knew the card
would reach her before I got back to my apartment, and I chuckled
as I thought about her reaction. Just as I had believed God's promise that I would win that pony when I mailed my postcard twenty
years earlier, I now held the same fervent belief that I would win
Karen's hand.

One day soon, we would be married.

Chapter 11
CONVINCING KAREN

✦

As soon as I arrived back in Birmingham, I knocked on Karen's door—and then impatiently knocked again. She was slow to answer, and when she did, she cracked the door open, leaving the chain on.

"Hi! I just got back," I said. "Did you get my postcard?"

"Uh-huh."

I was never good at reading her. "Well, aren't you happy?" I asked.

"I tore it up."

Her reaction surprised me. I thought she'd be happy for me, for us. "That's okay. God told me—"

She shut the door in my face.

"Well, can I come in?" I asked through the closed door.

"No!"

I heard her switch on her stereo and turn up the volume, which was my cue to leave—she was done talking.

When God told me he wanted me to marry Karen, I guess I'd assumed that he'd tell her the same thing.

Apparently, he hadn't.

✦ ✦ ✦

The last talk we'd had revolved around my spiritual questions, which Karen had patiently answered, but she'd followed it up by saying that we were "just friends." Now that I was under the impression we would be getting married, apparently I was coming on too strong. My approach made her uncomfortable. She was happy to be my guide to God, but now that I said I'd found him, she felt that her spiritual duty was over—and so was the relationship.

Also, in her mind, I was a nut job.

But my new faith emboldened me. I believed what God had told me, despite the fact he had decided not to reveal it to her yet. I was also a guy, which meant I could be pretty insensitive to the ways of women.

I gave her a day or two and then knocked again.

"I told you, I ripped up the card!" she said through the closed door.

"That's okay. I just want to talk."

But she refused to open the door.

Every night I knocked on her door, and every night some version of the same scene would play out. Some nights she responded, some nights she wasn't home, and some nights she turned out the lights and pretended she wasn't home.

Lesser men would have given up, but I had been a door-to-door book salesman. I knew what it was like to get rejected over and over, and as the twenty-sixth-best salesman out of six thousand book-sellers companywide, I'd learned how to take rejection and keep on knocking.

I also had complete faith that this was what God had planned for my life. I wanted to be persistent, not only in my pursuit of Karen, but also in my obedience to him.

So I kept knocking.

✦ ✦ ✦

My persistence paid off.

Karen answered the door one night and said I could come in if I helped her memorize the chapter she was studying for her Bible study.

"I will on one condition," I said.

"What's that?"

"You help me memorize it too."

I heard her sigh, and though her head was turned away from me, I had a feeling she was rolling her eyes at the thought. She obviously didn't think my conversion experience was real.

While we were studying, I hoped she would ask about the details of my experience, but she didn't. As the conversation allowed, I tried to fill her in on what happened to me, and I was disappointed at her indifference. I expected more reaction from her than I got. *Isn't this what she wanted? Isn't she happy that we are now both headed in the same direction spiritually?*

She attended Briarwood Presbyterian Church, where she led the female college group. She loved her church and often spoke about it. I'd been there once or twice. Now I looked forward to attending regularly with her. When I finished talking and she didn't have anything else to add, I finally asked her, "What time is church on Sunday?"

She looked startled. "Reggie—" she said and paused. I could hear in her voice that same tone of annoyance I'd heard in the past. "If you really want to pursue God—"

"I do!" I said enthusiastically.

"Then you need to pursue God on your *own*. In-de-pen-dent-ly."

I was crushed. I wanted to pursue God on my own, but I also wanted to pursue him with her. She'd been a willing guide before I believed in him, but it seemed as if she was done with me now. This wasn't turning out at all like I thought. Alone, I would cry out to God: *You've given me this vision; you've given me this promise, as well as this dream and desire for my life. Why is it so hard for her to understand?*

I refused to let her discouragement stop me from growing in my faith. I found another Presbyterian church and started attending regularly on my own.

✦ ✦ ✦

Karen was frightened by what she saw. She hadn't lived through the same experience I had; Jesus hadn't looked her in the eye and spoken to her heart. To her, it all seemed like a big put-on just so I could date her. Secretly, she also wondered if I might be a little crazy. So she continued to discourage me. The only time I could see her was when I helped her memorize Scripture.

Not only was *Karen* not reacting the way I expected, most of the *other* believers around me weren't either. I thought they would be praising God that I had found what they already had; instead, they seemed to doubt that what I said was true.

The memories of Jesus in the meadow were as real and as intense to me then as they were the day I woke up by my campfire. However, it was difficult for me to explain to other people what I'd experienced—and harder still for them to understand.

My frustrations drove me to learn more about him. I had an unquenchable desire to read the Bible. Knowing that he was as real as any of my friends or family members, I dove deeper into the Scriptures. In addition to going to church, I joined a Bible study for medical students. It was an outreach of Briarwood Presbyterian, Karen's church, and a man named Earl Carpenter led it.

The same week I signed up, R. C. Sproul came into town for an apologetics conference. Earl arranged for him to debate some of the campus intellectuals—great scientists from the medical school, some of whom had been my mentors. I attended, a little nervous about what these esteemed men might say.

At the beginning of the debate, I felt sorry for Sproul sitting alone with the intelligentsia of the medical college together on the opposite side. But I needn't have worried about Sproul being by himself. He was *in a class by himself.* I watched as he intellectually beat up on the professors I used to respect, while they squirmed, answerless, under his questions. Of course, he didn't have all the answers either, but if he had any holes in his arguments, God seemed to cover them. Like C. S. Lewis, Sproul was probably one of the greatest minds on the planet—and he was a Christian.

Sitting in the audience that night, I had another epiphany—I didn't have to be stupid to be a Christian. I'd once believed that. But watching the debate, I could see that everything takes faith. Even science requires a certain amount of faith. Walking out that night, I realized I could take my faith and bend in the direction of science alone or bend in the direction of the God who came for me.

I had already chosen God.

✦ ✦ ✦

I knew I needed to meet with Father Frank and let him know I wouldn't be getting confirmed. "I hate to tell you this after all you've done for me, but I don't want to be confirmed. I've found God, and we've worked out our relationship problems."

"See, I told you," he said. "You should go to seminary!"

We talked about the details of my experience and the things God had said to me. Father Frank said he understood what I was feeling. At that time, a sort of charismatic renewal was taking place in the Catholic Church, and I think he thought that's what was happening to me. Looking back, I suspect he was a charismatic Catholic. When we parted, he gave me his blessing.

He was a very cool guy, but we lost touch after I left medical school. However, I have every confidence that one day I will see him again.

✦ ✦ ✦

By the time summer ended, Karen and I were on better terms. We still hung out at her apartment only when she needed help studying, but our conversations were longer and more relaxed when we did. We had progressed to the stage where we would joke around and laugh a bit. Instead of saying we were "just friends," sometimes she actually said I was her friend. We both knew she was dating other guys; she'd recently attended a concert by B. J. Thomas—the pop singer known for hits like "Raindrops Keep Fallin' on My Head"— with one of them. "I wish you had been there with me!" she gushed about the concert afterward.

I wished I had too.

Our friendship was growing.

The Labor Day weekend was coming up, and most students were leaving town. I planned to visit my family in South Georgia, but Karen didn't have any plans. Though she'd rejected me hundreds of times, I couldn't help but try again. "My family is having a get-together in Georgia. We're going water-skiing over the break; would you like to come?"

She looked at me with one eyebrow raised.

"I know, we're not dating. My cousin and his wife have this big boat, and I just thought you might like to come along."

"I like to water-ski," she said. I could tell she was considering it.

"Well, come with me. What else are you going to do? Stay alone in Birmingham?"

Fortunately, she loved to water-ski as much as she loved to dance, and when she confirmed that everyone else she knew was busy or out of town, she agreed to come.

We had a great time talking in the car on the way down. My family was there, so she got to meet my mom and dad, as well as assorted aunts and uncles. When she was on her own with them, she got along with everyone and seemed to have a good time. But as a guy, I was clueless once again as to what was going on inside her head.

On the drive back, I could tell she was distracted. "What's on your mind?" I asked.

"I was thinking about how much I enjoyed talking to your mom," she said. "Your parents are really great Christians!"

I thought back to our first date and chuckled. "I know. I keep telling you that!"

Karen still seemed surprised. "When I prayed with your aunt, I felt the Spirit of God in that room, and I thought, *How can Reggie be from this family?*"

"Gee, thanks."

"I mean, you ask such basic questions about God. It's kind of shocking to think you grew up in a family with such a strong faith in the Lord."

Karen told me about a conversation she had with Mom while I was out. They'd talked about the details of the Alday Massacre and how the tragedy had affected me.

"You weren't making it up, were you?" Karen said. "It really hurt you."

"No, I didn't make it up," I said quietly.

Though Mom and I hadn't discussed my spiritual wandering much, she'd seen me go into the wilderness of rebellion seven years before. But now, Mom had told Karen that she had seen my countenance and attitude change when talking about spiritual things. My mom knew I had come back home.

"The Lord is the center of my parents' lives," I said. "I don't think either of them stopped praying for me until he was the center of mine, too."

Though it had been only weeks since I'd had the dream, I felt like the seven years of darkness that preceded it had happened a long time ago. I didn't like talking about it.

"Mom really liked you," I said, changing the subject. "She appreciates how strong you are in your faith."

Just then, we topped the hill from Montgomery to Birmingham, and there before us was the most incredible sunset I'd ever seen. I knew Karen saw it, too, because we both were quiet as we watched the baby-blue sky turn pink, then a deep rose color, as the final rays streaked across the sky. Slowly at first, the glowing sun began to recede behind the horizon. Then all at once, it slipped out of sight, and the sky gracefully faded to black.

Karen told me later it was at that moment she realized how creative God could be. If he could use colors and light to paint the sky with such splendor, perhaps he could creatively bring an agnostic to faith through evenings of memorizing Scripture. If God was that creative, she felt that she needed to be faithful to whatever his call was on her life—even if it meant stepping outside of her set expectations to look at a relationship she didn't see happening.

Later, she told me she felt as though God had a cattle prod on her, and the more he nudged her, the more she told him, "No, God, this isn't it. This isn't it!" The funny thing was, the closer she got to him, the closer she got to me.

On the farm, we say you can't make a silk purse out of a sow's ear, but as Karen looked at the magnificent colors in the sky that day, she wondered if God could. God was prodding her to get outside of her box of faith to see him at work in fresh ways. And one of those ways was taking an agnostic and turning him into a potential husband.

However, Karen knew that if she could prove I was faking my conversion, then she'd be off the hook, so she did the only thing she could—she put me to the test.

✦ ✦ ✦

At Briarwood Presbyterian, Curtis Tanner was the staff member who worked with volunteers like Karen. He helped run the college ministry and led a Bible study for the guys. Karen wanted me to meet him for lunch, and though she didn't tell me why, I knew. She wanted him to check out my story to see if I was legit.

Curtis met me at the medical building, and over a lunch of steak, potatoes, and green beans, it was my turn to get peppered with questions. "If you were raised a Christian, why did you leave God?" he asked.

I explained what happened to my cousins and how deeply that had affected me.

"Wow, I can understand that," he said. "So what brought you back to him?"

"He did." I explained the seven-year journey I'd been on. I told him about the dream and about all the things I was doing now to grow in my faith. "What happened to me in that dream was so real, and God forgave me so quickly and completely that I no longer have any guilt for the things he forgave me of."

Curtis seemed taken aback, so I tried to think how I could explain it differently. "I guess one day when I have kids, if they offend me and come to ask for my forgiveness, I'll say, 'For what?' If they say, 'Dad, remember?' I'll say, 'No, I don't.' I think that's what true redemption and true forgiveness look like. That's how completely God has forgiven me."

"I agree," Curtis said.

He called Karen after the meeting. "I think Reggie's conversion is for real."

"Are you sure?" she asked.

"I haven't run across too many Damascus Road conversions," he said, referencing Saul's dramatic conversion to Paul in the New Testament, "but I think Reggie is for real. So I would give my blessing to y'all dating."

It wasn't what she wanted to hear, but out of obedience to what she felt God was calling her to do, she reluctantly agreed.

Karen called and told me what Curtis said, and though she didn't explicitly say we could start dating, it was the first encouraging sign she'd ever given me.

Chapter 12
PAST, PRESENT, AND FUTURE GIFTS

✦

Karen and I started dating in September 1980. In October, I asked her when she wanted to get married.

"We just started dating! Can't you slow down a bit?"

Though she saw distinct changes in my heart and Curtis had confirmed their legitimacy, she still wasn't sure whether my conversion was real or not. "Three months isn't long enough. He could be faking it," she told Curtis and other mutual friends.

When she invited me to meet her parents during Christmas, I seized the chance to make our relationship official. In early December, I took all the money I had and bought her a ring. I knew I couldn't be turned down for a question I never asked, so a few nights later at her apartment, instead of getting down on bended knee and asking if she would marry me, I just handed it to her. I was young and naive and still assumed that God was going to reveal himself to her the way he had revealed himself to me.

"Okay," she said hesitantly when I handed her the velvet box with the ring inside. "But I won't wear it for at least two weeks."

"Why not?"

"I can't let the girls in my Bible study see me wearing it until I tell them I'm engaged, and I can't tell them I'm engaged yet."

"Why?"

"Well, I've been having them pray for this weird stalker guy, and now I have to tell them I'm engaged to the weird stalker guy. I can't just pop in wearing his ring." She looked me deep in the eyes, and I could see the pain in hers that I felt in mine. "I feel like I am supposed to marry you, but I am not in love with you."

Her words hurt, but once again I didn't let them stop me. We agreed to plan for a June wedding, but if she was not in love with me by March, we'd call it off.

She said she wanted to be cautious—she didn't want the girls in her study to get the wrong message. Although she was honest about that part, fortunately she was too kind to tell me the rest. She had taught her girls to choose a man who would be a spiritual leader of their home and marriage, but as I would later learn, she wasn't sure I could do that. She didn't think I fit the mold for the kind of godly guy she wanted her girls to marry.

But I took what I could get—a fiancée who didn't love me, who wouldn't wear my ring, and who planned to call off the wedding in three months. I had every reason to believe things wouldn't change—and only One to believe they would. God had made me a promise, and I trusted him to keep it.

✦　✦　✦

After I had given Karen the ring, I called Cotty, her dad, to ask for permission. When I told him that I had already asked her, he wanted to know what she had said.

"I think she said okay."

"Well, she knows you better than I do," Cotty said, since he and I had met only once. "If she said okay, then I guess it's fine with us."

His enthusiasm seemed to equal Karen's.

We spent Christmas with her family in St. Louis. There we went through all the motions that engaged couples go through, but without any of the exuberance. We found a church for the wedding and a hall for the reception, and we picked a date, June 13, which was six months away.

Karen eventually put on the ring, but she still hid it more than she showed it off. Though she had accepted my proposal out of obedience, it didn't seem like she really intended to go through with the marriage. She even started making future plans on her own—looking for a job in Missouri—though I had two more years of medical school in Birmingham. If she found a job, I obviously couldn't leave with her.

Though I lacked evidence, I believed what Jesus had told me: "You're going to marry Karen, and together you will have four children. All I have told you will come to pass. All you have to do is trust in me and in my words."

So I trusted.

But it was a painful time for both of us. I loved Karen passionately and *couldn't wait* to spend the rest of my life with her. But the best Karen could say was that she was *willing* to spend the rest of her life with me. And that was only because she was being obedient to God.

Our friendship had blossomed; in fact, Karen said we were best friends, but by March, it was clear she didn't love me and probably never would. She'd made no further wedding plans since Christmas, and her feelings for me hadn't grown at all. As she packed for a nutrition conference in Chicago, we both knew we had a decision to make when she got back.

Would we go through with the wedding or not?

I wanted to marry her, of course. I loved her! And I believed it was what God wanted for us. But I also knew that, if we did marry, we would be trapped in a lopsided love affair that wouldn't be fair to either of us.

✦ ✦ ✦

We prayed before she left for Chicago, and I prayed while she was gone. I wanted to marry Karen, but I wanted whatever God wanted for her more.

Unexpectedly, she called me from Chicago and said, "Reggie, I hate to do this over the phone, but I want you to know I've been thinking about you a lot . . ."

Her voice trailed off, and I thought I heard her choke back a sob. I stretched the phone cord from the kitchen to the couch, so I could sit down. I wanted to be prepared for whatever she said next.

"You're my best friend," she continued. "I've missed you so much, and today I realized . . . you know what? . . . I really do love you!"

I was so overwhelmed with emotion and gratitude that I could barely hear what she said next.

"I'm coming home from Chicago early. I don't have a wedding dress yet, and we don't have bridesmaid dresses, so I'm going to St. Louis for the weekend to shop and make plans for our wedding. I love you, Reggie!"

Having Karen as my *wife* was the blessing I'd longed for—the one God seemed to have promised me in my dream. But having Karen's *love* was a blessing I hadn't dared to imagine. It was a gift only she could give; there was nothing I could do to earn or deserve it. When I got off the phone, I wept tears of joy and relief.

Her words on the phone that day were also a reminder of God's love for me. His promises were not only true, but they were becoming reality in the greatest way imaginable. March, April, and May were some of the most incredible months of my life. As we prepared for our wedding, our mutual love grew and flourished. Karen had finally, and freely, given her love to me. *Finally, God! Finally! You showed her what you showed me. Thank you!*

By God's grace, less than a year after my dream, we were married on June 13, 1981, sealing the first of the events Jesus forecasted.

Two years later, I graduated from medical school and sealed the second: I was a doctor.

For graduation from medical school, my mother handed me perhaps the most precious gift anyone has ever given me. It was a framed child's drawing of a doctor with his arms wide open. He was wearing a head mirror and a huge smile. In a child's scrawl, the caption read, "When I Get Grown I am a Dr."

I recognized the artist, even before I read his name.

"Reggie Anderson. Second grade."

I remembered the assignment. Mrs. Baskins had asked us to draw what we envisioned we would be when we grew up. She wanted us to dream and dream big. Most of the students wanted to be farmers, policemen, or preachers. I don't know why I wanted to be a doctor.

But God did.

My Plan C was his Plan A for my life.

✦ ✦ ✦

My cousins' tragedy, and the dream that followed seven years later, showed me that God grants us insight into eternity. Those glances can provide comfort, healing, and anticipation for what comes next. They can also restore our broken hearts to a level of faith we never dreamed possible.

Just like they had mine.

Hearing God speak to me about the pony was the first time I remembered hearing his voice. But as my second-grade picture proved, God had continued to speak to me.

Now that I understood that God was real and that heaven was even more real than what we experience here, I wanted more glimpses of both. As a doctor, I now had a front-row seat to the parting of the veil. So I went into my profession open to seeing God at work in the patients I cared for. And I found him there.

But even with expectations of seeing him, what I learned surprised me: We don't spend our lives walking toward eternity—eternity walks alongside us.

Part 2:

COULD THESE BE GLIMPSES OF HEAVEN?

Chapter 13

DEPARTURES

✦

SUMMER 1983
JACKSON, TENNESSEE

I was in the call room when an ER nurse notified me that an ambulance was on the way with a new patient. "Apparently, the patient being transported has dementia, and she can't tell the paramedics what's wrong. However, the nursing-home staff sent her medical records along with her," the nurse said.

Most first-year residents dreaded nursing-home calls. We were the first ones to respond to the ER, and it was our job to perform all the grunt work, so the second- or third-year residents could come in after us. But when nursing-home patients arrived by ambulance, they were often so sick and confused that they couldn't tell us their own names, let alone their symptoms. These patients were mysteries waiting to be solved; unfortunately, there were often too few clues to interpret them quickly.

But as a first-year resident, I had an advantage.

✦ ✦ ✦

Karen and I had moved to Jackson, Tennessee, several months earlier so I could start my residency at the University of Tennessee (UT) Family Medicine Residency Program. I intentionally chose this program for several reasons. First of all, it was a rural program where I could receive the kind of training that would serve me for the rest of my career, especially the first few years while I repaid my financial obligation to the National Health Service Corps. It was also conveniently located within driving distance of both sets of parents. But most important, it meant that Jesus' promise to me in my dream—that I would be a country doctor in Tennessee—had come true.

We wanted our parents to be nearby, so they could be involved grandparents—Karen had gotten pregnant before we left Birmingham. This would have been the perfect time to tell her that Jesus also promised me that we would have four kids, but I was still hesitant to share that detail with Karen because of all the initial turmoil in our dating relationship. Things were finally going smoothly, and I didn't want to frighten her.

✦ ✦ ✦

Once in Jackson, one of my first rotations was geriatrics. As part of the rotation, our superiors assigned us our own patients at the nursing home. It was exciting for me to meet my very first patients and then to make rounds on a weekly or monthly basis, as their specific needs dictated.

Most of my patients were between eighty and ninety years old and suffering from senile dementia. I found that if I took my time while visiting them, held their hands, and listened to their stories, I not only got better information from them about their health, but I got to know who they were and what was important to them.

It took only a few visits for me to realize that these men and women were more than just the accumulation of diagnoses on their charts. They were magnificent people with fascinating stories. Though they couldn't tell me what they'd had for breakfast that morning, they recalled extraordinary details about past events in their lives, such as when they got married or the day they got out of the army. They remembered where they had met their spouses and what the weather was like on the day their children were born. To these gentle souls, time was a matter of opinion—usually theirs.

The home had more than three times as many women as men, and I affectionately began calling them my "Eighties Ladies."

The nurses would tell me that on the days I was expected to visit, the Eighties Ladies would quickly finish breakfast so they could dress "because Dr. Anderson is coming today!" They would then spend all morning getting ready. By the time I arrived, they would be decked out in their most colorful scarves and beads, wearing thick lipstick and an extra splash of perfume.

No matter how much paint they put on the barn, it was obvious their bodies were crumbling. Most of them had severe medical problems: heart disease, end-stage diabetes, kidney disease, multiple strokes.

Despite their deteriorating bodies, their personalities and their souls were intact.

✦ ✦ ✦

The ambulance arrived at the ER, and the crew unloaded the patient. While the nurses settled her in a room, someone handed me her chart. I was surprised to see it was Irene, one of my favorite Eighties Ladies. I'd gotten close to her over the past few months that I'd taken care of her. The last time we had visited, she'd said, "You remind me of my grandson!"

Like most of my patients, she was suffering from dementia and couldn't recall what she'd had to eat at her last meal, but she always had great stories about living overseas with her children while her husband was in the military. Photos of her three children and nine grandchildren were neatly displayed on the walls of her room. On holidays, freshly crayoned drawings and heartfelt notes scrawled in a child's hand would be hung on her door. Often, one or more family members would be visiting when I stopped in to check on her. It was obvious she was loved and had lived a full and joyous life.

I didn't have to look at the chart long. I already knew her history well. But I had no idea what symptoms had sent her to the ER or what the underlying medical condition might be. I hoped Irene would be lucid enough to explain her symptoms, but I knew that was unlikely.

I approached the right side of her bed and was prepared to introduce myself when she said, "Dr. Anderson! My favorite doctor!"

That was a good sign.

"How are you feeling?" I asked, taking her hand.

She beamed at me and said, "I'm a little short of breath. I feel like I'm being smothered."

Her face was gaunt, and she looked thinner than I remembered.

"Have you been eating?"

"Not much. I haven't been hungry."

I made note of her symptoms and ordered the appropriate tests, an EKG, and blood work.

With all her conditions, it could have taken a while to find the cause, but her initial test result immediately confirmed her diagnosis. Irene was having a massive myocardial infarction. It was doubtful she would survive the night.

It saddened me to have to give her the news.

I took her hand in mine and softly patted it. "Irene, you're having a heart attack."

She nodded silently.

From her records and past visits with her family, I knew she didn't want aggressive intervention, but her family requested she be kept peaceful and pain free as she passed.

"I'm going to admit you to the hospital, so we can watch you and keep you comfortable." Her lip trembled and a tear formed in the corner of her eye.

I recalled past conversations when she told me she was ready to go if Jesus called. As a believer, she couldn't wait to see him on the other side. Her husband had passed a few years earlier, and she longed to see him, too. When she did go, she would leave behind a legacy, and she would run to a lover.

I couldn't imagine a better way to go.

"They're going to put you in a room, and I'll come by in a little while and check on you," I said.

I advised the staff to call her family.

✦ ✦ ✦

The first time I was alone with someone who died, I was working on the cancer ward of the VA hospital in Birmingham. I was still a young medical student, and Dennis was in his sixties. He'd lived a hard life and had fought valiantly against the cancer that was taking him. His family, knowing his fight would soon be over, stood next to his bed as his adult son prayed.

"Dear God, we come to you with heavy hearts, because of the life that is leaving us. We thank you for the gift of our father, but we ask you now to take his hand and lead him the way home to be with you, so he may be free of the pain and suffering he has experienced far too long. In his absence, please give us your comfort. In Jesus' name. Amen."

My job was to stay at Dennis's bedside and call the resident physician as soon as it was all over; he would be the one to make the pronouncement of death.

The vigil passed ever so slowly that night. Prior to Dennis, all the deaths I'd witnessed as a medical student were in the ICU or the trauma unit, where students were kept in the background so we wouldn't get in the way of the professionals while they performed their jobs. But Dennis's death was different. It wasn't in a cold, sterile room with crash carts and machines. It was quiet and peaceful as a few family members stood around him.

As the night wore on, the family eventually retired to the waiting room, and I was alone with Dennis in the dimly lit room. His IV dripped like the sure and steady ticking of a clock. I watched for signs of death: decreased blood flow, mottled skin, or temperature changes in his body.

Sometimes he'd take a breath, and then it would be seconds before he took another, gasping for air when he did. Each time he struggled to catch his breath, I got nervous and checked the monitor.

Is he dead?

I was scared and unsure of what to expect. I'd already had a vision of heaven, but I wasn't sure I wanted to be there when Dennis made his journey. I assumed his death would be like it was in the movies—ghostly, dark, and creepy. This night had all the makings of that. His room wasn't well lit. The light from the hallway and the green glow of the monitors were the only light sources.

Like most hospital rooms, it was also cold. I shivered occasionally, though I'm not sure if it was from the temperature or the anticipation of what was to come.

When Dennis finally took his last breath and his heart stopped beating, I tried to keep mine from racing in fear. I switched off the monitors and looked closely at the motionless body in the bed. It was my first time alone with death.

Unexpectedly, I felt a warm sensation. At first, I thought it was my body temperature rising, but then I realized I could feel it not from within me but from outside of me. I distinctly felt it moving through the room, filling the entire space with warmth. I looked around for the source of the warmth, but the windows were closed and the curtains were drawn. It was too early in the season for it to be the heat. I couldn't figure out where it was coming from. I should have been alarmed, but it was surprisingly comforting compared to the chill I'd felt seconds earlier.

Just as I was getting used to the temperature change, a soft glow appeared above and to the right of the patient. *What was that?* The soft light was there, and then gone. *It must have been the monitor blinking.* I went to shut it off, and I realized the light couldn't have come from the monitor—it was silent and dark. I'd already switched it off.

What's going on here?

Puzzled, I sat down and looked again. Even if the monitor had still been on, the glow I'd seen couldn't have come from its screen.

The position was wrong. The glow was high and to the right; the monitor was lower than that and located on the other side of the bed. I tried to think of other explanations. The only time I remembered seeing a glow like that was Tinker Bell, a fairy from one of those Disney movies.

I looked again at Dennis's motionless body lying in the bed. His face had relaxed, and he seemed almost younger looking. I sensed a slight breeze mixing with the warm sensation and felt the warmth pass by my cheek. Though the temperature didn't change, the warmth seemed to be gone, leaving a fresh feeling lingering in the air.

I probably should have been frightened by the sensations I was experiencing, but I wasn't. Instead, I only felt a deep sense of peace and an embracing comfort.

Before Dennis died, I wanted to get out of there as quickly as I could, but now I wanted to linger in his room. I sensed the deepest peace I'd felt since the dream I had on my camping trip.

God's presence was in the room.

✦ ✦ ✦

Thoughts of that night with Dennis were on my mind as I walked to Irene's room. The nurses had put her at the end of the hall to give her and her family a place that was quiet and private. Still, once I arrived, several members of her family excused themselves. I understood. They were afraid of death. Before my experience with Dennis, I'd felt that way too. But ever since that night in the VA hospital, I wasn't afraid. I'd learned that there was nothing to fear; death can be a beautiful experience.

When I walked in, Irene was sitting up in bed. She had oxygen tubes in her nose and an IV that gave her morphine for pain. I'd also ordered some nitropaste for her chest to see if it would help her feel better. When she saw me, she once again remembered my name and beamed just like she'd done in the ER.

"Dr. Anderson!"

"How are you feeling?" I asked.

"Better," she said.

Irene was always dressed up when I saw her, so lying in the bed in a hospital gown made her look frailer than she had at the home. As I examined her and listened to her heart, her smile disappeared. She fidgeted with her hospital gown, and she seemed agitated or maybe even a bit nervous.

"Is there anything I can do for you?" I asked when I finished.

"Dr. Anderson, I don't want you to leave."

Her family had left and she was alone. "Why? Are you afraid?"

"I'm not afraid to die," she said quickly. Then she paused, and I could see her eyes darting up and to the right as she thought about it for a minute. Then she turned to look at me and whispered, "You see, Jesus is calling my name, and I need an escort to heaven. Will you be my escort?"

It was the first time I was invited to be with someone in life's final moments, and it was an honor to be asked. I could see she didn't want to die alone, and I was happy to stay with her. My own experience had taught me that even if we welcomed the destination, we could still be nervous about the journey.

In Irene's case, there wasn't much I could do to hold her here longer, and she wouldn't have wanted that even if I could. Irene understood the journey on which she was embarking; she just wanted someone to be with her as she departed. I felt honored to be that someone.

I pulled up a chair next to her bed and took her hand. My hands were always cool, and hers felt warm in relation to mine. Her fingers were thin and arthritic. I felt her pulse, and it grew weaker as we talked.

"I'm going to meet Jesus tonight," she said, her eyes shining.

"Yes, you are."

"And my sweetheart will be there waiting for me too."

Briefly, she told me about all the people she knew who had already gone to the other side whom she would soon meet again.

As her blood pressure drifted downward and she got too tired to talk, I reclined her bed so she could rest easier. Occasionally, I would pat her hand. Less frequently, she would respond by nodding to let me know she was still there.

The room was quiet, and above her bed, a single lightbulb shone. As she continued to grow weaker, I gave her permission to go. "You've lived a great life, Irene, and there is nothing left for you to accomplish here. You've been a faithful servant to the Lord and to your family, and so it is well for you to go."

Her breathing changed. She would take a long, drawn-out breath, followed by a similar shorter breath, then a series of short, shallow breaths followed by an absence of breath, and then the abnormal breathing pattern would repeat. This is called Cheyne-Stokes respiration. It's a neurological term for a specific type of labored breathing followed by erratic quick breaths and then the absence of breath. It often signals that the end is near.

I watched her struggle for air, and I could tell she didn't have long. Several family members came in and said their good-byes, and then drifted back out to the waiting room where they held each other and cried.

It took less than an hour before her body grew cooler, and her pulse stopped. She let out her last breath, a quiet exhale—the last breath is always out, never in. I watched her body relax. It was easy to see that life had drained from her.

Alone in the room with Irene's body, suddenly the same warmth I'd felt with Dennis filled the room. It was like the warm breeze of spring when you open the door, and it catches your breath. The whole room seemed to respond to it. Once again, a brief glow appeared above and to the right of the patient's body. It was longer than a blink, but not long enough for me to really see it. Then it faded away.

Irene hadn't been connected to any monitors. And I looked around to see if I could find the source of the glow, but there was nothing else in the room that could have caused the illumination. I remembered being in Dennis's room and having some of the same experiences more than a year earlier.

A cool breeze interrupted my thoughts, and I felt it mix with the warmth. The best way I can describe it is to say it felt as if something were being gathered up and prepared for a journey. The once stagnant air of the room now smelled fresh. The room was filled with the lightest of scents. I inhaled deeply, and the fragrance of lilac and citrus seemed to fill me like it filled the room. The fragrance seemed vaguely familiar.

I've smelled this before.

With a flash of insight, it came to me. It was the same fresh scent I'd smelled in my dream in the mountains. With joy, I inhaled it again and closed my eyes, longing to be swept up in it. Instead, I felt the warmth pass by me and join with another warm sensation, like when two bodies enter a room and you can sense the heat from each one. I opened my eyes; I knew it was her soul carried on a fresh breeze slipping to the other side into the warmth of God's presence.

Death was a feverish child reaching out, and heaven was his mother's cool embrace.

Heaven had arrived to carry Irene home.

✦ ✦ ✦

I looked at my watch and made a notation as to the time of death. Then I went out to tell her relatives.

Many people want to shy away from the word *death*, and instead use terms like "She's passed," or "She's gone on." As a doctor, I just tried to read the family and see where they were emotionally— whether they wanted frank words or something softer.

On this night, I didn't have to use any words. When I got to the waiting room, they looked at me and burst into tears. They already knew, and I didn't have to say anything more than "I'm sorry."

And I was. I knew the pain they were feeling. Irene had been an integral part of their family up until the day she died. I put my arm around her eldest daughter and said, "If there is anything I can do . . ." But I knew there probably wasn't.

As soon as a doctor informs the family that their loved one has died, they stop listening, and no condolences can help at that point. They're involved in their own sorrow and mourning.

+ + +

Irene was *my patient*—one of my first patients—and my favorite. She was also my first patient to die. On the night of her death, I got to feel God's presence during the precise moment she crossed over.

I would say that it was a coincidence that I was the one who happened to be on call that night, but I no longer believed in coincidences.

God had me there for a reason.

Chapter 14
BORN INTO
A NEW WORLD

✦

A first date, a first kiss, a first child—firsts are often unforgettable. During residency, I probably delivered close to one hundred babies, and before that as a student, I'd probably done eighty. But the ones I remembered the most were the firsts. The first baby I delivered. The first time I lost a baby. And the first baby of my own. These were significant, not only because they were *my* firsts but because each of them helped me see God in new ways.

✦ ✦ ✦

The petite Chinese lady doubled over in pain. "*Ohhhh,*" she groaned. It was the first noise she'd made since she arrived—and I froze. I knew what I was supposed to do, at least I thought I did, but her urgent cries made me forget.

I'd spent the previous day shadowing a resident who showed me how a typical labor and delivery should progress, but now I couldn't remember anything I'd learned. I tried not to panic, but her contractions were obviously coming faster. She screamed again, "*Ahhhhh!*"

Something in her cry jogged a memory. The resident's advice from the day before came back to me. "For thousands of years, women have made this journey without a doctor coaching them. The best thing you can do is just let it happen and only intervene when necessary."

As medical students, we were the "baby catchers." If it was a run-of-the-mill delivery—in Birmingham, that meant the woman was full-term, in labor, and likely poor—then our job was to be there to catch the baby after the mother pushed him out. The residents were there to handle the more difficult, high-risk cases.

On this day, I had checked the mom, and everything was progressing nicely. The resident also examined the mother and agreed with me. "Her heart rate is good. You can catch this one on your own; I've got a C-section to do. If you need anything, I'll be down the hall."

And with that, he was gone, and I was on my own.

The Chinese lady didn't speak much English. It was probably a good thing we didn't share a common language. It only would have made it more obvious that we shared the same fear of what was about to happen.

The woman hadn't received much, if any, prenatal care, and she was in a lot of pain. She found some relief with narcotics through her IV, but as the labor progressed, I could tell she was having a hard time. In the beginning, her breaths were deep, but now they seemed quicker and more shallow. It was almost as if she were panting, blowing the air through her lips, and then moaning as each contraction seized her body. When the pain got bad enough, she'd cry out, "*Ahhhh!*" With each anguished scream, I'd watch her eyes widen in fear, and I wondered if mine were doing the same.

More panting, more screaming, and more fear. No one was with her to translate, to hold her hand, or to guide her through the breathing. She seemed lost and alone. She was as ill-prepared for the birth as I was. Fortunately, the delivery nurse had been coaching both new moms and new doctors for more than twenty years. She was the only one in the room who wasn't concerned.

The Chinese lady's water broke.

When she was fully dilated, it was time to go. I did my best to communicate with her. "You push," I said making an exaggerated pushing motion with my hands. Then I pointed to myself, held my hands out, and rounded them. "I'll catch."

I'm sure the delivery nurse thought I was brilliant. Who else would push? And what kind of doctor says, "I'll catch the baby," to a mom about to give birth? I was doing such a poor job of communicating; I knew the Chinese lady had to be confused. She probably thought my pushing and large circular gestures meant I wanted her to get out of bed and get me a large pizza!

Fortunately, as the contractions continued, the nurse stepped up to the patient's bedside and took control of the situation—and, thankfully, the communication. The nurse took the mom's hand, looked her in the eyes, and with each contraction began to model the proper breathing.

Breathe, pant, pant, pant.

Soon the lady was following her lead. Breathe, pant, pant, pant.

The mother finally seemed to understand what was happening because when I said, "Push!" she pushed. Soon, a patch of dark hair crowned, and the pushing became more fervent. It took only a minute or two before the infant's head came through. I reached in to guide the shoulders, and a dark-haired baby boy squirted out. I clamped the cord and cut it, and then handed the baby to the nurse. He was crying, which was a good sign.

I wasn't, which was also a good sign.

After letting the mom briefly hold the baby, the nurse quickly checked him and informed me that his Apgar score—a newborn's measure of health—was a ten. Perfect.

I went back to work to deliver the placenta and to check for any retained products from the delivery. The placenta looked intact when I delivered it, but I'd been taught to always feel to make sure nothing was left inside. I pushed down on her abdomen expecting to feel a postpartum uterus, but for some reason, it felt larger than I expected.

What could I have missed?

I was embarrassed.

It was my first solo delivery and I didn't want to make a mistake, but there was an obvious problem. I went through the delivery checklists in my head and couldn't think of anything I'd overlooked. I grabbed the fetoscope and listened to the women's abdomen. That's when I heard it—a second heartbeat!

"There's another baby in here!"

The nurse's eyes were now as wide as the mother's had been earlier. "I'll call the resident," she said.

Of course, the mother was still in the throes of labor. She was in pain *and* aware of the tension building in the room. I had to tell her something. I pointed at her stomach, and then held up two fingers. Her eyes grew huge, and it was obvious that this time my sign language was *very* clear.

Before the OB resident could even wash and gown, baby boy number two came kicking and screaming into the world. I caught him just as I had his brother, and all of us celebrated the arrival of not one but two healthy boys.

Although every delivery has the same sense of wonder, this one—my *first* one—was extra special. I didn't know she was having twins. The resident obviously didn't know she was having twins. Even *she* didn't know she was having twins.

But God did.

And he chose me to be a part of it.

✦ ✦ ✦

Each birth is miraculous and special in its own way. Attending deliveries is one of the happiest things I get to do as a doctor. When that wriggling newborn takes his or her first breath, that cry is celebrated. It means the baby has arrived, is healthy, and is breathing on its own. There is a congratulatory mood in the room. The parents are ecstatic at the arrival of their little one. I'm always deeply grateful to have once again peered through the open veil to welcome a new soul into the world and be the first on this side to hold him or her. Even jaded labor and delivery nurses, who've been through thousands of births, are happy and smiling.

But sometimes when the veil opens, it doesn't close. The baby takes a breath or two, and the veil stays parted, waiting for the soul to return to heaven.

There is no celebration in those moments.

✦ ✦ ✦

It was Sandra's third pregnancy, and at twenty-four weeks, she was in premature labor. Even today, it's difficult for such a premature baby to survive. If Sandra gave birth—at that time and at that hospital—there was very little hope. The baby would weigh less than a pound, and the chances of survival would be very slim.

As the resident in charge, I did everything I could to keep Sandra from delivering. Sandra did too. But at two o'clock in the morning, our best efforts failed, and Sandra went into active labor.

When the baby arrived, it was without the usual fanfare. Sandra was a single mom, so there wasn't a father standing beside her and cheering her on. Sandra also knew the risks for such a premature baby, so she was crying, not so much from the pain, as from the sadness of what she was experiencing.

As the baby slid out, I quietly said, "It's a boy."

He was so tiny! With my outstretched fingers, I could cradle him in the palm of my hand. I assumed he wouldn't live long enough to take a breath, yet against all odds, I watched him struggle and succeed. Cupping him in my hands, he managed to get out a pitiful little cry, followed by a couple of short breaths. It was a valiant effort, and it took everything he had in him.

"Is he okay?" Sandra asked, sounding concerned.

"He's so frail. He's very, very young," I said, trying to keep my voice steady.

I asked the nurse to update the neonatologist and her obstetrician. They hadn't come in because neither one expected the baby to take a breath.

"Can I hold him?"

I knew how much she wanted this baby. I took him to her and sat next to her while she held him. To make Sandra and her baby more comfortable, the nurse turned down all the lights except for a lamp in the corner. For the next fifteen minutes, I sat in a chair next to Sandra's bed and watched her weep over her baby. As I sat there, I sensed a warmth on my skin. It almost felt like I was sweating, but my skin remained dry.

The last time I felt this same warm sensation, I was in Irene's hospital room. I'd felt it with Dennis, too. That's when I knew God was keeping the veil open for Sandra's son to return to him.

My heart broke for Sandra. For the previous twenty-four hours, she'd done everything she could not to go into labor. She was exhausted, hungry, and hurting.

And now this.

The tiny baby began to pant as he struggled to breathe. I thought about how Sandra had struggled with her own breath just minutes before to bring him into this world. Their patterns weren't that different. Breathe, pant, pant, pant. Her labored breathing was to bring forth life. His labored breathing was meant to keep him alive. I thought of the end-of-life breathing—the abnormal pattern referred to as Cheyne-Stokes respiration, something I'd witnessed so many times before—and marveled at the connection between the two.

Sandra cried softly over her son as he took his last breath. I watched when his little body relaxed and went limp in her hands. As she began to whimper, I felt the warmth of God's presence, filling the room and bringing comfort. He had been present through the delivery, and he was with Sandra and her son now.

As she cried harder, I cried with her.

✦　✦　✦

A very thin veil of breaths separates this world from the next. Sometimes, the curtain blows open to let a soul come through. Sometimes, it remains open to accept a soul back in. I don't know what all was wrong with Sandra's baby, but I know he would have faced a mountain of insurmountable illnesses had he lived through the day; even then, there were no guarantees that he would have survived for long.

There are millions of babies who are never born into this world. As many as a third of all pregnancies end in miscarriage. Often, the mother thinks her menstrual cycle is just a week or two off. She has no idea that a baby is forming in her womb. I know that God holds *every* life precious and that babies who aren't born into this world are born directly into heaven. In those cases, *God* is the ultimate baby catcher.

As painful as it was for me to watch Sandra's baby leave his mother's bosom and go to God's bosom, it was a reminder to me of divine sovereignty. God gives, and God takes. But when God takes, he is taking to himself, to a place that is better than this fallen world we are born into.

Our loss is heaven's gain.

✦ ✦ ✦

Every woman who gives birth is a hero. She is the star of the show—at least until the baby is born and takes that honor away. But for Karen, being "the star of the show" took on new meaning.

We hadn't been in Jackson that long, and we didn't know many people, so each week when we attended our Lamaze class, it was fun to get to know the other couples. One day a single man showed up to the class and asked the teacher if he could speak to her in the hall. When they returned, the man introduced himself as a producer for the local news.

"We're doing a special on natural childbirth, and we're looking for a couple to feature as part of our show. If you'd be willing to have a camera crew follow you in labor, we'll give you a keepsake videotape of your child's birth."

I thought it sounded like a great idea. This was long before the days of portable video cameras, and even longer before everyone could shoot a video with their phones. I also loved the idea of educating a television audience about natural childbirth. Plus, did I mention *we'd get a free videotape?*

As soon as he asked for volunteers, my hand shot up.

Just as quickly, Karen's hand shot out and punched me in the upper arm. "But we get a free videotape!" I whispered, with my hand still waving wildly in the air.

"I don't want a free videotape!" she said. I knew she meant it.

It was too late; the man had already seen my hand. In front of everyone, he asked for our name and contact information, as well as our due date. I provided him with the details, and he wrote them down. I could tell Karen was fuming. When we left class an hour later, Karen was still mad.

"What's the big deal?" I asked. "It will be an opportunity to educate a lot of people, and *we'll get a free videotape!*"

Through gritted teeth, she said, "I'm just going to ask you one question: Who do you think they'll be filming? *You?*"

It was a good point and one I hadn't considered. As a green doctor and an even greener husband, I learned an important lesson that day—always listen to the patient.

Especially when she's your wife.

Fortunately, the crew had asked for two couples to volunteer in case one didn't work out. Since the other couple was due before we were, I figured I didn't have much to worry about. And I was right. They went into labor a week ahead of us.

Unfortunately, they needed a C-section.

We were back on the news.

✦ ✦ ✦

Karen's labor was typical for a first pregnancy—long and hard. Even the Lamaze breathing didn't speed things up. Of course, the camera crew was there to film the entire thing, which made it seem even longer than it was. Though everyone was appropriately discreet, Karen wasn't happy with me. As I helped her with her breathing, I found myself apologizing.

Breathe, pant, pant.

"I will never do this again."

Breathe, pant, pant.

"I am so sorry."

Breathe, pant, pant.

"You're right, and next time I will listen."

As a husband, labor coach, and soon-to-be new father, I was beyond excited. I'd been present for a lot of births, and every one of them was special to me. But this one was different. This baby was *mine*. I would be the one responsible for him or her. This is the one I'd put my life on the line for.

In the delivery room I paid attention to everything that was happening medically. Sometimes knowing too much is a bad thing because I considered everything that could go wrong. When the doctor saw our baby crowning, I knew we were in the homestretch—Karen's labor was about to end.

This was a critical part in the delivery. As a doctor, I usually wanted to deliver the baby fast because the placenta was tearing away and oxygen was no longer being delivered to the infant. If the baby gets stuck in transition for too long, there is a chance of the oxygen level dropping. It's important to get the baby out so he can take his first breath. At the same time, doctors don't want the mom's tissue to tear or to find the umbilical cord wrapped around the baby's neck. So delivery is always a delicate dance of speed and safety.

From having delivered more than one hundred babies, I knew what a special—but also tense—moment this was. This was the last point where the doctor could tell the mother to hold on or to push. It was also the last moment the baby had in the womb before entering this world.

By now Karen's contractions were so intense that even she couldn't control the urgency of her labor. She squeezed my hand, bore down, and squeezed out our first child.

"It's a girl!" the doctor said.

I'd said those same words many times before, but they had never sounded so sweet. When they placed our precious daughter on Karen's chest, I marveled over her little pink body and kitten-like cry.

There is something about a new soul entering this world that can't be explained by biology. Only God can take the credit. I joined Karen in tears of happiness celebrating our new little bundle. Watching my wife with our beautiful baby girl on her chest, I felt like I was the luckiest man who had ever lived. I had two miracles! The first was getting Karen to be my wife, and now having our precious daughter.

I felt a warm glow in the room and a connection with heaven unlike any I had felt before. I knew the veil had opened again, this time to allow a little, pink, writhing, kicking, screaming baby girl into our lives and our hearts.

We recognized that she was a gift from God. While I had always seen each new life as a miracle, I'd never felt the pleasure of that miracle as much as I did that day.

We called her Kristen Michelle, and we also were thankful that we could call this miracle *ours.*

✦ ✦ ✦

The news story turned out even better than we expected. A few people from our church and Bible study who saw it congratulated us on a job well done. Even Karen was pleased with the videotape. When it turned out better than she expected, she forgave me for volunteering us—although she told me she *never* wanted to do anything like that again.

I thought she had been amazing. And now I had the videotape to prove it.

Chapter 15
GOD'S PROVISION

✦

"Somebody help me! My baby can't breathe!"

I had turned to say good-bye to the trauma center staff in the sleepy town of Lexington when I heard the mother's terrifying cries coming from the parking lot.

"Help me, please! My baby, my baby!"

I'd heard that wail before. It's the sound a mother makes when she loses her child to heaven's gate. It's a horrifying sound forever branded on your heart and soul.

It was my second year of residency, and I was winding down one of my first-ever overnight shifts in the ER. It was scary being a young doctor and in charge. I'd just been telling myself what a great job I'd done making it through my first night without a single true emergency. It had mostly been a no-hitter in the one-room, one-bed trauma center. I'd even had a chance to nap in the on-call room. The only action I'd seen had been much earlier in the evening when I'd stitched up a couple of cuts.

That changed in an instant as I faced the worst nightmare for a new resident—in fact, for any doctor: a dying baby. I could tell from the anguish in the mother's wail that if it hadn't happened yet, it was about to.

My hair stood on end.

✦ ✦ ✦

As resident doctors, we were on the front lines of medicine each time we took shifts in the backwoods towns that surrounded Jackson. We treated small emergencies in our facilities and readied big emergencies for transport to the hospital. Most of these trauma centers had only a single bed or two in the emergency room. Regardless of the facilities the residents worked in, these young doctors were the patients' lifelines to the specialists who worked in Jackson. Often, we were the only doctors standing between a patient's life and death.

Those opportunities to be in the ER served *us*, too. As residents in the Family Medicine Program, our pay was not enough for most of us to live on. The money we made working those overnight shifts in the little trauma centers around Jackson made the difference between living barely above the poverty line and being able to feed and clothe our families. Now that Karen and I had two girls (Ashley followed Kristen in 1985), I'd started moonlighting to cover the costs of diapers and baby food.

However, those of us who were moonlighting were worried. We'd heard that our superiors thought we were more interested in the money than in learning. They felt that overnight shifts in the ER took too much time away from our regular training and left us sluggish the next day. Rumors circulated that those in charge were going to end the practice of moonlighting. If that happened, I didn't know how my family was going to make it.

✦ ✦ ✦

The mother burst through the doors of the trauma center and ran toward the nurses' desk.

"My baby! My baby! Please help my baby!"

In her arms was a little boy, probably nine or ten months old. He was blue. She handed the child to a nurse, who in turn handed him to me—a limp and lifeless baby. I could feel my emotions welling up and threatening to spill over.

Keep it together, I told myself.

With two kids of my own at home, this one felt personal. This blond-haired, blue-eyed boy could have passed as my girls' baby brother. I swallowed hard, trying to choke back my emotions and regain my professionalism.

I'm the one in charge here, I reminded myself. *I've got to take control.*

"What's going on?" I asked.

"He was *fine*," the mother insisted between breathless sobs. "I just turned my back for a minute!"

"It's okay. Tell me what happened," I said, trying to calm her.

"He was in the high chair," she said, gasping for air. "I was feeding him breakfast, and I turned around to grab his cereal. When I turned back, he was choking! I just picked him up and ran over here." She grabbed my arm. "Please, you've got to save him! He's my entire life!"

From the boy's color, I could tell that whatever had caused the choking was completely obstructing his airway. I tried not to panic as I laid the baby on a cot and listened for any sounds of breathing. None. I did a sweep of his throat with my finger. Nothing.

I could hear the mother praying, "Oh, Jesus, please, sweet Jesus."

My mind exploded in a thousand directions as I tried to determine what I should do first. *What were the details of the pediatric advanced life support course I took before I started working in the ER?* While working to clear the airway, I tried to think ahead.

A: Airway

B: Breathing

C: Circulation

D: . . .

What was D?

Suddenly, those acronyms weren't just textbook mnemonics or theories on a blackboard. They were the cues I needed to save this beautiful, limp baby. Other questions quickly followed.

Should I assemble a code team?

Should I perform a tracheotomy?

Should I ask the mother to leave?

The mother stood in the corner crying and begging both God and me to do something. I glanced up at her terror-filled eyes. She was trembling.

"Assemble the code team," I whispered to the nurse.

I knew it would take her a minute or two to round them up from the rest of the trauma center. I wasn't even sure we had enough time to wait for them. I was out of my league here. *What else can I do for him? For his mother?* It was up to God now. I began to pray a prayer similar to the mother's cries. *Oh, God, please help me save this baby.* And I prayed it over and over as I tried to figure out what to do next.

Suddenly, a warm breeze blew through the stagnant hospital room. The sensation told me God was present, and I felt God's hands on me. Knowing that gave me confidence beyond my medical training.

I grabbed the laryngoscope, a metal tool with a hook-like head that would give me a view of the larynx. I stuck it in the baby's throat and looked around. Nothing.

Though it had only been a minute or two at the most, I knew the baby had been without air for too long.

"Get a tracheotomy tray," I said to the nurse.

But as I said it, God spoke to me. It wasn't an audible voice. It was more like I *felt* his words inside of my head. *You won't need it.*

As I looked through the laryngoscope again, something caught my eye. It was almost as if something moved. *Is there something in there? Had I seen something?* I looked again. *I had!* It looked like a ball bobbing back and forth.

The hard back of the laryngoscope dislodged it enough, and the baby was able to take one quick breath. It gave us a moment to breathe as well, but I still had to get it out.

"Hemostat," I said to the nurse.

She handed me the clamp-like device. Holding the laryngoscope in my left hand and the long hemostat in my right, I reached in and grabbed the object. I pulled out a small square of plastic with a notch out of one side.

A bread clip.

The baby took a deep breath and started crying. Frightened by the people surrounding him, or maybe by the doctor's face, he started searching for his mother. I'd never been so happy to reunite a baby with his momma.

"I'm sending you to Jackson," I told her. "Just to get everything checked and make sure he's okay."

+ + +

An hour or so later, I got ready to leave the Lexington trauma center for the second time that day.

"Great job!" said one of the nurses as I walked out the door.

It had been such an exhilarating experience to hand a healthy, breathing baby back to his mother. Unlike earlier in the day, I wasn't patting myself on the back because I did it. Instead, I was thinking how any number of circumstances could have changed the outcome. If I hadn't seen the piece of plastic, if it had been smaller, if his throat had been larger and the clip had gone down farther, if I'd still been in the on-call room instead of standing at the door, if the mom had not lived across the street, if it had been raining and she'd slipped in the parking lot—if any of those "ifs" had occurred, the baby could have died in my arms.

There are an infinite number of ifs in medicine and in life that I had no control over. But God did.

I'd felt his hand guiding me throughout the whole event. He was the one who kept me calm and free of panic. He was the one who helped me see the plastic lodged in the baby's throat. He was the one who helped me grab the moving object at the right time, and I was so thankful he had!

The next morning when I arrived at the Jackson hospital for rounds, I saw the mom and her baby boy leaving to head back to Lexington. She ran up and hugged me—her thanks were profuse and heartfelt.

I understood exactly how she felt. I felt that same gratitude toward God. It was his miracle, and I was just grateful to have played a part.

✦ ✦ ✦

Early one Monday morning about six months before finishing my residency, I was having a cup of coffee before I left the house to make rounds. The phone rang, and it was the director of the residents program. As one of two chief residents that year, I wasn't surprised to get a call from the medical director on a Monday morning, but as soon as I answered, his tone told me this one was different.

"I need to see you and Tim in the conference room near my office right away."

"Yes, sir," I replied. His sense of urgency caught me off guard. "We'll be right over after the morning report."

"And I want the other residents to come with you."

It was an unusual request; we rarely met together as a group and never on such short notice. "We'll be there," I said.

Karen walked into the kitchen. She was wearing her bathrobe and looked sleepy.

"The director of the program just called. He wants to meet with me and the other residents this morning. I'm afraid they're going to cut out all the moonlighting."

"Oh, no! What will we do without the extra money?" She looked worried.

"I don't know; I'll think of something. In the meantime, let's just pray."

I was thankful I had married a frugal wife. Karen knew how to stretch a dollar, and she spent money wisely. Even so, with two little girls and a resident's salary, money was tight.

Our family was in God's hands, but I felt the responsibility of providing for them. Growing up poor, I wanted more for my girls, and for Karen, too. *How will we manage without the extra income?*

Karen and I said a quick prayer together over our coffee, and then I left for the hospital.

✦ ✦ ✦

Tim was the other chief resident, and he'd gotten the same call. I was worried. Taking away our ability to moonlight would be bad enough, but could there be something even worse planned? As we walked across the parking lot that separated the hospital from the UT family practice clinic, I quizzed him. "Have you heard anything new that we need to be prepared for?"

Tim shook his head.

Maybe I should try to make a medical case for why moonlighting is important. I thought about the baby who, weeks earlier, had choked on the bread clip. *Where would that mother be if there hadn't been a doctor in the emergency room that morning?* We reached the conference room and were told to wait for all the other residents to arrive. Through the glass door, I could see that the hospital administrator was also there, and he seemed to be having an animated conversation with the director. Now I was really scared. The administrator was there only when serious problems arose. Either somebody had really screwed up or there were potential legal issues involved.

While Tim and I waited for the other residents to arrive, neither of us spoke. I felt as if I were back in junior high waiting to see the principal. *God, I need you now*, I prayed. *Please help the director see how much we need the extra income, and if not, please give me peace and strength to deal with whatever happens next.*

Once the residents had all arrived, the director opened the conference room door and said, "Come in and have a seat."

We filed in and each took a seat around the table.

The director appeared nervous as he cleared his throat. "Boys, the hospital is in a bit of a predicament. I know all of you are working on the side, outside this hospital. You've been moonlighting."

I looked again at the residents. Some of them had just finished overnight shifts and looked sleepy. Most of them needed the money as badly as I did. Many of them had wives with babies at home. Once again I said a quick prayer. This time it wasn't only for me; it was for all of us. *What will we tell our wives?*

"We're going to need your help. Due to some hiccups in contract negotiations, the hospital is without ER doctors," the director said.

My head had been down, waiting for the ax to fall, but now I looked up to see what he was talking about.

"We're going to need your help to cover the ER on nights and weekends until you finish the program. And we know that is asking a lot." He paused and looked at the administrator. "So we're going to pay you double what you're making now if you'll agree to help us out."

Every resident's jaw, including mine, dropped in disbelief.

This was not what I expected at all. I knew who was responsible, and I bowed my head in thankfulness. It was an answer to prayer beyond anything I could ever have imagined.

Chapter 16
STAB IN THE DARK

✦

The radio crackled. "Trauma one, this is 452 en route to your facility."

I didn't pay much attention to the nurse taking the call from the ambulance driver until she said, "Dr. Anderson, I think you need to hear this."

She was referring to the radio that ambulance drivers used to communicate with the hospital to give us a heads-up.

"Please repeat, 452," she said.

"We have a twenty-four-year-old male with a trauma code in progress. Stab wound to the left anterior chest wall. There is no blood pressure. No pulse. Monitor shows EMD."

EMD, electromechanical dissociation, meant that although electrical activity showed in the patient's heart, the heart itself wasn't contracting. This could indicate a rupture in the heart. Though it wasn't a good sign, it was consistent with what I'd expect to see from someone who had been stabbed in the chest.

"He was intubated with two large-bore IVs hanging wide open with lactated Ringer's solution. Repeat: no pulse, BP, or spontaneous respirations. Arrival at your facility in approximately three minutes."

✦ ✦ ✦

Our residency training was paying off. In the ER, we no longer had to stop to think about each step. We knew what to do, and we just reacted. As the residents stepped up to fill the vacancies left by the departing ER doctors, the codes and calls all became second nature. Of course, we were on a first-name basis with the interventional cardiologist and trauma surgeons, since they were the ones who pulled us out of any tailspin we might find ourselves in. But medically speaking, we were handling things well.

At home, our wives were also pleased with the increased and more predictable income, but they weren't as fond of our absences. The new shifts in the ER were a mixed blessing. Instead of moonlighting only on weekends, we were now working weeknights, too. The hospital in Jackson was so busy that we no longer had those occasional no-hitters we had in the rural trauma centers. In other words, we weren't getting much sleep. We may have been making twice the money, but we were earning every penny of it. Now we prayed to survive until the end of our shifts, and sometimes that our patients would too.

Every night I worked in the ER, I worked in the foyer of heaven. From that first incredible night when I felt heaven's presence in the hospital room after Dennis died, I'd begun to look for God in every situation, and I often recognized signs that he was there. When the door between this world and the next was cracked open, even slightly, the sights, sounds, and smells from the other side would blow into the emergency room. I'd feel the warmth of a soul passing while heaven's breeze welcomed the soul in with a light fragrance of citrus and lilac.

Each time this happened, I'd sense the overwhelming love and comfort I'd experienced in my dream, and I'd long to go too.

✦　✦　✦

Three minutes is either an eternity or merely a single grain of sand in the hourglass of time. It all depends on your perspective. That night it was both. I grabbed a long gown, gloves, and a mask, and I ordered the nurses who would be assisting me to do the same. The universal precautions were followed out of self-preservation. AIDS was just making headlines, and while there was a lot we didn't know, one thing we knew for sure was that anyone who was bleeding was a threat to our lives.

I checked the room and made sure the instruments I might need were available. Then I rechecked again. I began making lists in my head. The first was the ABCs of a trauma code. *Airway.* He was already intubated. *Breathing.* The EMTs had started this, and the respiratory therapist was standing by. *Circulation.* He had no circulation, no pulse, no blood pressure.

But he still has electrical activity in the monitor?

Basically, the electricity was working, but the mechanisms of his heart weren't. When there was a disassociation between the electrical and the mechanical functions of the heart, I had to figure out what was causing it—something physical was keeping the heart from expanding. I paced as I considered what the cause could be. There were at least two possibilities. The first was a collapsed lung, called a tension pneumothorax. The second was cardiac tamponade—the heart was compressed due to fluid in the pericardium, the sac around the heart.

Up to this point, most of the patients I had personally dealt with who had died in the ER were very ill or very elderly. Their deaths were expected. This one wasn't. It troubled me to think a man around my own age was losing his life so tragically. It also brought up some of the same questions I'd asked years earlier when I so violently lost my cousins. *Why, God? Why would you allow this to happen?*

I could feel emotions rising from deep within me, and I needed to get control. If I didn't, my mask would start fogging up, and I wouldn't be able to see. Then everyone would know how nervous and emotional I was. I began to pray. *I need you right now. I need your healing hands to be used through me. Please guide me through this process . . .*

✦ ✦ ✦

When the patient arrived in the ER, I could tell that the EMTs had been accurate in their assessment.

Trauma resuscitations hardly ever succeed, but I knew I had to try. Fortunately, he was already intubated, and his sucking chest wound was sealed by a Vaseline gauze.

The staff surrounded the ambulance stretcher, and on my count, they slid him to our gurney. I began to examine his airway and breathing, while the nurse took over bagging—using a handheld device to ventilate him—from the emergency medical technician. I mentally moved through the checklist and ended my initial exam with a thorough inspection of his stab wound.

I looked down at his dark skin and chest hairs, now matted with blood. The ambulance had picked him up in a bad area of town, and the driver speculated that the patient may have been involved with a drug deal gone bad. But my exam didn't show any of the usual signs of an addict. There were no needle tracks, and he wasn't underweight.

In an otherwise healthy man, I was pretty sure it would be one of the two things, if not both, that I'd considered before the ambulance arrived: He either had a collapsed lung or blood in the sac surrounding his heart.

I decided to go with the collapsed lung. In order to fix that, ironically, the only treatment that could save him was the same thing that brought him to us in the first place—a stab to the chest. This time with a needle.

The lung was under pressure, causing it to deflate. A needle with a one-way valve would release the air and allow the lungs to fill back up. Once the lung was inflated, the man would be able to breathe, and his blood pressure and pulse should return to normal. To do it properly, I had to stick the needle in exactly the right spot between the lungs and the ribs, in the pleural space. "Hold the dressing in place," I instructed the nurse, "and keep that wound sealed."

I inserted the needle into the money spot and heard the unmistakable hiss. The bagging suddenly became easier, and he was obviously breathing better. But he still had no blood pressure. The tension pneumothorax was relieved, but something else was wrong.

What can it be? The lung was inflated and working. He was now breathing easier. We'd done CPR all along. I could see the stab wound, and it wasn't that. The only possible explanation was that he also had a cardiac tamponade. My heart sank as I thought about what I would have to do—stab him again.

This time in the heart.

This was his last chance. If I missed, if I was wrong about the cause, if anything was off by the tiniest bit, he would not be coming back.

I could hear crying and wailing outside the ER doors. "What's going on out there?" I asked.

"It's his family. They've arrived, and they're gathering in the waiting area," one of the nurses said.

Not only were there a lot of them, but they sounded distraught. Several women were crying. A few of the men seemed to be yelling loudly, though I couldn't comprehend what they were saying. Each time someone new came in, their hysterics would rise to new levels. I knew they were worried.

So was I.

"Spinal needle, with a twenty CC syringe, please."

I was standing on the left side of the patient almost parallel to his shoulder. My right hand was trembling as I took the syringe from the nurse. I hoped she didn't notice. It wasn't good to have shaking hands when what I was about to do required such precision. *Into the pericardial space and no farther*, I reminded myself, as I raised the needle high enough above his heart to make sure I could hit the mark with enough pressure to stab him.

But then I stopped.

Please, Lord, hold my hand. I can't do this one on my own, I prayed. The prayer seemed to lift me out of my chaotic environment. I took a deep breath and felt my heart slow ever so slightly as my hands grew steadier.

Once again, I lifted the needle.

This time in a quick downward motion, I stabbed the patient's heart.

Suddenly, I felt a calming breeze. An air current from heaven seemed to blow all around me. Nonclotting blood rushed into the syringe, and as I held it in place, I looked up and to the right and felt a slight brush of wind on my cheek. The ever-present veil—so thin, yet thick enough to separate us from the next world—was flowing freely in a heavenly breeze. Then I felt the warmth of his soul. Before anything else was said, before I looked at the machines, I knew. He was coming back.

"Doctor! We have a pulse!"

Her words pulled me back to the operating room.

"Call the thoracic surgeon and tell the OR to prepare a room. Then prepare to roll him up."

I took off my mask and gloves and tried to collect myself. *Thank you, God, for holding my hand while I made that puncture. I couldn't have done it without you.*

✦   ✦   ✦

The situation was still grave but hopeful.

The mother cried while I held her hands and told her that her son, DeWayne, was dead on arrival, but through God's grace we'd been able to restore his blood pressure and his breathing.

I didn't tell her all the details of how God had been with me. How could I explain them? But from our conversation, I could see this was a woman who prayed for her family. She was a single mother who was doing the best she could despite her circumstances. "I just want you to know, I felt God's presence in the room with us, and I think he's going to be okay."

I explained how the thoracic surgeon had DeWayne in surgery, and we would know more after the surgeon examined him. I suggested she move to the surgical waiting room where that staff would keep her informed.

The women with her were all younger. I couldn't tell if they were friends or family, but they circled around the weeping mother and helped her to the surgical wing. The men who had been so noisy earlier seemed subdued, and they followed behind.

My shift ended before the surgery, so it wasn't until the next day that I learned the details of what the thoracic surgeon found. The stab wound to DeWayne's chest had nicked the sac surrounding his heart, and one of the blood vessels had filled the sac with fluid.

I felt as if I'd had another direct encounter with heaven, just when I needed it most. But at the time, I didn't know the half of it.

+   +   +

I visited DeWayne on my daily rounds that day and each day for the duration of his hospital stay. Three days after he was admitted, he was sitting up in his bed and feeling better.

"What's up, Dr. Anderson?" he said when I walked in.

"Looks like you are!"

I pulled up a chair to talk. I was concerned and wanted to make sure he understood the enormity of what had happened to him.

"Do you remember what happened the night they brought you to the ER?" I asked.

"A little," he said.

"You were DOA. Dead on arrival. You had no pulse, no blood pressure, and you weren't breathing on your own." I wanted him to know that the lifestyle he'd been leading had consequences that could have cost him his life.

"I remember that," DeWayne said. "But after I got to the hospital and you moved me onto that other bed in the room with all the bright lights, you took care of me, Doc."

"You remember us moving you?"

"Yeah, sure, that was right before you stabbed me the first time."

"You remember me stabbing you?"

"Yeah. Twice."

I was surprised he could recall those events. "What else do you remember?"

He described the nurse who had worked with me and the respiratory therapist. "Doc, would you please tell them thank you for saving my life?"

I was stunned at the clarity and detail of his memories.

"Were you in pain at all?"

"No, I didn't feel a thing," DeWayne said. "But I was real scared."

I didn't tell him that I was too.

"But then I saw my granny."

"You saw your granny?" I asked. I tried to remember if I had seen her too. I'd talked to his mother, and there were other, much younger women in the waiting room when I'd spoken to her. But there wasn't anyone that I would have considered old enough to be his grandmother.

"That's when I knew I was going to be all right."

"When did you know?" I was confused.

"When I saw my granny," he repeated. "She was sitting in the corner of the room, until you let her come over."

"I let her come over?"

"Yeah, don't you remember?"

I didn't, but that didn't mean it didn't happen. I'd had enough wow moments to know that God worked in some pretty unexpected ways.

I wanted to know more. "What did your granny say?" I asked.

"She held my hand and said, 'You're going to be all right.' That's when I knew I didn't have to be afraid no more."

"Do you remember what I was doing?"

"Oh, yeah, that's when you were staring at something. It was up and to my right, kind of far off in the distance. It was like you were listening real hard for something."

I smiled. Heaven's breath had been in the room that night, and we'd both experienced it differently. As I stood up, I said, "If everything looks good, you'll be able to go home tomorrow."

On my way out, I told one of the nurses what he'd said.

"That's odd," the nurse said.

"That's God," I said.

I closed the chart and handed it to her. "I'll stop by tomorrow, and I'm hopeful he'll be ready to be discharged."

✦ ✦ ✦

I couldn't get DeWayne's words out of my mind. I'd heard reports of patients who hovered between life and death observing what was going on in an emergency room, but to my knowledge, I'd never had a patient who had experienced it. DeWayne, however, had clearly been dead when they brought him in. Without a pulse and a heartbeat, he shouldn't have had a working mind and been able to observe the things he observed.

The next morning I picked up his chart at the nurses' station and checked the notes for any signs of confusion. There were none. He looked good, and he was certainly coherent and lucid.

I cleared DeWayne to go home and returned to the nurses' station to write up his discharge instructions. A familiar voice interrupted me.

"Dr. Anderson, I'm glad I caught you!"

It was Kathy, the nurse I'd talked to the previous day.

"I wanted to tell you that DeWayne's mom visited yesterday after you left, and so I asked her if DeWayne's granny had been in the ER the night they brought him in. His mother said his granny passed away in her sleep. She's been dead for four years. She thought Granny must have visited DeWayne from the other side."

Though DeWayne knew his granny was dead, he wasn't alarmed when he saw her. While growing up, he'd heard stories of people who had also seen deceased loved ones in the room with them. At the time, his experience left me with a lot of questions. However, I'd later be present when others had similar encounters.

✦ ✦ ✦

I've spent a lot of hours marveling about what DeWayne and I each experienced that night in the ER. I don't have all the answers, but what I've come to understand is that God sent DeWayne's granny to be with him that night. Though his granny was dead, she'd been sent to restore DeWayne's life and his spirit and to calm his soul, just like my cousins had done for me.

It seems to me that, in rare cases, God allows dreams or visions of people we have loved, those who have gone on to the other side, to help us know and accomplish our purposes here on earth. During those moments when the veil blows freely, I know that God is at work.

Chapter 17
MOVING CONFIRMATIONS

✦

My third year of residency was the final chapter in my formal training. It was both frightening and exciting. No longer were decisions made by teams or committees; I was now the sole decision maker.

Although I obviously felt the responsibility for the medical decisions I made each day, another decision also weighed heavily on my shoulders—where I would practice medicine once I finished.

I had an obligation to repay my scholarship to the National Health Service Corps (NHSC). In exchange for their paying for my education, I had agreed to practice as a primary care doctor in an underserved area. But I still had to choose a location from their approved list, a decision that would affect my family and me for the rest of our lives. Walking the halls of the hospital, I'd find myself getting lost in my thoughts, distracted by all the considerations of choosing a new location. At night, I had a hard time falling asleep as I struggled through all the issues involved. The only way I found I could carry it was on my knees, allowing God to lift it for me.

✦   ✦   ✦

Early in my third year, one of my final rotations was rural medicine. Mine was located in Dickson, Tennessee, where I worked alongside Dr. Bill Jackson, another graduate of the UT Family Medicine Residency Program. Bill was the heir apparent to the medical center in

Dickson County started by his father, Dr. Jimmy, and his two uncles, who were also doctors. I loved working with Bill and Dr. Jimmy, but even more important, I loved working with the patients in the area.

Not long after I arrived, talk began about creating a satellite location in Cheatham County, to the east. With more than twenty thousand people and only two doctors, Cheatham was a doctor-deficient county with a ratio that was ten times what was considered optimal and safe. Dr. Jimmy had befriended one of the doctors there, and Bill began discussions to build the first new hospital in the state in more than twenty years. I found the conversation interesting, but I didn't participate in it.

One day, Dr. Jimmy pulled me into his office. "There's a great need for doctors in this area," he said. "We'd like you to partner with us on this new endeavor."

As he filled me in on the details, I could feel the enthusiasm building within me. I'd already fallen in love with the locals. How could I say no to the opportunity of starting a new hospital in such a needy place? In addition, Ashland City, Tennessee, had been on the NHSC list for five years running.

Karen and I prayed about it and discussed it at length. This opportunity filled all our needs and was an answer to our prayers. We both agreed this was where God was calling us. It was good to know I would finish out my third year of residency with a plan for my career, my family, and our future. I felt as if God had reached down and lifted the burden of my future from my shoulders.

+ + +

By late April, I was only weeks away from finishing my residency when the envelope from the NHSC arrived. I opened it, planning to fill out the paperwork so I could turn it in and check one more thing off my growing to-do list.

Pen in hand, I scanned the list for Ashland City and didn't see it on my first pass. I read it again, more slowly the second time. It wasn't there.

"What am I missing?" I asked, handing Karen the list. "Do you see Ashland City?"

She looked carefully; then she looked at me, puzzled. "It's not on here," she said.

I read the paperwork more closely and saw their recommendation was a little place in Alabama. It was an odd recommendation. There were already enough physicians in that location. "Why wouldn't they want us to go to Ashland City where there aren't nearly enough doctors?"

It was hard to understand. Ashland City had been on the list for years. I had done my rural rotation in the area, I'd been recruited to go there as part of the program, and now there were plans to build a much-needed hospital. *What went wrong?* The weight I felt God had so easily lifted was back on my shoulders—and heavier than ever.

I was scared and confused. This wasn't what Karen and I had planned, and it certainly was not where we thought God had called us. *Has your will for us changed? Did we miss it somehow? I thought you were behind all this.* If Ashland City wasn't on the list, it was obvious God must have wanted us to serve somewhere else, but where? Until I received the paperwork, everything Karen and I had prayed about seemed to lead us to Ashland City. Now, we were in a real predicament. Not only did we *not* have a plan or a place to go, but apparently we had completely misinterpreted what God had been trying to tell us. The last part concerned me more than anything. How could Karen and I reconcile what we thought we'd heard from him with what the evidence revealed?

"I'd better call Dr. Jimmy," I said, dragging myself to the phone. "It's going to be hard to break the news to him."

I called the practice in Dickson and got Bill on the phone first. I told him about the paperwork I'd received. He also found it incomprehensible. "Let me put Dad on the phone," he said.

Dr. Jimmy answered, and I explained once again.

"No way! I'll check on this and get back to you," he said and hung up.

I chuckled at the thought of Dr. Jimmy, a good ol' country boy, going up against the NHSC, but it was a classic response from the elder doctor.

+ + +

I had only a couple of weeks before I needed to make a decision, so each night Karen and I pored over the list they'd sent us and tried to decipher where it was that God wanted us to go. It was even harder to hear his voice, knowing that we must have missed it when he spoke before. The only thing we consistently heard from him was a faint whisper in our ears, *The needs of the many outweigh the needs of the few.* But we had no idea what that meant.

We investigated several NHSC-approved opportunities, but they each had more doctors and less need than Ashland City—or all of Cheatham County, for that matter. It didn't make medical sense, and it didn't add up when the only thing we were hearing from God was to *serve the many.* So we continued to research available opportunities without clear direction.

+ + +

Two weeks before the deadline, I received a late-night call from Dr. Jimmy. "Meet us at the Nashville airport in the morning," he growled in his Southern drawl. "We have a meeting to discuss the hospital in Ashland City. The flight leaves at seven."

"Where are we going?"

"DC!" he barked and then hung up.

I had to call his secretary to get the rest of the details.

The next morning, I met Dr. Jimmy at the airport. He introduced me to the chief of staff from Goodlark Regional Medical Center in Dickson and the hospital's attorney.

"I've already arranged for you to meet with Congressman Don Sundquist, Senator Jim Sasser, and Senator Al Gore," said Dr. Jimmy.

I realized he didn't have a suitcase with him. "Aren't you going?"

"Nope. These guys can handle it. And you tell Senator Gore that

I said hello. His daddy was a great senator, and he helped us when we were starting out. I trust his son will do the same." Dr. Jimmy looked me in the eye and shook my hand. "I'm counting on you, and Cheatham County is depending on you."

I was representing the project to these politicians? I tried not to show how nervous I was. "Thank you, sir," I said. But I'm sure he heard my voice tremble. I'd never even met the men I was traveling with, and I had no idea what to say to these important politicians. I began to pray *hard*.

Once in DC, we moved from government building to government building, describing the great need in Ashland City. We explained how necessary it was to have another doctor in place, and that without one, the new hospital building was in jeopardy. Without the hospital, the medical needs of so many would go unmet.

I particularly remember the meeting with Senator Gore. He was extremely charming, and he listened patiently and asked insightful questions. When we neared the end of our conversation, Senator Gore picked up the phone and said, "Can you get the head of the NHSC on the phone, please?"

When the call came through, Senator Gore got right to the point. "We have a young doctor who needs to go to Ashland City. Will you see what you can do?"

I was awestruck at his power, and it must have shown in my face. The senator chuckled. Then holding his hand over the mouthpiece so the other person couldn't hear, he reminded us that he was on a committee that had influence over the NHSC.

Karen and I had both been praying, before I left and while I was gone. We believed God was calling us to Ashland City. By the time I left DC, I was told by several people that Ashland City was back on the list!

✦   ✦   ✦

But it wasn't.

I returned home. A few days later, I received a call from the regional director at the NHSC. "You haven't informed us of your choice yet, and it's getting down to the wire."

"I'm going to Ashland City," I announced proudly.

Apparently, he hadn't gotten the memo. "I'm sorry; Ashland City isn't on the list. If you choose to go there, you know there will be penalties."

Indeed, I did. We'd been through this conversation several times before. Even though Ashland City was even more underserved than some of the places listed, if it wasn't on *the* list, it didn't count. I would be in default of my loan.

The penalty would be either to accept an assignment of their choice or to pay back three times the loan amount plus prime interest (about 20 percent at the time). Conservatively, Karen and I estimated this to be about $300,000.

"Let me talk to my wife and call you back," I said.

I felt so deflated. *What is going on?* Karen and I felt that God was clearly calling us to Ashland City. We'd thought that from the beginning. More recently, we'd felt that we heard God confirm it when he had said, *The needs of the many outweigh the needs of the few.* I'd even seen him work among the power brokers in DC to accomplish what I thought was his will. How could Ashland City not be on the list, if it was so clearly what God wanted?

Lord, do you want me to have to pay back $300,000? How can I ever do that on a country doctor's salary? More than anything, I want what you want, but I have no idea how to do what you're asking.

I spoke with Karen that night. We both believed that Ashland City was where God was calling us despite the obstacles, and together we agreed that we'd take the consequences for doing what we believed was God's will.

My fingers shook the next day as I dialed the regional representative. When he answered I said, "I believe in something much bigger than this list. My wife and I have prayed about it, and we feel God is leading us to Ashland City, regardless of the cost. The need for a doctor there is greater than where you want to send me."

The director tried to talk me out of it. "If you don't go to the recommended place in Alabama, you know you could get sent to an Indian reservation out west, right?"

"I understand, but we'd refuse to go. We're heading to Ashland City."

"All right, then I will mark you down as in default of your loan. You should get the paperwork from us in the next couple of weeks."

It wasn't an easy decision—and I didn't tell anyone how terrified I was—but Karen and I both knew it was the right one. The relief we felt from having made our choice, however, was replaced with another burden. How would I pay back all that money on a rural doctor's salary? Fortunately, Karen was fearless. Every time I tried to discuss it, she'd say the same thing: "It's in God's hands, Reggie."

✦ ✦ ✦

June in Jackson was warm. I was finishing my residency and looking forward to having a couple of weeks off to visit our families before moving to Ashland City. I was home when the postman rang the doorbell.

"Certified letter for Reginald Anderson," he said. "Sign here."

He handed me the letter, and I could see it was from the NHSC. I took his pen, and my hand was so sweaty and shaky I could barely sign my name. Even for a doctor, it was illegible.

"Thank you," I said and closed the door behind him. I leaned my back against the wall. Though the house was air-conditioned, I was sweating profusely. With shaky hands, I opened the envelope, expecting to see orders to report to the Indian Health Service or to a prison to work with an inmate population. At the least, I expected to see a very large bill I wouldn't be able to pay back.

I pulled the letter out, gasped for air, slid down the wall to the floor, and cried.

"Who was at the door?" Karen asked as she entered the hallway. "Are you okay?"

I looked up into her beautiful, trusting face as she came over to check on me. With hands that were still trembling, I handed her the now tearstained letter. "Read this," I said, choking on my words.

She read out loud, "Congratulations! You have been assigned to Ashland City, Tennessee. Your service will begin July 1, 1986. If you do not appear for service on that date and in that location, you will be held in default."

We laughed, and we cried. We had been faithful to what we thought had been God's calling, and now we clearly had his blessing (and the NHSC's) to serve him where we'd heard his call all along. While we never uncovered the source of the mix-up, we knew the source of the blessing.

✦　✦　✦

Karen and I packed up the girls and moved to our new home in Ashland City. Once we were settled, I had to get about the business of starting my practice and taking on new patients. In big cities, patients might come from referrals or networking, but in Ashland City, they came when people showed up needing medical care. They would come back if I earned their trust.

In my first week of practice, I saw several elderly people and a few walk-ins—people with chronic illnesses, a diabetic, a teen with asthma, some middle-aged adults with high blood pressure, and a newborn who needed a pediatrician.

Even more than my assignment letter from the NHSC, being able to care for babies, the elderly who didn't want to go to "the big city," or those who needed regular medical care and were so thankful for my local services—it all proved to me that our family was in the right place.

✦　✦　✦

Ashland City quickly became home for Karen and our girls, Kristen and Ashley. Karen had told me earlier that Jesus would let us know when our quiver was full and we were done having children. Apparently, it wasn't full yet.

Less than three years after moving to Ashland City, we welcomed Julia into our home, and a year later, David followed. David was born with a cleft palate and required a lot of medical attention. Karen was busy shuttling him to specialists' appointments in Nashville, as well as taking care of the three girls. I was busy at my practice and working at the new Cheatham Medical Center, which was just a few years old at the time. After several particularly hard days, Karen and I talked and then prayed before deciding that David would be our last child.

Our quiver was now full.

A few days later, I was driving through the lush green Tennessee countryside and spotted a stream near the road. In a flash of memory, I recalled a detail about my dream, a prophecy I had long since forgotten. God had told me I would marry Karen and we would have *four* children, and now we did! I couldn't wait to tell Karen the detail I'd kept from her for so long that even I had forgotten it.

I was so overcome by God's love that I teared up and was afraid I'd have to stop driving, but a cool breeze dried my tears. I don't know if it was heaven's breath or the wind coming in my open truck window. It didn't matter. It was obvious that God was there with me.

I thought about the other things he'd said in my dream—that I would be a doctor, and I would practice in a rural Tennessee town. Though it all hadn't happened immediately, over time it had all come true, just as he'd promised. And now, I was living only three hours west of the place where that dream had occurred.

Late that night, as I lay in bed next to Karen—the wife I still couldn't believe I had—I thanked God for our four precious and healthy children and for the job that I loved. Then I turned to Karen and said, "Honey, there's something I've got to tell you. Remember the dream I had by the campfire? The dream that started all this?"

"Mm-hmm."

"Well, there's one small thing I've never told you. . . ."

Chapter 18
HEALING TOUCH

✦

A year before the NHSC mix-up, the National Health Service Corps brought Dr. Jeffrey Lundy to Ashland City, and when I arrived, we became partners. Before the hospital was completed, we would get occasional requests to visit shut-ins and the elderly. Often, they were too sick to make it to the clinic or too stubborn to go to the hospital in Nashville, which was about thirty miles away. The locals didn't trust people in "the big city." As a result, I occasionally got to follow in the footsteps of my television hero—Marcus Welby M.D., the fictional hometown doctor who still made house calls.

One of these visits was to see a lady named Mary, who lived out in the countryside. Whenever she got sick, she sent a family member to "fetch a doctor."

On this day, her granddaughter came into the clinic and said, "Granny's getting sicker every day. Now she won't even get up off the couch. Can you come visit her?"

"What's wrong with her?" I asked.

"She's coughing up blood and running a fever. Can you check on her this afternoon?"

Clinic hours ran from eight to eight, Monday through Friday, and nine to three on Saturday. The only day Dr. Lundy and I had off was Sunday. However, we'd worked out a rotation, so it wasn't twelve hours a day, every day, for both of us. On most days, one of us would work from eight to two and the other would work from two to eight. Then, at night, we alternated overnight shifts in the ER. On that particular day, I was scheduled to be off early.

Despite my schedule, I was young, idealistic, and still entertaining the Marcus Welby fantasies from my youth. "Sure, I'll come visit your granny." I had her write down the address and said, "I'll be there around three."

When my shift ended, I packed a few things I thought I might need into my black leather doctor's bag and walked to the car where Karen was waiting to pick me up. She had the kids in the car with her.

+ + +

The street name was the first indication that I should have been worried—or that I should have turned around. Shotgun Road was a long, winding dirt road with century-old oaks that canopied both sides of the drive. Along the way we saw deer, turkey, and geese. I even pointed out a beautiful hawk to the kids. But the area wasn't used just for hunting animals. Later, I'd learn that this stretch of road came by its name honestly—the last shooting of a *human* had happened only a few months prior.

When Karen stopped the car, I grabbed my bag and got out. Suddenly, a pit bull appeared and snarled at me. I froze, not sure what to do next. Without warning, he lunged, and I jumped away. I was getting ready to hightail it back to the car when the chain he was on, still secured to a nearby tree, jerked him back. Fortunately, the length of the chain stopped him just short of reaching me.

He was a mean-looking scoundrel of a dog, and I could feel my body trembling as I watched him. "Stay in the car and keep the girls in their seats," I warned Karen through the closed car window. I wanted her to be ready in case anything happened and we needed to make a quick getaway.

The dog stood between me and the front porch, blocking my path to the door. *How am I supposed to get in?* I tried to quickly assess the situation. Mary lived on the side of a hill in what could only be called a shack. *Maybe there's a door around back.*

Keeping my eye on the snarling dog, I cautiously navigated around the pit bull toward the back of the house. Thankfully, there was a back entrance. As I knocked on the screen door, it banged against the frame.

"Who's there?" a gruff-sounding older man asked.

"Dr. Anderson."

"C'mon in. Mary's in the front room."

I opened the door and entered. As it snapped shut behind me, I paused to give my eyes time to adjust to the dimly lit room. I could hear Mary wheezing; she was obviously in respiratory distress.

As I gingerly stepped around the mattresses on the floor, it was easy to see that five or six people lived in the three-room shack. That would have been enough, but animals were also living inside. Cats slept in the windowsills, and chickens freely roamed in and out of the propped-open front door.

Mary was lying on the couch that doubled as her bed. I sat down beside her and held her hand.

We were taught in medical school that if you listen to patients, they will tell you their diagnosis. I believe that when a doctor touches the patient, he or she is given confirmation to what the ill person expresses in words. I often found myself "listening" with my hands, so I could feel what my patient feels. Just as a mother develops a sensitivity or an instinct for her child's pain or illness, I felt that God gave me a similar gift that only increased with my medical training.

Mary started to say something and couldn't finish because she began choking. She was breathing fast and hard. I touched her forehead, and I could tell she was running a high fever. Something in the way she looked and felt told me this was serious.

Oh, no, could she have TB? I thought of Karen and the kids in the car. With a small practice in the country, we didn't always have all the newest high-tech tools that specialists in the city had. And when making house calls, I didn't even have the basics. I couldn't order a chest X-ray for more information; I simply had to trust what I discovered during my examination.

"When's the last time she's seen a doctor?" I asked an older man in the room.

"It's been years," he said.

"Any idea how many?"

"Maybe thirty?" said her son Billy.

Mary continued to cough, and she coughed up the foulest of sputum into a towel. She opened it to show me evidence of blood. I pulled out my stethoscope and listened to her heart and chest. There were obvious rales—the clicking, rattling, or crackling noises that often indicate pneumonia.

"Have you been coughing up blood for long?" I asked her.

"I saved some other ones for you," Mary said, reaching for a large plastic container full of balled-up pieces of toilet paper. They contained further evidence that she had been doing it for a while.

"I don't need to see them; I really don't." I once again touched her burning forehead with my cool hands. "I'm almost positive you have pneumonia. We need to get you to the hospital." Since the local hospital hadn't been built yet, she had only one option—Nashville.

"No way, Doc. I don't trust those city folks. Going to the hospital will kill ya," she said before launching into another coughing spell.

I waited for her to finish, then I said, "Mary, you're very, very sick. Your temperature is *very* high. With a fever and pneumonia, you really need to be in the hospital."

"Well, I ain't going, so what else ya got?"

"We ain't takin' her to no hospital in Nashville," said the older man. "Billy had a friend who went there once, and he ain't never come home!"

"I understand," I said. And I did. Those living out in the country who'd never traveled farther than their rifles could shoot often viewed a Nashville hospital as a scary place. But I had to try. "The problem is, this illness is very serious. If she stays here, she could die."

"Well, if that's the Lord's will, then that's what's going to happen," the man said.

He didn't say it with callousness but with simple faith.

Billy asked, "Can't ya do *anything* for her?"

"Tell you what, I'll give her a shot of antibiotics, and then I'll give you a prescription for more. You can take these down to Empson Drugs, and they'll fill it for you." Empson was a local drugstore that had been in Ashland City for nearly fifty years and had been handed down through generations of family druggists. Until we opened the clinic, they were one of the few trusted health care resources available to the locals.

"All right," the older man said. "We'll get it filled, but we want you to come back and check on her."

Mary was the poorest of the poor in our community, and she didn't have many options. People like her were one of the reasons I had come to Ashland City. I was happy to continue to check on her.

Though her lifestyle was outside my comfort zone, it was also quite familiar to me. I had grown up in a community of poor people, and I knew families just like Mary's when I was a young boy. If I had never left my hometown, I could have been Mary.

"I'll be back at this time tomorrow."

✦ ✦ ✦

Every day for a week, I made the trip out to Shotgun Road to check on Mary. As sick as she was, she should have been in the hospital. I was worried about how well she would recover at home; but slowly, she seemed to regain her strength. The day she met me at the screen door and smiled a toothless grin, I knew she was going to recover completely.

Going to the hospital may have been the first recommendation I gave Mary that she refused to follow, but it wouldn't be the last. She and her family had their own way of doing things, and they were willing to stand by their beliefs—even if that meant that they died doing it.

Despite her stubbornness, Mary eventually got well enough to come see me in the office. I'm not sure if her family ever understood what a miracle it was that she recovered. Had Mary passed away, her family would certainly have missed her, but they would rather it happened at home than in a hospital.

I suspect that Mary's kin, like many of us who grew up in the country, had always lived with several generations of people. Together, they witnessed the life cycle of both humans and animals, including the deaths of grandparents and the births of grandchildren, and they understood that livestock were sometimes bred to die for their dinner. Mary and her family understood something about the inevitability of the life cycle that their city counterparts didn't. Depending on the weather for crops causes country folks to lean on God in ways that factory workers don't have to. Mary's family understood that God was in control. Had she died, they wouldn't have been destroyed; they would have just leaned on God and continued doing what they needed to do.

Over the years, I think I eventually treated all of Mary's kin. Most of them had never had consistent health care before—not only because it was financially out of reach but because they weren't sure they could trust the provider.

Mary paid me for my services with her gratitude, a few fresh eggs, and more important, her family's *trust*. Rural primary-care doctors may not have all the same diagnostic equipment or receive the same pay and perks that specialists in the cities do, but when I hold my patients' hands, I think the rewards are greater when medicine is as high-touch as it is high-tech.

✦ ✦ ✦

Growing up on the farm, I learned from Leroy, Big John, and Uncle Luther how to touch a watermelon and know whether it was ripe or not. Eventually, I could identify ripe melons even if I was blindfolded. In the winter, we pruned the peach trees. The dead and diseased limbs wouldn't be able to support fruit the following summer, so they needed to be pruned back. The only way to tell which limbs were dead was to feel them. Often the healthy branches and the dying branches looked the same; it was only by touching them that we could tell the difference.

In much the same way, my hands became my eyes and ears in the examination room. For thousands of years before CT scans, X-rays, and MRIs, healers had to rely on their hands to tell them what was going on inside someone. It was one of the first and only diagnostic tools they had. The elderly often comment on the coolness of my hands, and I simply say, "That's because I have a warm heart." But I think the temperature of my hands is a gift. When I hold hands with a patient or examine them with my hands, I can feel something. Sometimes clues about their pains or diseases come to mind and lead me to explore things that their symptoms might not have suggested. While I think this ability is a gift, I don't think it is that unusual.

One time, I met a friend of my mother's. When I shook hands with her, I felt something different in her grip. Like the dying branches on a tree, her skin had a subtle dry and scaly feeling.

Later, I discreetly asked her, "Are you having any thyroid problems?"

"Not that I am aware of," she said, laughing.

"Well, I might be wrong, but I just have a sense there may be something going on with your endocrine system. You may want to have your doctor check it out next time you see him."

She laughed it off again but thanked me in that "bless your heart" kind of way that old ladies do.

A few weeks later, she called my mom and asked, "How did your son know what was wrong with me? Even my doctor said I didn't have any of the usual symptoms, but the lab work confirmed I was having a thyroid problem!"

I didn't think there was anything special in that moment; to me, it was just like pruning tree limbs. Over time, you know how things are supposed to look and feel, and you expect certain things. At times, I've seen a patient whose symptoms all pointed to an obvious diagnosis, such as vague abdominal pain that suggested a gallbladder problem. Without knowing why, I've ordered a more specific test looking for a completely different problem that was less obvious to detect—like cancer. Often, my hunch would prove correct.

Something about the coolness in my hands seemed to give me a clue as to where the pain or disease was centered in a patient. When I am examining a patient and my hands suddenly warm up, I know something is awry. When that happens, I start my search for a diagnosis where my hands felt the warmest. Patients seem to appreciate my high-touch diagnostic skills, and the more I utilized them, the more I began to recognize that they are a God-given gift.

Make no mistake—as a doctor, I can't heal anyone. God heals. At best, I can only hope to guide a patient toward better health.

✦ ✦ ✦

During one quiet overnight shift in the ER in Ashland City's newly built two-bed emergency room, I went to the on-call room to take a nap. I hadn't been there long when I was called down to see a young boy who'd fallen. His mom brought him in because she was worried.

She introduced herself and told me the story behind their visit. Apparently, her son had fallen and bumped his head earlier in the evening. He seemed fine, so she put him to bed at his regular bed-time. A few hours later, he woke up and vomited.

"I heard that throwing up after hitting your head is a bad thing, so I brought him in," she said.

The mom was calm. She was fully dressed and completely made up, and it was 1:30 in the morning. *If she had time to dress, how serious could it be?* The little boy with her seemed quiet, but he understood everything his mom said. I asked her to put him on the table, and I began my exam.

His pupils were equal and reactive. He was attentive and easily followed my directions. "Where did you hurt your head?" I asked.

He pointed to the spot, and I felt it.

It was a normal neural exam. He was a normal kid who'd gotten a bump on his head. I turned to write up his report, and I planned to ask the nurse to give the mother a head injury instruction sheet.

"Well, his exam looks good, but I think we should send him to Vanderbilt Children's Hospital to get a CT scan of his head."

I had no idea why I said that. I wasn't *intending* to say it, but the words slipped out of my mouth. I looked at the nurse. She stared back at me like I was a lunatic. Even the mother looked a bit confused.

In that moment, I knew something more was going on.

I left the examination room, and the nurse followed me. "Why are you sending a healthy child down there?"

I knew why she was asking. It was a big deal to find a neurosurgeon in the middle of the night. We would have to locate one who was on call and hope he called us back. Then we'd have to call Vanderbilt and make arrangements there. The nurse would have to order an ambulance to take them, and there was a ton of paperwork involved.

"I don't know," I responded honestly. "God just told me to send him."

The exam and all the evidence showed that the boy was fine. I couldn't put my finger on it, literally or figuratively. It wasn't as specific as a bump or a lesion; it was vague, like a temperature change while my fingers palpated the area of his injury. To this day, I'm not sure why I sent him, other than I'd touched him and felt something. Although I had no objective data to back up my referral, I had a sense that something was happening that only God could explain.

✦ ✦ ✦

If I were a betting man, I would have laid all my money that night on the likelihood that the neurosurgeon would call and say the boy was fine.

Four hours later, he phoned. "I'm not sure why you sent him," the neurosurgeon said.

"I'm not sure either," I confessed.

"Well, I'm glad you did. I just got out of surgery. We evacuated a hematoma from his brain. If you hadn't gotten him here in time, he would have died."

It was God who'd sent that boy to Vanderbilt, and he'd used my hands to make it happen. I thanked him not only for saving that boy's life but for allowing me to be a part of his healing.

Chapter 19
GLASS HEART
IN ASHLAND CITY

+

Cheatham Medical Center kept me busy in the ER nights and weekends, and during the week, I saw patients in my clinic. I was working hard, and my practice was growing. So were my kids. Kristen started school, and Ashley soon followed. As our family increased with Julia and David, we needed more room than we had in our house in Ashland City. We also needed more privacy. As one of only three doctors in the county, I was a minor celebrity. Patients would drive by the house and take pictures of me mowing the grass! We needed distance between our home and my work.

We found a house about twenty minutes from my practice, in a subdivision in Kingston Springs. The kids made friends in the area, and Karen stayed busy chauffeuring them to and from playdates, sports, and lessons. Our family joined a local athletic club so the kids could swim on its team and Karen and I could work out while they practiced. I tried to get to the gym as much as my schedule allowed. Often, we'd go out for a family dinner afterward.

I was running late one Wednesday, and I knew Karen would be waiting for me. I'd have to hurry if I wanted to get my workout in—the kids would soon be finished swimming. *They're going to be hungry*, I thought.

I entered the club and picked up a pen to sign in. Suddenly, a strange feeling washed over me, interrupting my thoughts. I could almost feel tension in the foyer and an indescribable smell of panic. *Something is up.*

When I'd originally experienced being in the presence of dying patients—the fragrance of lilacs and citrus along with the sensations of warmth followed by cool breezes—I'd discussed it with Karen. She'd been my spiritual guide when I was seeking God, and now we were spiritual partners as we continued to see him in new ways.

Karen and I never shied away from talking about our spiritual experiences, so our kids were always eager to hear the stories I told them about how God was working in the lives of my patients. But each time I experienced something new at work, I couldn't wait to talk to Karen about it first. She helped me get better at recognizing these appointments with heaven and understanding their significance. Eventually, I came to understand that the warmth I felt was the soul leaving the body, and the breeze was the wind of heaven welcoming new souls—or occasionally, pushing them back to earth. The smells reminded me of all that awaits us there.

So when I smelled panic in the air that day, I recognized something spiritual at work. I stopped midway through signing my name and listened for God's voice to tell me what to do.

I noticed a wide-eyed receptionist staring at the tennis court. She looked at me with fear in her eyes. "Aren't you a doctor?"

"Yes, why?"

She pointed. "That man just collapsed! Can you help him?"

I turned toward the glass separating us from the indoor tennis court, where a middle-aged man was lying on the floor. "Call an ambulance!" I shouted as I dropped my gym bag and raced inside.

I wasn't sure what was about to happen, but whatever it was, I didn't want it to be visible to families entering and exiting the sports club. So as I entered the court, I quickly pulled the tall, vinyl curtain across the glass to block the view from the lobby.

The symbolism wasn't lost on me.

As I drew the curtain to close off the court, somewhere else a heavenly curtain was opening.

I definitely sensed God's presence as I ran toward the man. I could see he wasn't breathing. His soul had already left his body, and I didn't know whether or not it would be returning. Two worlds, present and future, were colliding for him.

Players from a neighboring tennis court also ran to the man's aid. The three of us reached him at the same time. "I'm a doctor," I said, kneeling down to feel the man's pulse.

"So are we," the taller of the two men said.

"He doesn't have a pulse." I put my hand on his chest and couldn't feel anything. "And there are no respirations. We're going to have to do CPR."

"I'll help," said the other man. He knelt beside me.

"Make sure the ambulance is on the way," I said to the other.

We didn't have any tools or instruments with us, and we all knew his chances weren't good.

+ + +

When doctors on TV perform CPR, nine times out of ten the characters on the show walk out of the hospital and carry on with their lives as if nothing happened. But in real life, the opposite is true. About 90 percent of the time, CPR ends in *death*. When CPR is given outside of the hospital, the percentage increases to 99 percent. In either setting, the small percent of patients who survive CPR rarely come out unscathed. They usually have major disabilities, which is one reason the American Heart Association advocates automated external defibrillators (AEDs) in public places.

Even though I didn't know the other doctors, I knew they had to be aware of the statistics. Most doctors were. Those statistics were the reason most physicians didn't want heroic measures used on them should something happen. They know the chances of more damage being done are higher than the odds of surviving without problems. As doctors, we saw patients every day who were trapped between life and death, kept alive only by machines. In the doctors' lounge, away from patients and their family members, doctors discuss how they don't want to end up like that. That's why so many doctors have do not resuscitate (DNR) orders.

On TV and in the movies, death is defeated daily. But in reality, things are much messier.

+ + +

Despite our knowledge of the futility of CPR, doctors always go through extraordinary means to save the lives of their patients, unless there is a DNR or a living will in place. That's what we were trained to do. So on the tennis court that day, the three of us did everything we could to save the man.

We had been keeping him alive through CPR breathing and compressions for approximately eight minutes when the EMTs entered with their emergency equipment. I identified myself and so did the others.

"ER doctor at Cheatham Medical Center. Looks like a heart attack."

"Cardiologist, St. Thomas Hospital in Nashville," the first doctor said.

"Anesthesiologist, Baptist Hospital, Nashville," the second said.

"Three doctors?" the EMT asked in disbelief. "What do you guys need? We'll let you handle this one!"

The cardiologist grabbed the defibrillator. The anesthesiologist procured the IV equipment. I took the intubation equipment to insert a tube through the man's mouth and down his throat, which would allow mechanical ventilation into his lungs.

Since our patient was flat on the ground, I was practically standing on my head as I tried to figure out how to intubate him on the tennis court. Typically when you intubate, the head is below the point of insertion, so you can see the tube as it slips through the vocal cords. But because the man was lying flat on the tennis court, I would essentially have to do the insert blind. I knew it could take several tries to get it right, and if I missed, I could do a lot of damage.

Several minutes passed while we worked. A small crowd of club employees and management gathered. I also sensed God's presence. Despite the chaos, as the defibrillator charged and the anesthesiologist prepared the IV, I felt a sense of calm come over me. The circumstances were trying, and I did my best as I lay next to the patient with my ear on the ground, hoping I could see the tube go in.

It didn't work.

I still couldn't see what I needed to see in order to slip the tube past his vocal cords. *God, you have got to be my eyes here!* The anesthesiologist inserted a femoral central line as the cardiologist charged the defibrillator. Another minute passed, and I looked again. I still couldn't get a visual on what I needed to see. I would have to do it blind. *Please guide my hand*, I prayed and pushed it in.

It worked on the first try!

Everything fell into place just as it was supposed to. The defibrillator charged to 360 joules as the endotracheal tube slid into his trachea, and the femoral line began flowing freely. Suddenly, I felt a cool breeze on my cheek. The cardiologist shocked the dead man's heart, and miraculously it started beating on its own. I knew the patient would live, though I didn't yet know what damage he may have suffered.

God had masterminded an astounding series of events to allow this man to be revived. So much could have gone wrong, statistically speaking—in fact, so much usually *did go wrong*. But God's hand had reached through the veil and held ours as we helped bring the dead man back.

It was hard to believe that within seconds of his heart stopping, the patient had three doctors reviving him. Eight minutes later, each doctor used his special skills to try to save the man's life. Then within fifteen minutes of his heart attack, the man's heart had started beating again.

God had not only orchestrated the events of the day to bring three doctors to the club at the very same time the man's heart gave out, but he had been with each of us through the CPR. I'd felt him guide me through possibly the ugliest intubation I'd ever performed. Now, instead of tallying up all the things that went wrong, we were marveling at all the things that had gone right. Obviously, God had a reason for sending this man back.

✦ ✦ ✦

The cardiologist decided to ride with the patient to the hospital. "I'll admit him to my service, and we'll see what happens."

We all knew that the man had a ways to go before he was out of danger, but we had every reason to believe he would make it. While the staff cleaned up the area, the anesthesiologist and I walked out front and talked about what an extraordinary thing had just happened. We shook hands at the front door, and he left.

As I picked up my gym bag near the sign-in sheet, Karen walked out.

"There you are! The kids are hungry. Do you mind skipping your workout tonight to go straight to dinner?"

"That'll be fine. I've already finished what I came here to do."

✦ ✦ ✦

In the days following the collapse of the man on the tennis court, I prayed for him often. And I questioned God, *Why did you send him back?*

A couple of weeks later, I was home with Karen and the kids. We'd just finished dinner when there was a knock at the door. That wasn't unusual. When we lived at our house in Ashland City, patients would sometimes come by the house if they needed something. I didn't encourage it, but I never turned them away either.

I opened the door.

"Are you Dr. Anderson?" an attractive woman asked.

"Yes, can I help you?"

"My name is Jeanna. You took care of my husband, Michael, a few weeks ago."

I was usually pretty good with patients' names, but I couldn't remember anyone by the name of Michael. Fortunately, she continued. "My husband was playing tennis, and he had a heart attack on the court."

"Yes, of course! Come on in," I said, showing her to the living room, where Karen joined us.

"How is he doing? I've been praying for him."

"He's doing great," she said, with a big smile. "He had open-heart surgery and had to have a four-vessel bypass."

"Four?" I asked.

She nodded. "Four."

"It's a miracle he's still alive. Were there any complications?"

I held my breath as I waited for her response.

"Nope, he's doing great!"

I exhaled. I was so happy to know that he'd not only survived the CPR, but apparently after getting the medical treatment he needed, he continued to thrive.

"That's why I'm here. I wanted to thank you for helping save him."

"You don't need to thank me. Thank God above."

"I do every day," she said. "But still, I have something I want to give you." She held out an elegantly wrapped box.

"Thank you," I said, as I untied the silk ribbon and lifted the lid off. Inside was a beautiful, handblown glass ornament.

It was in the shape of a heart.

We talked a bit more about the timing of the events that day and how God had arranged to have three doctors at her husband's side when his heart stopped beating. Then, without knowing it, she answered the question I'd wondered about since that day: *Why had heaven's breath blown Michael's soul back to earth?*

"He's been at home recovering for the past two weeks, and they've been some of the best weeks of our lives. I don't know what I would have done without him. Since he's been home, our marriage is stronger than ever, and we're both growing in our faith and enjoying renewed fellowship with God. I'm just so grateful."

✦ ✦ ✦

Nearly every week, I witness or hear about a healing that seemingly defies medical explanation. Occasionally, as with Michael, I get to be used as God's hands here on earth.

Some people have asked why I have been privileged to see Jesus and they haven't. I don't know the answer to that. I do know that I have kept my eyes open for glimpses of heaven. I've said, "Okay, Lord, use me however you want," no matter how strange or crazy it seemed. As a result, I started to see evidence of his handiwork everywhere. Of course, being in the medical profession, I often get to see people at the beginning or the end of their lives—the times they are closest to heaven. However, I suspect that if we all slowed down, kept our eyes open, and listened more attentively, we would frequently recognize heavenly experiences happening all around us.

Through those early years, he used me in some extraordinary circumstances. I had seen his presence in women giving birth and felt his presence as my patients passed. But that day on the tennis court was a reminder that he was also found in life's ordinary circumstances. I never expected to sign into an athletic club and find God guiding a team of off-duty doctors through the steps that would save a man's life. Yet he was there.

I certainly never expected to see him line up everything so perfectly and in such a timely way that a man's life would be spared within minutes of losing it so he could rejoin his wife and together they could pursue God even more intimately. But God gives and God takes away. This time, he gave Michael his life back—and gave Jeanna her husband back—purely for his glory.

To me this was one more confirmation of how God is real and very much alive. He's still healing people just as he did two thousand years ago, and sometimes he even uses doctors to help in that healing. The handblown glass heart that sits on my office shelf reminds me that at the perfect time and place, under his guidance and direction, my God-blown fragile heart will cease to beat, and I will be allowed to enter into heaven, where I'll remain with him always.

Chapter 20
QUEEN ELIZABETH

✦

"Good morning, Elizabeth!" I said.

Beth didn't respond. She couldn't. She'd been in a coma for months. But I didn't let her silence stop me. I continued talking as I examined her.

"It's a gorgeous day outside. A little cold, but then I guess it should be since it's December. Can you believe we're only weeks away from Christmas?"

I've always spoken to my comatose patients as if they could speak back. Early in my career, one of my mentors explained that we don't always know what is getting through and what isn't. I took that to mean I should continue to treat my comatose patients with the same dignity and respect I would give anyone else. That's why I talk to patients like Beth as if they could answer me. But I had another reason for speaking to this patient—she was one of my favorites.

Her name was Beth, but I had taken to calling her "Queen Elizabeth" because she was so regal. Though she was in her early eighties, she made it clear that she was in charge and I was merely a servant to do her bidding. Whenever she visited my office, one or more of her three daughters chauffeured her, and she arrived in style. She was always impeccably dressed with coordinating accessories, manicured nails, and a splash of perfume. She had a keen mind and often carried a list of questions for me—sometimes answering them herself without waiting for my input.

Despite some mild hypertension, elevated cholesterol, and a family history of stroke, she was otherwise in good health. During her office visits, she would entertain me with stories about her great-grandkids and their recent accomplishments. I could only hope my parents and in-laws were as proud of their grandchildren as she was of hers.

This morning as I looked at her lying in bed, unable to speak or eat, I remembered how sprightly she'd been during her last visit to my office, only a few months prior.

✦ ✦ ✦

"Dr. Anderson, I've outlived all my relatives," Beth said.

"That's a blessing," I responded.

But I could tell from the way she squared her shoulders and looked at me that something was bothering her. She cleared her throat. "My mother and father and two of my brothers—they all died from strokes. I just know I'm going to be next."

Her eyes narrowed as she spoke. I could see how concerned she was. *Your patients will tell you what is wrong with them.* Those words from medical school echoed in my mind while I listened to Beth's concerns.

"You're right," I told her. "You do have some risk factors, but we're doing all we can to minimize them. Simply controlling your blood pressure and cholesterol reduces your risk by half." I tried to think of anything else I could do to help reassure her. "You're still taking that baby aspirin, aren't you?"

"Every day," she said. "And I had the two tests you ordered. Did my results come in?"

"Yes, I have the carotid Doppler and echo reports right here. Your heart is in fine shape. There's no problem with the valve or the rhythm, and there are no blocked arteries to your brain. Everything looks good."

She reminded me once again of her family history. "Most of my family died within a few hours of their strokes, but my oldest brother, Larry, lingered on the edge of glory for more than five years. If that happens to me, I just hope and pray I don't hang around like Larry did."

I took her hands in mine and looked her in the eyes. "You're going to be fine. I look forward to seeing you in three months and hearing more stories about your great-grandkids."

+ + +

A few days later, one of Beth's daughters called me at the office.

"Dr. Anderson, I came by to check on Mama this morning, and I couldn't wake her up. I called 911, and the ambulance is on its way. Can you meet us in the ER?"

I was shocked. Beth had been fine just a few days earlier, and I had the test results to prove it. *What did I miss?*

In the ER, the stroke team had been called, but treating her with tissue plasminogen activator (tPA), a blood clot dissolver, wasn't an option. It had to be given within four hours of having the stroke. Beth had been home alone for an undetermined length of time, so she didn't qualify. Plus, her age placed her in a high-risk category. Since she fell outside the window of all the protocols, the only thing we could do was admit her to the ICU and pray while we waited it out.

A CT scan and an MRI soon confirmed our suspicions: she'd had a small embolic stroke that had left her in a semicomatose state and unable to communicate. Her lab work and vital signs were perfect, and she was breathing fine on her own.

I was standing in the ICU room talking with Beth's three daughters when the neurologist strode in. He quickly evaluated her and ordered physical and occupational therapies, as well as a speech evaluation. "Continue her on aspirin therapy," he recommended. Then he signed off the case. "Not much else I can do here. Looks like a skilled nursing facility is in her future."

He left as abruptly as he'd entered.

The neurologist's assessment didn't leave much room for hope. A week earlier, Queen Elizabeth had been in charge and ordering us all around. Now she lay in a vegetative state in the ICU. I looked at her three daughters. They were as speechless as their mother.

"I'm sorry he was so blunt," I said. "But I'm afraid he is probably right. Unless there is some kind of miracle, the area of her brain that controls communication has been permanently damaged."

I explained that she'd likely never be able to speak or understand language and that, as long as she was in a coma, she wouldn't even be able to eat food on her own.

"So what do we do now?" one of her daughters asked.

"Did she leave any instructions regarding what she wanted you to do if something like this ever happened? Maybe a living will or a DNR?"

Her daughters weren't sure and decided they would check her house before making any more decisions.

A day later we once again stood by Beth's bedside.

"We looked all over the house, and we didn't see anything," the youngest daughter said. "But I know she didn't want to die like Uncle Larry did. Can you guide us on what to do next? We really have no idea what to expect."

We agreed to meet later that afternoon to discuss her care options.

✦ ✦ ✦

Some people believe that having a DNR or a living will means a doctor won't try to save them if something happens. They're squeamish about filling one out when they're healthy, and they're superstitious about filling one out before a medical procedure, thinking that having a DNR might somehow jinx them. Nothing could be further from the truth. A Do Not Resuscitate (DNR) order is not an all-or-nothing document. Essentially, these papers merely provide medical professionals with documentation of the patient's wishes.

Just as many pregnant women put together a birthing plan that includes where and how they want to deliver their baby and what medications they do or don't want to take, a DNR or a living will is just a written plan for how a patient wants to pass. It basically answers these questions: *When you get ready to die, how do you want to go? And how much intervention do you want on your way out?* The default answer is that you will get every treatment available unless you or your representatives choose otherwise.

For example, I have chosen not to be resuscitated. I don't want to be kept alive by machines and feeding tubes. But if I didn't have a DNR readily available, the EMTs and ER doctors would do everything they could to save me following a heart attack. That's why I make sure everyone around me—my wife and kids, as well as the people I work with—all know my wishes. My DNR hangs on the bulletin board in my office, so it is immediately accessible should someone need it.

I understand not everyone feels the way I do, and that's okay. But even if others don't have the same desires I do, they still have some idea of what they do and do not want.

Do they want any intervention?

Do they want to be intubated? How about a ventilator?

Do they want drugs or not? If so, what kind?

Would they rather have surgery or be treated with nonsurgical techniques?

Do they want to be on a feeding tube if they can't eat? If so, for how long?

These are the questions that a DNR and a living will can answer, and it's ideal if the patient has decided these things *before* something happens. Without this paperwork in place, the patient's loved ones or the person who has power of attorney must make those decisions. This can be quite a burden for family members trying to second-guess what the patient would want. When everyone is on the same page, the business of dying can be very peaceful.

In my experience, when believers near the end of their lives, they're ready to go. Sometimes, this conflicts with the desires of the family. Because I work with a lot of geriatric patients, I frequently see families who want to extend the dying process because *they're* not ready to let go. Sometimes they want to keep Granny alive for their own pleasure—they love her and will miss her when she's gone. But just as often, they keep her here because of their own guilt. Maybe they weren't the best children or grandchildren, and they want those stolen moments either for reconciliation or because they can't detach themselves. My job as a physician is not to make the decision for them, or even to influence them; rather, my job is to help them understand the consequences of the choices they make.

But as a compassionate friend who is on the journey with them, I also want them to know that dying isn't the worst thing that can happen to somebody.

✦ ✦ ✦

I met with Beth's daughters and helped prepare them for what to expect.

"We have some decisions to make. Depending on what you decide, your mom could die naturally in a few days, maybe a few weeks at most, or we can do some things to prolong her life. If we do that, your mom will be moved to a skilled nursing home. I can recommend several good ones for you. If you choose that option, I'll continue to be her doctor, stopping by weekly or as needed to manage her care."

The women nodded. Tears glistened in their eyes.

I handed them each a copy of the DNR form, so they could follow along as we talked about it. "These are the questions I ask everyone in this situation, and I want you to know that there are no right or wrong answers."

I started with questions about resuscitation. "If your mom's heart stops beating, do you want her to have CPR?" The women discussed the question and finally concluded that wasn't what their mother would want. As we made our way through the checklist, they also agreed that their mom wouldn't want to be intubated or put on a ventilator.

As I continued to ask questions, I could tell they were having a hard time. One dabbed her eyes with a tissue, and the other two cried openly.

"I'm sorry. I know this is hard, but you're doing great. Would your mom want to be fed by either a PEG tube or an NG tube?"

I explained that the percutaneous endoscopic gastrostomy (PEG) tube was placed directly in the wall of the abdomen, while a naso-gastric (NG) tube went in through the nose, down the throat, and into the stomach. Each had its own indications for use and possible complications. The women looked at one another. They had easily decided on all the other questions, but this one posed more of a dilemma for them. The answer to this question would determine the course of their mother's treatment.

Finally, one of them asked, "What should we do?"

"Let me just say that this is the question people struggle with the most. And once again, I want you to know there is no right or wrong answer here. Basically, all we're asking is whether or not you want your mom to get food and water through an artificial tube in either her nose or her stomach. Fifty years ago these tubes didn't exist, and we wouldn't even be asking this question. God would have welcomed her home sooner rather than later. But now we have the technology and you have the option."

"I don't know," said one daughter. "It seems cruel not to feed her. But she definitely doesn't want to be in a coma, lying around for five years like Uncle Larry."

They understood what was at stake. Without a feeding tube, their mother would die in the hospital within days. With it, she would likely go on living for weeks, months, or even years, like her brother. They knew as well as I did that she didn't want that.

"Why don't you three think about this a little while longer? Give yourselves some time to pray about it, and we can talk again in the morning."

By the next morning, they had an answer.

"Dr. Anderson, we talked about it, and we just don't feel that we can let Mama starve to death," the oldest said. "We don't want her to get CPR, intubation, or ventilation, but we want her to have IVs and antibiotics as she needs them, and we want her to get the PEG tube."

"Good. I'll get the GI doctor to put the PEG tube in tomorrow. We'll have her in a nursing home by the end of the week."

✦ ✦ ✦

By now, Beth had been in the nursing home for months. I looked at her frail body, wasting away in the bed. For a woman who liked to be giving orders, she was no longer in charge of anything. She couldn't even speak. Her hair was long, her skin was pale, and she no longer wore makeup. She looked more ghostly than alive. She certainly wasn't as regal as she had once been. But otherwise she was healthy. I feared she could linger for years. *Should I have done something differently for you, Queen Elizabeth? Should I have made you fill out the DNR when you were in my office that day? Should I have advocated more strongly for your wishes to your daughters? How could I have been a better doctor for you?*

Doctors are used to making these kinds of calls and moving on, but sometimes we have moments when we ask ourselves if we made the *right* call. This was one of those moments for me. *Lord, did I guide this family in the right direction? Is this what you wanted?*

A nurse came into the room and saw me staring at Beth. I glanced at her and then back at Beth. "I don't want to end up like this," I said.

She nodded in agreement. "Me neither."

I handed her Beth's chart. "No changes. I'll be back next week to check on her again."

As Christmas approached, I often thought about Beth and her daughters. But I'd resigned myself to the fact that there was nothing I could do for my Queen Elizabeth.

She was truly in God's hands now.

✦ ✦ ✦

It was a few days before Christmas, and the nursing home appeared more festive than usual. The daughters must have put a tree and lights in her room. I thought about how much Elizabeth would have liked to see the decorations.

"Can we open the blinds to get a little more light in here?" I asked the nurse who came in with me for Beth's examination. I walked to Beth's bedside and took her limp hand in mine.

"Good morning, Elizabeth."

"Good morning, Dr. Anderson."

It was such a soft whisper, I thought at first that perhaps it was wishful thinking on my part. I looked at the nurse. Her eyes were wide with surprise; she'd obviously heard it too. I leaned in closer to Beth's bedside and asked, "Did you hear me, Beth?"

"Yes, I did."

I was flabbergasted. Beth had spoken! Despite the trauma to her brain, the damage to her communications center, and the months of lying in a coma, the queen was back!

She was tired and didn't feel like talking much.

As I examined her, I found nothing remarkable. Her vitals hadn't changed, her breathing was normal, and her medicines were the same. I could find no medical explanation for why she got better, other than that it was a miracle.

That day, I made one of the happiest calls of my life to Beth's eldest daughter.

And it had to be an especially joyful Christmas that year as her family gathered in her room. Over the next few weeks, as Elizabeth grew stronger, she also became more vocal. Soon, Elizabeth was back to herself, hair coifed, giving orders to the staff and other residents. To everyone's surprise, she walked out of the nursing home and went on to live another two years!

✦ ✦ ✦

The next time Elizabeth came to see me in the office, she was carrying some papers. She had a blank copy of a DNR, and she wanted me to help her fill it out. "I was close enough to heaven that I could taste its sweetness," she said. "If I ever get that close again, I don't want anyone to stop me!"

"Yes, ma'am. I understand."

Together, we filled out the form. She said no to CPR, intubation, ventilators, and tube feeding. "I love my family, and I'm glad to be here with them. But I don't want to miss a minute of heaven!"

Elizabeth's progression from comatose to talking, to being active in life, was another reminder that there are no right or wrong answers. Once again, God had proved to me that it isn't medicine or treatment decisions that determine our final days.

He does.

Chapter 21

THE SMELL OF
GOOD AND EVIL

✦

Developmental psychologists claim that, within two months, babies can recognize familiar faces and voices, but it takes only a week for them to recognize their mother's smell. The olfactory powers, even in a newborn, are that strong and well developed. I've always been sensitive to smells. Some of my earliest memories are connected to specific scents, and even today, a whiff of certain smells will take me back to my childhood.

That's true for most people. The aroma of baking bread reminds them of their mothers, a sniff of engine oil reminds them of their fathers working on the car, or the fragrance of a particular hair spray or perfume brings back memories of their grandmothers.

Perhaps that's also why some people don't like the smell of hospitals or nursing homes. At first whiff, these places often reek of the chemicals used to clean them. But these same chemical smells are also found in places that are less objectionable to our olfactory senses—like schools. So why do people say they don't like the smell of hospitals or nursing homes?

It's possible that when they refer to the objectionable smell, they are referring to less dominant scents, such as body odor or the smell of blood, urine, or human waste—stenches the chemicals were meant to mask.

But if these people have sensitive noses, they may also be detecting another odor, one that is harder to describe and something they may not even be consciously aware of. When a person is dying, there is an earthy, almost musty scent associated with the process. Other medical professionals have described it as "sickly sweet" or the smell of acetone.

It's the malodor of the body breaking down. Some refer to it as the smell of death.

The scents associated with the body's deterioration seem to linger in places where there is a high concentration of deaths. Even patients who have been freshly bathed by a nurse produce this distinctive mustiness when their bodies are shutting down. Often when I make rounds in the hospital, even before I can see signs of a patient's decline, I can smell it—sometimes before entering his or her room.

The smell of heaven is completely different. Nothing on earth is quite like it. It is both citrusy and flowery, yet neither bouquet overpowers the other. It's so light and fresh, with hints of lilac and citrus, like the smell of spring as it teases the senses before bursting into its fullest fragrance.

The first time I smelled heaven in a patient's room, it was so startling that it immediately took me back to the only other place I'd experienced that sweet aroma—in the dream I had while camping. From that moment on, anytime I was with a dying patient and caught even the slightest whiff of heaven's scent, I tried to drink it in as deeply as I could. In those brief moments of holding the sweet fragrance inside me, I felt the experience of being in heaven all over again. The world seemed crisper, brighter, and more solid—like the first time I put on glasses and saw all I had been missing. Life was no longer fuzzy.

Inhaling the scent of heaven, I felt the peace and stillness I'd felt as a boy when I would lie on my back and gaze at the Alabama sky. The warmth in the room was like being hugged by the sun while an aromatic spring breeze tickled my face.

But it wasn't only the smell. There were other sensations, like the glow that appeared above and to the right of the patient. It made the room brighter and warmer before it quickly faded away. These and other signs from heaven made me long for the time when I would be the one to cross over.

+ + +

On the rare occasions when I talked with other doctors about these glimpses of heaven, their condescending smiles suggested I'd been out in the country a little too long.

They thought I was like the pilot who saw a UFO. Either they didn't believe me, or they thought I should know better than to talk about it in public.

Although doctors weren't receptive to hearing about my experiences, I found that my dying patients often were. With them, the conversations came up naturally.

When my patients were getting ready to pass, it became my job to help them make the transition. Once they knew they didn't have much time left, I tried to help them assess where they were and where they were going, not just physically but also emotionally and spiritually. I asked a lot of questions, about their illnesses and their lives. I wanted to help them through the shock of being terminal by talking about the next steps they needed to take.

I'd start by asking them, "How do you want to die?"

We'd talk about alternatives, such as dying in a hospital or at home, with or without aggressive intervention. Sometimes, I would help them fill out a DNR order. Next, I'd ask about their support system. Did they have friends or family around to care for them physically and emotionally?

I'd try to understand their current emotional state and whether or not they felt they needed to get things in order before they died. For some people, this meant taking care of things financially. For others, it meant healing past relationships. Regardless of what it meant for each patient, I wanted to make sure he or she had the time to take care of any unfinished business before it was too late.

Typically, toward the end of the conversation, I would also ask them, "What do you think happens after you die?"

I wasn't as interested in their answers as I was in knowing whether they *had* an answer. If they had questions, I wanted them to know they could talk to me. If they didn't feel comfortable talking to me, I offered to arrange for a clergyman to help them get their spiritual lives in order.

Most of the people I cared for believed they were going to heaven and looked forward to seeing loved ones on the other side. Sometimes patients asked me what I thought would happen when they got there. Questions like that gave me the opportunity to share with them some of the things that I had witnessed. They often wanted to know more about those experiences, and I was happy to share with them as I felt it was appropriate.

For most of my patients who were believers, the closer they got to death, the more peaceful they became. It was as if they had accepted it and couldn't wait to slip quietly to the other side.

But that wasn't the case with everyone.

+ + +

Eddie winced as he sat down on the exam table in my office. He was obviously in a lot of pain. It was the third time I'd seen him in the past few weeks, and our conversation that day mostly followed the pattern of the previous two visits.

"Have you had a fever?"

"I'm not sure, but I had the chills yesterday."

"Are you coughing?"

"Sometimes I have hacking spells. It's worse when I get up in the morning."

"How about nausea or other stomach pains?"

"Yes, my stomach hurts all the time. I'm in a lot of pain. I need something stronger than what you've been giving me."

Eddie was in his early sixties but looked as if he could have been in his late seventies. He had an aggressive form of lung cancer, and it was growing rapidly. He'd been diagnosed only a couple of weeks earlier, but I was pretty sure he wouldn't live much longer. We'd talked about it, so he knew this was his fate, but the speed of his body's deterioration surprised even me.

"I'm afraid I'm going to have to admit you to the hospital. If you're an inpatient, I can do more to help you with your pain and to ease your physical suffering."

While I'd been treating Eddie for only a few months, I knew a lot about him. He had a reputation in the community for being a bad man. A heavy smoker, he'd abused his own body as well as abusing others. Whenever I saw his name on the appointment sheet, I dreaded his visit. He had a horrible temper, and his personality was as aggressive as his cancer. He'd physically and sexually abused his wife and his kids in the past. He was a troublemaker who, after drinking too much, got into fights, sometimes with his fists and sometimes with a knife. His victims were left bleeding, with broken bones, along the sides of roads, in bars, or wherever the fight happened to take place. He treated his children horribly and didn't care whether they lived or died.

I don't write this lightly, but Eddie was truly *evil*. He thrived on being mean and hurting others. I knew this firsthand because I had been treating his victims for years.

But I also believed deathbed conversions were possible. While I don't have the ability to look into another man's heart or soul and know where his relationship stands with God, I believed that no matter where he was spiritually, redemption was available. God had rescued me from the godless life I'd once been living, and I believed he could, and did, rescue others—even up until the moment of death.

In the book of Luke, there's a passage about two criminals hanging on crosses on either side of Jesus. One of the criminals was unrepentant, but the other acknowledged Jesus as the Son of God: "'Jesus, remember me when you come into your Kingdom.' And Jesus replied, 'I assure you, today you will be with me in paradise'" (Luke 23:42-43).

I wanted Eddie to know Jesus, to experience God's great love and forgiveness, and to spend eternity in paradise, like the penitent criminal had. Every time I had an opportunity, I tried to talk to Eddie about spiritual things. This day was no different.

After completing his examination, I asked, "Spiritually, are you good with God?"

As he'd done in all our previous visits, he quickly and soundly rebuffed my attempts at spiritual conversation with, "Shut up, and just treat the cancer! I don't want to waste my time talking about something that doesn't exist."

I admitted Eddie into the hospital as a hospice patient so we could keep him comfortable until he died. I knew he was hurting, not only physically but also emotionally and spiritually. While he was in the hospital, no one came to visit or to say good-bye. If folks knew that he was sick, they didn't seem upset to hear it.

Every day for the next two weeks, I'd stop by Eddie's room and try to talk to him about God. His response was always the same: "Shut up, and take care of my cancer. And if you can't take care of my cancer, then just shut up and give me pain medicine."

He was unrepentant until the day he died.

✦   ✦   ✦

Each death is different, just as each person is different, but I noticed that there were some recognizable patterns associated with dying. For example, I remember one of the first times I walked into the room of a dying patient. The man was looking up and to the right, staring off into space. But there was something different about his gaze; it was relaxed and peaceful, with an almost otherworldly quality to it. He seemed to be seeing something I couldn't. His stare looked past the people in the room, even beyond the walls of the hospital.

I took out my penlight and examined his eyes. His pupils were still reactive, so I knew he wasn't physically gone, but he was definitely somewhere else.

He died a few hours later.

I started seeing this same gaze in other patients. It was always up and to the right, and it always happened shortly before they died. It's hard to describe what I've seen in words because the experience transcends the tangible. In those moments, what I sense is that my patients are preparing for a journey. It's almost as if they are seeing a preview of where they are going.

The signs of this gaze are so distinctive and recognizable that they could easily be confused with mental illness. During my early years, if the patients who exhibited this gaze were young and healthy, I'd have probably said they were schizophrenic, because they didn't look at me—they looked *through* me. But with time and experience, I've come to realize that this is just one more sign that heaven is near. The patient senses that someone else is present in the room with us. Sometimes I can feel the presence behind me or even somewhere farther beyond the room itself, in a place I can't see or grasp with my earthly vision.

I call this peaceful stare "the gaze of glory," and it is often a sign that the patient is ready to cross to the other side of the veil.

✦　✦　✦

I was sitting at Eddie's bedside, praying for him as he made the transition from this world to the next. The room was sparse; there were no flowers, cards, or balloons. Although it was well lit, it was devoid of warmth—very much like his life—functional, but containing no obvious signs of relationships or connection to others. In all our conversations, Eddie never acknowledged that he had a soul, and he didn't seem to think there was any kind of afterlife.

As I sat with him, Eddie began to stare off into the distance. But it wasn't like the gaze of glory I'd seen with other patients. Eddie's stare was different. He seemed to be staring off into a great chasm. His eyes grew wide, he was restless, maybe even anxious, and I detected a look of fear on his face.

The Cheyne-Stokes respiration signaled that death was near, and

I listened to him as he struggled to take each breath. Unlike many of the believers I'd witnessed who had crossed silently and peacefully, Eddie seemed to be struggling. He made grunting noises and clung to each breath as if it were his last. Eventually, his breathing slowed, and the grunts became less frequent. When his last breath finally came, it wasn't the same peaceful exhale that I'd become so familiar with in my other dying patients. Eddie fought to take a final breath, and then his pulse and heart stopped.

His last breath was a grunt.

Suddenly, I felt some type of dark cloud present in the room. The lights grew dimmer, and the temperature plummeted. The room was freezing cold as though the temperature had instantly dropped 100 degrees. The warmth I'd come to expect when heaven's door opened seemed to have been replaced by the opening of a liquid nitrogen canister. The room appeared dark and shadowy, as if it were being swallowed by a black abyss. That's when I smelled sulfur and diesel. The air felt heavy, and it got harder to breathe. I remembered the same smell from Donalsonville after the Alday murders. Memories of those dark days flooded my mind. I was terrified. Though I had no rational reason to feel this way, I was afraid I would get trapped and be unable to leave. I wanted to get out as fast as I could. Evil had entered the room.

I quickly made the death pronouncement and left.

I hurried down the hall to the sink. I turned the water on as hot as it would go. While I waited for it to heat up, I lathered my hands. Then I frantically scrubbed my forearms. As soon as the water was hot, I held my hands and arms under the steamy faucet until they turned red. I wanted to wash the darkness off me. *Lord, please keep me from that evil in the future. Thank you for rescuing me from that. Because if you hadn't come after me, that's where I'd be too.*

✦　✦　✦

Everything about the room that day was the antithesis of heaven—no warmth, no breezes. Just a stagnant coldness. For weeks afterward, every time I passed that room, I noticed that it reeked of death and that the sulfuric odor lingered. The fear I experienced that day stuck with me like a bad memory that refused to leave. Although I have visited countless other patients in that same room since Eddie died, I still get a strange sensation when I walk in that door. My experience the day Eddie died was that traumatic.

I believe that when Eddie crossed over to the other side, he didn't like what he found. But I also believe he could have made a different decision at any time before he died.

His death made me even more thankful that I know where I'm going. But it also made me more intentional about making sure others knew where they were going too. I have never wanted any of my patients to go through what I experienced in Eddie's room, or what I fear Eddie is experiencing now.

After Eddie's death, I became more determined than ever for people to know what *heaven* is like.

Chapter 22
LAUREN

✦

My kids stared up at me as though they had no idea what I was talking about. So I repeated myself, this time with emphasis. "I don't want to *ever* catch you turning the hood of a car upside down and pulling it with a tractor!"

"Why would we want to do that?" Julia asked.

"So you can have a sled," I said.

"But we have real sleds in the garage."

"Besides, we hardly get any snow in Tennessee," Ashley added.

"We have a tractor?" David asked.

"No, David. We don't have a tractor," Kristen, my oldest, said. "Dad just had a bad day at work."

"Well, don't use someone else's tractor or any other vehicle either," I emphasized, hoping I sounded like I meant it.

"What are you talking about, Reggie?" Karen had walked into the room and caught the tail end of my sermon. I already knew it was a waste of time. The kids weren't interested in sleds, cars in our neighborhood didn't have unattached hoods, and the kids probably wouldn't have thought of the idea if I hadn't brought it up first.

"Kids, why don't you go outside and play until dinner. It will be ready in a few minutes," Karen said.

"Stay away from the street," I called after them. Again, as soon as the words slipped out of my mouth, I realized how dumb they sounded. The kids never went near the street, and even if they did, we lived in a quiet neighborhood without through traffic. Still, I always felt better if I warned them of the dangers.

"You must have had a bad day," Karen said. "What happened at work?"

Being married to an ER doctor has a few perks, like never having to go to the emergency room if your kids are sick. But it also has a few drawbacks. As ER physicians, we're exposed to the craziest things that can happen to a human being. Tragic car accidents. A kid putting something unusual in his mouth and choking on it. Accidental poisonings. Or the worst, the consequences of impulsive teenage decision making. The things I saw at the hospital scared me. I was on a crusade to keep my kids safe, so I was constantly telling them all the things they shouldn't do.

"Some boys were dragging an upside-down car hood behind a tractor," I told Karen. "They were using it as a sled. When the tractor went too fast, the hood whipped over on top of them."

"Oh, no!" Karen said. "Are they okay?"

"I had to stitch up three of the boys, and I sent the fourth one to the pediatric trauma unit in Nashville. He has a severe brain injury and is unconscious. I'm not sure if he'll make it."

"Oh, honey, I am so sorry," Karen said, hugging me. "But do you really think *our* kids would do that?"

"No. But maybe under the right circumstances . . . I don't know. The truth is, I didn't think *any* kids would do that, but they *did*—and now there's a boy who might not live. I just want to protect our kids."

But even as I spoke those words, I knew they were as useless as my earlier safety lecture. There was only so much I could do to protect our kids. What happened in their future was ultimately up to them, and to God.

✦ ✦ ✦

When I thought about our girls growing up, I didn't want them to be like some of the impulsive kids I saw in the ER. I wanted them to be like Lauren.

Lauren had been a patient of mine since she was a little girl. Everyone in town seemed to know her. She was the captain of the cheerleaders at the high school. She was pretty and popular and had been elected homecoming queen her senior year. More important, she was a good girl who loved the Lord, loved her family, and was a good friend to many. She was also smart and had received a full scholarship to a large state university.

I was so proud of Lauren.

So were her parents. They were excited for her future. They adored her and had attended all her high school activities. Like a flower whose petals opened in the sun, Lauren's life was blossoming before our eyes. I wasn't the only one who looked forward to seeing what else life would bring this special girl.

At night when Karen and I prayed for our children, we asked God to accomplish whatever he planned for each of their lives. But secretly, I sometimes prayed that my girls' lives would turn out just like Lauren's.

✦ ✦ ✦

"Cheatham ER, this is Cheatham One EMS en route to your facility." The radio crackled, and I heard only pieces of what was said next. "Emergency traffic. Arrival in five minutes. Single vehicle rollover. Trauma CPR in progress."

The radio went silent.

Dropped calls like this were all too common in the hills and hollows that surrounded our tiny outpost hospital in middle Tennessee. Even years later when cellular service replaced the radios, calls still dropped frequently. Unfortunately, it seemed we lost communications at the most inopportune times—like in the middle of an important EMT transmission.

Despite the communication interruption, I knew this was going to be a bad one. Trauma CPRs are very difficult cases, and most of the time, the patient doesn't survive. If someone is in an accident and is physically injured enough for his or her heart to stop, it is usually fatal.

I told the staff to prepare for the worst. "But let's pray for the best."

The ambulance arrived, and I met the EMT outside.

"Sorry, Doc, we couldn't get you back on the radio to give you much heads-up," the emergency medical technician said. He filled me in on the details as he and the driver rolled the gurney into the ER and I hurried behind.

"Patient drove her car off that big curve on Johnson's Creek Road. She had this sweet red convertible, and she totaled it. Car landed upside down in the creek at the bottom of the ravine."

"What was her condition when you arrived?" I asked, as we rolled through the ER doors.

"She was strapped in upside down. We were able to get her out and thought we caught a pulse at the scene, but we lost it. She just turned eighteen. Graduated high school today and was running late for her graduation party. Parents were at the scene. They'd been following behind her when it happened, so they saw everything."

"How horrible," I said. Silently, I prayed for the girl and her family.

We arrived in the room, and I stepped back so the EMT and the nurses could transfer her from the stretcher to our bed.

"One, two, three, move!"

The young lady's body was limp, except for her back where the spinal board was still in place from the transport.

"Sad thing is," the EMT continued, "the parents were the ones who bought the car for her. They gave it to her today as a graduation gift."

I stepped up to the head of the bed to get my first good look at the girl.

"Oh, no!" A heavy feeling settled in the bottom of my stomach. I recognized the beautiful but bruised and swollen face.

It was Lauren.

The story the EMT told was sad enough, but now that I could see it was Lauren, I was devastated. *God, you have got to help me.*

The breathing tube was secured to keep Lauren's airway open. I listened, and I could hear breathing sounds from both lungs as the EMTs manually assisted her breathing. But when we got to circulation, we hit a snag—she had no blood flow, except for the CPR compressions. It didn't look promising.

The nurses were doing their own assessment and calling out any unusual findings. "Core temperature 94," one nurse reported.

It was a flicker of hope in an otherwise dismal outlook. Sometimes, with cold temperatures, the heart shuts down in order to try to protect itself from further damage.

"Let's warm her up," I said.

Silently, I kept praying. This was a long shot. While we waited, we continued the CPR, but it wasn't having any effect. Her temperature rose, but nothing changed.

I attempted every standard protocol, plus anything I could think of, to coax her back to life. Nothing seemed to be working.

I continued CPR much longer than I usually would.

I knew her friends and family were gathering in the waiting room. Every part of me wanted to go out there and tell them she'd be fine, that she would soon rejoin them. But it was becoming clear that it wasn't God's plan for Lauren. When I did a secondary check of her body, I felt the back of her head and realized she had broken her neck. At the crash site, the veil had opened instantly to receive Lauren's soul, and it had quickly closed behind her. She wouldn't be returning to this world.

I had no doubt about where Lauren was now, but I also knew the pain that her death would bring to those who loved her. My heart ached at the thought of telling her family. My job shifted from trying to heal Lauren to trying to comfort her parents.

✦ ✦ ✦

The waiting room was filled with family, high school friends, and crying cheerleaders. I paused just outside it to pray.

God, please take care of her up there. And please give me your words to pass on to the family, so I can comfort them any way I can.

When I walked in, everyone stopped what they were doing. The room was still, and all eyes were focused on the man in the white coat—me. Lauren's mom was sitting in the middle of the room, with her husband standing next to her. I could see them searching my face for any sign of hope. When they didn't see it, their eyes quickly filled with tears.

I knelt in front of Lauren's mom and took her hand, and I said the words that no parent wants to hear. "I'm truly sorry, but she didn't make it."

"No! No, no, no!" she screamed. Her other hand covered her mouth in disbelief.

As the words sank in, Lauren's mother began that wail, and the room filled with sounds of friends and family members joining her in grief. It was one of the saddest moments of my life, hearing their raw pain and knowing there was nothing I could do to help them or to fix it. Most disheartening of all, I was powerless to bring their daughter back.

Teenage girls hugged each other and cried. A few adults gathered into a group and prayed. Others sat staring blankly ahead, obviously in shock. But above all the other noises was that awful, distinctive sound of a mother weeping for her daughter.

✦ ✦ ✦

"I'm so deeply, deeply sorry," I said, when she stopped crying. "I can't give you an answer as to why this happened, but I can tell you that she died instantly at the scene and that she didn't feel any pain."

"Are you sure?" her father asked.

"I'm sure," I said, trying not to choke up. "Her neck was broken in the accident, and she went to be with the Lord right there at the scene. There was nothing anyone could have done to save her."

Perhaps the most important thing I said to Lauren's parents that night was that she didn't suffer. At the time, I didn't understand the comfort those words would bring. But I've since learned that even if believers know their final destination and look forward to it, they have questions and concerns about the transition that takes place getting from here to there. As tragic as Lauren's broken neck was, knowing that she passed quickly and painlessly brought great comfort to her parents.

I hugged her mother and said, "If there is anything I can do, anything at all . . ."

Eventually the waiting room cleared. Only empty tissue boxes and half-empty soda cans remained. Before I left for home, I took one more look at the room and thought about how much I'd wanted my girls to end up like Lauren. Now, I realized it was only by God's grace that they hadn't.

✦ ✦ ✦

A few weeks later, I ran into Lauren's parents and asked how they were.

"It hurts," they said.

"I understand your pain, but if you have a minute, I'd like to tell you something."

We found a bench and sat down. I briefly told them about my cousins' deaths and then talked about the dream and my experiences in heaven where I was reunited with them.

"I like to think about Lauren walking through that meadow," I said. "I'm jealous as I think about her drinking from the icy-blue stream or perhaps sitting on the rock, soaking in that rainbow of color. It makes me long to go too."

"Do you really think that's where she is?" her mother asked.

"I think that's where she started. But then, I believe she was met by friends and family who've gone before. I think they waited for her at the edge of the meadow, so they could escort her back to a place that is even more wonderful than the things I've seen and described to you."

"I bet my mother was in that crowd, waiting to greet her," Lauren's father said.

"I'm sure she was. There is such a great sense of peace that it's hard to describe. It's unlike anything I've felt here. Everyone is happy and whole. There are no scars, no diseases, and no disabilities. Lauren won't have that scar on her arm from falling off her bike, her neck won't be broken, and her face will be even more beautiful than it was before her accident."

Her mom teared up, and I handed her a tissue. "That sounds nice."

I told her about meeting Jesus and the instantaneous, overwhelming, unconditional, and abundant love that only he could offer. "I've never felt so loved before or since. Everyone is so happy and whole. Once you've been there, you would never wish for loved ones to come back. You just want to join them on the other side."

I told them about other glimpses I'd had of heaven through a touch, a temperature change, or a smell. "I didn't have those experiences the night that Lauren died because her soul had passed at the accident site. But I definitely felt God's presence in the ER." Had it not been for God's strength holding me up that night, I would have crumbled too.

By the time our conversation ended, I knew I hadn't taken away the pain of losing Lauren, but I prayed that the hope of heaven at least partially filled the hole in their hearts left by her absence.

✦ ✦ ✦

Lauren's death was a defining moment for me, and not just because a young patient I cared about died. It was also transformative because it led me to look at my job differently. God revealed to me that not only had he given me the gift of being a doctor to help heal patients, but he had also given me the privilege of standing beside people and holding their hands through some of life's most difficult transitions. I do this by sharing my glimpses into heaven and explaining how I know that our longings to see our loved ones will, one day, be majestically fulfilled.

Like a butterfly that struggles to break free of its chrysalis, the struggles through the transitions of this life make us stronger. At some point, we'll leave our worn sheath behind. We'll transition to a world that is bigger, brighter, and more loving than anything we've ever imagined.

Chapter 23
ANGEL TIME

+

I adopted a whole new crew of Eighties Ladies as soon as I started making monthly rounds at the nursing home in Ashland City.

Or maybe I should say *they* adopted *me*.

One of the residents I most enjoyed seeing was a woman named Lois. She told the nurses that her favorite day of the month was the day I made rounds. When I arrived, she'd be waiting for me at the nurses' station. She was always dressed in her finest clothes and jewelry—sometimes they even matched. Her coral lipstick was occasionally smeared, but even then, it couldn't hide her big, bright smile.

"Oh, Dr. Anderson, I'm so delighted to see you!" she'd say. Her choice of words always struck me because Lois couldn't *see* anything. She'd been blind since birth.

As soon as I signed in, she'd ask me to escort her back to her room for a private consultation. While the nurse pushed her wheelchair, Lois would insist on holding my hand all the way down the hall and back to her room.

"Doctor, do you know who you remind me of?"

"Who?" I asked.

The nurse winked at me. We both knew what Lois was going to say. She'd been saying it every month since I first started rounds several years earlier.

"You remind me of Clark Gable!"

"I do?"

"Yes! He's my favorite movie star, you know."

Lois was a flirtatious schoolgirl trapped in an elderly woman's failing body. Since her blindness prevented her from knowing the truth, I often wanted to tell her that I looked just like Gable. But I never did. I figured the nurse's laugh would give me away.

✦ ✦ ✦

One day when I arrived at the home for my regularly scheduled rounds, I didn't see Lois waiting in her usual spot near the nurses' station. In fact, I didn't see her anywhere.

"She's not doing well," a nurse said. "She's in bed and running a fever this morning." The nurse led me back to her room.

"Good morning, Lois. It's Dr. Anderson," I said, as I approached her bedside and took her hand.

"There's my Clark Gable doctor!" She smiled in my direction. "I'm not feeling so well today."

"Tell me what's wrong."

"I'm not sure. I was fine yesterday. But today my stomach and back ache, and I feel kind of nauseated."

I did a quick examination. "Your heart rate is up and so is your blood pressure. Have you been urinating?"

"Yes, but it hurts when I go."

"I think we should admit you to the hospital so we can run some tests. I don't think it's anything serious, but I just want to be sure."

Lois was transferred to the hospital where the tests I ordered confirmed my suspicion—pyelonephritis, a kidney infection. I ordered IV antibiotics and stopped by later that afternoon.

"How are you doing?" I asked as I took her hand.

"I'm feeling a little better," Lois said. "That's Sissy over there," she said, pointing to the patient in the next bed. "Sissy, this is my Clark Gable doctor!"

Sissy didn't respond. I later learned she had senile dementia and didn't talk much.

"I'm glad you're feeling better," I told Lois. "My plan is to keep you here for another day or two while we give you antibiotics. When you feel better and your appetite returns, we'll send you back to your room at the home, but until then I want to keep an eye on you."

We talked a little longer, and then I had to go. "I'll check on you in the morning," I said before I left.

+ + +

The next morning, I had several patients to visit during rounds. Lois's room was at the end of the hall, so she was my last stop. As I neared her door, I could hear her raised voice.

"Keep them away from me. Please keep them away from me!"

When I opened the door and walked in, I could see her trying to push something away—but nothing was there. Lois's daughter was at her bedside attempting to calm her down.

"What's wrong?" I asked.

"I don't know what happened; she just went crazy all of a sudden."

"Please! Don't let them get any closer to me!" Lois cried out. She was clearly agitated and determined to keep the invisible away.

"Lois, it's Dr. Anderson," I said and grabbed her hands. I held them securely in mine, hoping it would comfort her. "What's wrong?"

"Don't you see them? There are so many of them. Their brilliant lights are hurting my eyes!"

She jerked her hands out of mine and began making a shoving motion. She seemed to be shooing something away, something none of us could see, which was ironic because Lois was the only one in the room who couldn't see.

"Please get them away from me!"

Both her daughter and I tried to calm her down. We spoke to her in soothing tones and tried to engage her in conversation, but she was fixated on whatever it was that she saw. We tried gently touching her and placing our hands on her arms or legs, hoping that despite her blindness and confusion, she would understand that she wasn't alone, that we were right there with her. But she only became more frantic. "Their colors are so bright. They're hurting my eyes! Please, tell them to leave. It's not my time yet. It's not my time . . ."

Lois's daughter looked fearful. She'd obviously never seen her mother act in such a way, and she wasn't sure what to do.

Lois's frustration increased, and she began tearing her sheets away from her bed. "Please tell them to stay away from me. Tell them it's not my time!"

Her daughter reached over to help pull her mother's covers back, when without warning, Lois reached out and slapped her daughter on the side of the head.

The daughter jumped back and looked as if she might cry.

"She didn't mean it. She's hallucinating," I said. "This can happen when people get sick. They get a little confused. I'll order a sedative to help her relax." Lois continued pushing invisible things away and protesting the proximity of whatever she was seeing in her head. "Please make them go away!"

I could hear her as I walked down the hall.

The nurses' station was forty or fifty feet away. Lois's cries faded as I neared it. I realized she was probably suffering from sundowner syndrome. It is a common condition among the elderly; they become disoriented when placed in unfamiliar surroundings. Typically, the symptoms occur at night. *Maybe because she's blind, her body can't tell the difference?*

Once inside the nurses' station, I picked up Lois's chart to write my orders. Before I could even click my pen, I heard the alert, "Code ten, room two!"

Code ten meant that CPR was in progress.

Room two was the room I'd just left.

Lois is coding!

I dropped the chart on the counter and sprinted back down the hall. *What had I missed?* As I raced toward her room, thoughts of what caused this to happen darted through my mind. *An AMI?* An acute myocardial infarction, a heart attack, was possible. She'd certainly been upset when I left her. *Possibly a PE?* Though it seemed unlikely, a pulmonary embolism, or blood clot to the lung, could have happened that quickly. *Maybe she's gone into septic shock from the kidney infection.*

The door was closed, and Lois's daughter was standing outside, biting her nails while tears ran down her cheeks. I knew she had to be scared, but I didn't stop to talk to her. During an emergency, it was protocol to clear the room of everyone except medical professionals.

I pushed open the door and closed it behind me, stopping right inside the door. I tried to make sense of what was happening. The crash cart was there, and the nurses were readying the patient, but the patient requiring CPR was in bed *one*.

Lois was in bed *two*.

Lois wasn't having a heart attack—it was Sissy, her roommate!

With a code ten, time is of the essence. Since there wasn't enough time to move the patient's bed out, the nurses had asked Lois's daughter to leave and then drawn the curtain around Lois's bed while they worked on Sissy.

My instincts kicked in, and immediately I joined the nurses in running the code.

I intubated Sissy while the nurses charged the defibrillator. We shocked her. Nothing happened. "One milligram of epinephrine. Push the EPI!" We continued CPR and then shocked her again. The monitors remained flat. "An amp of sodium bicarbonate. Continue CPR."

Together, we tried to pull Sissy back from the veil before she passed through. It was noisy and chaotic while we did everything we knew to do. At one point, I thought of Lois and wondered if she was still upset. *This noise and commotion must be frightening her.* She was in a strange place and was already confused. I couldn't imagine how worked up she would be now that her daughter had been asked to leave the room. In addition, I knew she could hear the commotion, but she couldn't see what was happening. However, at that moment, we were so busy working on Sissy, I couldn't worry about Lois.

After nearly thirty minutes of CPR, Sissy's heart failed to beat on its own. We knew it was useless to continue much longer. Her doctor arrived and said we could stop, and he pronounced her dead. We all took a step back. Silently, I said a quick prayer for the woman's family. The nurses began clearing the equipment and cleaning up the room from the battle that had just taken place.

That's when I remembered Lois.

I slowly pulled the curtain back, expecting to see her in the same state I'd left her, but instead she appeared calm.

I took her hand in mine. "Lois? Are you okay? It's Dr. Anderson."

"They're gone now, Doctor."

"Who's gone?"

"The angels. They're not flying over my bed anymore; they've gone with Sissy. They've taken her away."

"What did they look like?"

"Like bright lights. There were so many of them darting around. They hurt my eyes."

God had sent a band of angels to escort Sissy home, and he'd allowed a blind woman to see them.

As I recalled all the things Lois had said when she thought the angels were coming for her, I was reminded of the night Dennis died. It was the first time I saw a glow in the hospital room after a patient passed. Something in the light that night had reminded me of Tinker Bell. I smiled as I thought about Lois pushing away a bunch of flying and brightly lit angels, only to discover they weren't there for her. They were there to escort her roommate to heaven.

I did a quick examination, and her vitals were perfect; nothing was elevated. I could see her face was serene as she spoke, and she seemed surprisingly calm despite all that had happened to her in the past hour.

"I'm glad you're okay. I'll send your daughter back in. If you're still feeling good tomorrow, we'll let you go back to the nursing home."

"Dr. Anderson?"

"Yes?"

"You still remind me of Clark Gable."

I decided not to order the sedative—she obviously didn't need it.

✦   ✦   ✦

Lois was blind.

And she claimed to have seen angels.

It would have been easy to dismiss her story. In fact, many doctors would have assumed that she was hallucinating and ordered a sedative, adjusted her medications, or made a note in her chart about possible dementia. But as a doctor, I think we fail our patients when we don't take the time to really talk with them and listen to what they're saying.

I believed Lois. I believe she really had seen angels coming to take Sissy home. If I hadn't known her as a person before this happened, I could have come to very different conclusions. But as a family physician, I'd had the opportunity to come in contact with people of all ages, and through the years I've noticed a curious parallel: children and the elderly both have the same kind of faith.

The very young have clarity of vision that has not yet been clouded by the things of this world. They see God and his work more clearly than the rest of us. On some level, I believe they recognize that where they came from is a very real place and that it still exists. They believe without effort, and they're willing to talk freely about their spiritual experiences.

Likewise, the elderly seem to have this same clarity. As the very old near death, their physical bodies grow weaker, and their vision begins to dim. Whether the cause is cataracts, glaucoma, or just old age, they can't see as well as they once did. But their inability to see as clearly as before has some positive benefits. For the first time in their adult lives, they're able to slow down.

As the sights and sounds of this world start to fade, they tune their eyes and ears toward heaven. It suddenly seems much closer than they'd previously realized. They start to reflect more, and they begin to see and hear from God in ways they'd never been able to before. Their spiritual side somehow is being awakened to new levels of insight and perception after having lain dormant for years. The elderly often reach a stage where their spiritual vision improves, even as their physical vision fails. They experience things—such as dreams or visions—that they've never experienced before, and they're more emboldened to share with others what they've seen. In other words, they become more childlike in their faith.

It's easy for medical professionals to chalk this up to dementia or senility, and in some cases those conditions do exist. The problem, however, is that those who make medical decisions for the elderly are usually in the middle years of life, too busy to stop and really listen, too quick to dismiss anything they haven't seen before or can't independently prove. During this middle stage of life, people often seem to have lost the spiritual vision they were born with, the insight that may return when they grow older. As a result, they're often impatient with both children and the elderly who have experiences they don't have. Irritated, they react by becoming more cynical and sarcastic, quick to explain why certain things "couldn't happen."

So I can't help but wonder, *What if the faith we had as children continued throughout our entire lives?*

Several times in the New Testament, Jesus is quoted as saying that we must become like little children if we want to enter the Kingdom of Heaven. I think he's talking about the faith I've seen in both the young and the elderly. They are the ones closest to the veil; either they've just come through on arrival, or they'll soon be departing. Heaven feels nearer to them than it does to those basking in the middle years of life. Or perhaps the very young and the very old are just more willing to see heaven.

I think I know why Jesus asked us to care for the widows and the orphans, and I don't think it's only because they need us to provide for them. Certainly, throughout history, these populations have been "the least of these"—at risk for poverty, sickness, and victimization. Jesus was clear to his followers about taking care of the least of these. But I think there is another reason why he asked us to care for the most vulnerable. I think it was to help *us*. When we spend time with widows and orphans, we are able to see him better.

If we want to know God, we need to learn from those who know him best, and who is closer to his heart than widows and children? They can provide the lenses we need to see both this life and the next with more clarity. So it makes perfect sense to me that an elderly blind woman would be the one to see God's angels. She had better vision than the rest of us, who were distracted by the sights and sounds of this physical world. Lois was focused on another world, one that is even more real than where we now live.

✦ ✦ ✦

Throughout my career, I've come to understand this clarity of vision possessed by the very young and the very old, and now the blind.

I've deliberately tried to spend more time with those people who see God with more clarity than I do. It's also why I want to be at the bedside of dying patients. No one is closer to heaven than someone who just has or is about to cross over.

When I'm holding the hands of dying patients as they take their final breath, I'm standing in the foyer of heaven, watching them enter the spirit world that lies beyond my vision.

In those moments, it is as if I'm standing in the narthex of a large cathedral. The elegant architecture and design that surround me lead me to believe that the inner sanctuary must be exquisite. I've never seen the inner rooms, but I've gotten glimpses of a place where the lighting is better—everything seems brighter and clearer. While the foyer is welcoming and pleasant, I know this is only a hint of what is inside. The smells of heaven leak into the foyer, but the source of that fragrance comes from somewhere beyond, offering just a whiff of the banquet to come.

Knowing how much more there is to experience, I've often told

God that I'd be happy simply to be a footman in the foyer of heaven welcoming new souls upon arrival. I can't wait to be able to stay there!

In the meantime, I want to see life like Lois, the elderly, and children see it—blinded to this world, knowing that the soft glow and the bright twinkling colors here are the navigational lights pointing toward what comes next.

Chapter 24
PAIRED FOR LIFE

✦

State Industries, the world's largest hot water heater manufacturer, has a plant in Ashland City that employs more than two thousand workers. Two of those workers were Alice and Robert. They graduated from high school, got married, and went to work at State.

Twenty years later their son, Robert Jr., known as Bobby, graduated from high school and joined them at State. Alice and Robert beamed with pride. Though Bobby started on the maintenance crew, they hoped that one day he would get his own rig and join the family hauling water heaters across the country—maybe even replacing his mother so she could work part-time.

About a year after Bobby started at State, a driving rain and an unseen hole in the roof flooded one of the main buildings, making it impossible for the workers to do their jobs. The factory lines were shut down, and hundreds of jobs and thousands of dollars were at risk. The maintenance crew on the scene checked the roof for the breach. Though he was a novice, Bobby was eager to do his best to keep the factory running. Through the pouring rain, he searched for the hole and was the first to find it. The source of the deluge was several inches wide near a clogged drain on the roof's edge. Bobby took a step closer to investigate.

The roof gave way.

He instantly fell thirty feet to the concrete floor below.

Witnesses said his head smacked first.

✦ ✦ ✦

When they brought Bobby into the ER, he was boarded and collared, the traditional transport method designed to protect the spinal cord and neck from further damage. The EMT in charge updated me on his status. "Right pupil blown. Skull fracture. Brain tissue leaking from the scalp laceration. Snoring respirations, so we couldn't intubate. We just bagged him until we got here. The parents are on their way."

I'd never known anyone to survive a fall like that, so my first thoughts weren't about saving his life—they were about how I would tell Alice and Robert that their son was gone. I began working on his obstructed airway. Blood—probably a result of his fractured teeth—was filling his oral pharynx as fast as we could suction it. The only thing left to do was nasal intubation. I'd only done that once, years before, in the early part of my training.

This time I didn't pray silently. "God," I prayed aloud, "you have got to help me with this one."

I placed my hand on the right side of Bobby's head to correctly position it and immediately jerked my hand back. His skull was crushed, and brain matter was protruding. I moved to the left side, and I slid the breathing tube into Bobby's nostril and prayed for him to take a breath. "One more breath, Lord, please."

Intubation without a clear line of sight depends on listening for the distant sound of the vocal chords opening. All I needed to secure the airway was just a split second for them to open as the tube neared. "Please, Lord, let it go past!" As I listened for Bobby's breath, I held mine and slipped the tube in.

I inflated the cuff on the breathing tube to open the airway and prevent aspiration of any other blood or gastrointestinal material. Death was not cheated, but at least it was placed on hold. Instead of opening the veil, God had opened an airway—at least temporarily.

We called the trauma unit at Vanderbilt to tell them what we had. They confirmed we were on the right path, but we likely weren't clear yet. They would send air transport, but it was still questionable whether or not Bobby would be alive when it arrived.

Our job was to keep him alive until LifeFlight arrived. We bagged Bobby so he could breathe. The room was quiet except for the gentle hum of the machines. I prayed silently. *Please, God. Please help us help him!* I heard a voice. It was barely audible—or maybe it wasn't audible, and I just felt it. "This is *my* child."

For the next twenty-three minutes, we bagged Bobby to keep him alive, and I heard the whisper over and over again, "This is *my* child."

Suddenly, the whisper was interrupted by a great commotion coming from the waiting room. It was only thirty feet away, so I could hear everything that was said.

"Where is my child? Where is my child?" the woman cried. "I have to know! Is he dead?" I knew it had to be Bobby's mother.

While the nurses tried to calm her down and stop her screaming, I was struck by the similarity of her words, "Where is my child?" with what I'd been hearing: "This is *my* child."

God, he is your child, but temporarily, he is also hers. Please help me know what to say to her.

Things were under control in the ER, so I left to talk to the parents. As soon as I opened the door to the waiting room, Alice and Robert's eyes met mine. "How bad is it, Doc? We heard he was dead. Is he?" his mother asked.

"It's bad. But he's still alive. We're breathing for him, and LifeFlight is on the way. He's had a skull fracture and a traumatic brain injury. Only God can tell us what the final outcome will be, but we'll continue to pray for God's hands to guide him as they've guided us."

✦   ✦   ✦

Bobby survived.

The days passed. Weeks turned into months. Summer became fall and slipped into winter before I finally got the call I'd been praying for. "Bobby's being released to Stallworth, the rehab unit. He'll need a follow-up appointment with you to continue outpatient therapy." The skull fracture actually had enlarged the space available and had given his brain room to swell.

That fracture probably saved his life.

+ + +

I visited Bobby in the rehab center, and he greeted me with a left-handed high five. His right arm wasn't working as well.

"How are you feeling?" I asked.

He grinned and said, "Fuh, fuh-ine."

In the beginning, even talking was an arduous task for Bobby. But he worked hard in rehab and continued to make progress. On another visit, I asked him if he remembered anything from the night of the accident. "No, Doc. Some days I have trouble remembering what I ate for breakfast."

"That's okay," I said. I explained how we had all thought he was going to die and how his brain had literally been leaking from his skull. I also told him about the whisper I'd heard, "This is *my* child," just minutes before his mother ran in screaming, "Where is my child?"

"God saved you for a purpose, Bobby. I don't know what it is, but I look forward to finding out."

+ + +

Bobby eventually went back to work at the factory, though this time he stayed on the ground. Through the years I would see his parents, and they would update me on his progress.

"He's still a little slow," his mother told me one day, "but he's got a new girlfriend!"

A few months later she said, "Bobby Jr.'s getting married in June. The wedding's out west in Wyoming. Looks like he's going to move there permanently."

We talked about how hard it was to let go of our kids, but Alice assured me that she and Robert would see their miracle son often. "One of our routes goes right by there."

Eighteen months later, Robert and Alice stopped by my office one afternoon. "Bobby wanted us to show this to you."

Robert held out a photo, and I took it from him. It was of a brand-new baby boy. Puzzled, I looked up and saw Alice and Robert beaming—as only new grandparents could.

"Congratulations!" I said, hugging them both. "You tell Bobby I said a child is very precious and a special gift from God."

"Well, he's got a message for you, too, Doc," Robert said. "Turn it over."

I turned the photo over. On the back, Bobby had written, "This is *my* child."

✦ ✦ ✦

It was fall. The leaves were lazily falling from the trees, and the cooler breezes hinted at the chill that was to come. Autumn is typically a slow time of year in the emergency room. In the summer there are always accidents, cuts, and broken bones. In the winter there are victims of flu and pneumonia, and their resulting complications. But the fall is usually a little more relaxed.

In my earliest days in Ashland City, Dr. Lundy and I had alternated days on call for the ER, but we didn't stay at the hospital. We'd sit by the phone at home and rush over when a call came in. As Ashland City grew, so did the demands on the ER. By the time of this particular call, the ER had a full nursing staff and 24/7 staffing by a physician.

I'd just finished with my last patient. No one else remained in the emergency room, so I'd gone back up to the on-call room to put my feet up and relax. I wasn't there more than five minutes when the nurse called, "Can you come back down? CPR in progress. The ambulance will be here in five minutes." I jumped up and headed back down to the ER to make sure I was prepped.

I'd barely put on my mask and gloves by the time the ambulance arrived. The team was in place and ready to receive the patient. The gurney rolled through the doors.

"White female. Seventy-nine years. Collapsed at home. 911 called. She was intubated on-site and IV placed. She had asystole on the monitor. However, we continued CPR en route since we were so close."

Asystole was a dire form of cardiac arrest—the heart completely stops beating, and no electrical activity can be detected on the monitor. It is usually a serious and life-ending heart attack.

Betty Sue hadn't responded to any of the EMTs' initial interventions. The survival rate for her age and lack of response was less than one percent. Things didn't look good. But a one percent chance was better than no chance at all.

We moved her into the two-bed emergency room to see what we could do. The EMTs had been doing masked breathing, so we moved her from their portable machine to our larger one. No activity registered on the monitor.

"Continue CPR. Push the EPI."

Still nothing.

"One amp of bicarb. Continue CPR."

Nothing.

"Charge the paddles."

We shocked her heart. Still nothing.

The ambulance attendant poked his head in the room and said, "Her husband, William, is outside."

"We're busy working on Betty Sue. Tell him I'll be out when I can to talk to him. It will probably be a few minutes."

"I don't think you understand," the EMT said. "*She* called us for *him*. William is the one who had a heart attack first. He's in the hall, and we're doing CPR on him."

"What?" I looked up in time to see my nurse's jaw drop.

The EMT explained that the husband had collapsed at home and the wife had called 911, but by the time the ambulance arrived, William and Betty Sue were both lying on the floor.

"Well, bring him in and put him in cot two!" I said.

Running two codes at once in our tiny ER was unprecedented. I continued to work on Betty Sue while the EMTs and nurses set up William in the adjoining bed.

I strongly sensed God's presence inside the ER. I felt his warmth as intensely as I'd ever felt it. The divine scents calmed me as I felt the veil parting for one or both of these precious souls.

"Their children are on the way and should be here in five minutes," the nurse said.

"Continue CPR on both patients until they arrive."

Handling one code was challenging enough, but trying to keep up with two at the same time was impossible without God's intervention. Thankfully, I felt him directing my attention between the two patients and keeping me focused as I supervised the nurses.

Once William was hooked up to his monitor, I could see that his heart wasn't registering any activity either. Like his wife, he was flatlined.

I intubated him, and we started mechanical breathing. Still no signs of heart activity. "Let's try to shock him."

I didn't think that shocking him would work any better than it had with Betty Sue, but I had to do something for the adult children who were about to learn they'd lost both parents within minutes of each other.

"Charge the paddles."

I turned to look at Betty Sue's monitor one last time before I shocked William, but as soon as I turned toward her bed, his nurse said something that made me turn right back.

"Doctor, something's happening here."

She pointed to the monitor where it showed a hint of activity. Then, even before we could shock his heart, we saw a single heartbeat. *Blip.*

"Hold the paddles," I said. "I think we're getting a pulse. He's coming back."

Then there was another. *Blip.* Only this second blip wasn't from William's monitor; it came from somewhere behind me. I turned to see what was happening, and I realized it was on his *wife's* monitor!

Blip. A second beat on William's monitor.

Blip. Another beat on Betty Sue's monitor.

Blip, blip, blip went William's monitor, and Betty Sue's echoed with a *blip, blip, blip.* It was like a game of Ping-Pong. I turned my head to watch each volley of heartbeats as they registered on both patients' monitors.

Without intervention, William's heart had begun to beat regularly, and then his wife's followed! Soon the two heartbeats were beating in a synchronized rhythm.

It was the most unusual thing I'd ever seen, and it nearly took my breath away. The activity in the room, which had been so busy and chaotic while we were trying to run two codes, had ceased. All the medical professionals were speechless as we stood in awe and listened to the monitors amplifying the sounds of two hearts beating in unison.

✦ ✦ ✦

It was one of the most marvelous miracles I'd ever witnessed. But the couple wasn't out of the woods yet. Both patients were intubated and had heartbeats and blood pressure, but they were still unconscious. I would need to send them to Nashville for further care by a cardiologist.

When their four adult children arrived, I told them what had happened. The kids were amazed, but they didn't seem surprised. They told us that their mom and dad had not spent a night apart in sixty years! Their parents' marriage was obviously a source of pride in the family.

I explained that we would need to transfer them to the ICU in Nashville, and that since they were in a frail state, anything could happen. The kids agreed that their parents were obviously in God's hands and that he wasn't finished with them yet. But they also agreed to a DNR. If their parents left again, the kids didn't want extraordinary means used to try to bring them back.

William and Betty Sue left Ashland City in separate ambulances. Their kids followed behind in cars.

I called the Nashville hospital and spoke to the cardiologist on call, Dr. Peter Scully, who was originally from Australia. I updated him on the medical situation of the two patients, and I also described what had happened in the ER. He was intrigued. "I've heard of a case similar to this in the outback, but that was years ago."

Dr. Scully promised to keep me updated on their progress.

+ + +

Days later, I received a phone call.

"I have an interesting story to tell you about your patients," Dr. Scully said. "They arrived in the ER, and I had the same conversation with the kids that you did. They wanted the ventilators kept in to help them breathe, but they decided they didn't want any further heroics. If their hearts stopped, we weren't supposed to start them again. I admitted both patients and put them in separate rooms in the same cardiac unit."

Nothing he said up to this point surprised me. But Dr. Scully wasn't finished.

"This morning during rounds, I was standing at William's bed when his monitor flatlined. Since we weren't going to resuscitate him, I called time of death, and then went down the hall to the nurses' station to write, "Discharged to a funeral home," in his chart. While I was writing, I happened to look up at the monitors in front of me, and I noticed Betty Sue's. While I was watching, hers flatlined too!"

+ + +

There have been medical reports of "broken heart" syndrome, where people who have lost a loved one have had stress-induced cardiomyopathy. But in this case, Betty Sue didn't intellectually know that William's heart had stopped beating and that he'd passed. She was in a separate room, unconscious. Yet within seconds of his heart stopping, hers had stopped too.

How could something like this be explained?

When we're young, we often get the impression from adults that heaven is light-years away, off in space somewhere, or at the very least, up in the clouds. But over the years some of my glimpses have convinced me otherwise. How else would I have heard God whispering in my ear when Bobby Jr. was in the emergency room? I'd certainly felt heaven in the warmth and in the cool breezes in my dying patients' rooms. I'd even smelled it. It's hard to feel and smell something from a distance.

If heaven was closer than I thought, would that explain how, when God called William home, Betty Sue heard him and responded too? Or did William, with one foot in heaven, stretch out his hand to his wife's soul, so she could come with him? How close does heaven have to be for us to reach out and touch our loved ones, or for our loved ones to reach out and touch us?

We often think of heaven as an end point or a final stop on a journey. We look at life on earth as if it begins and ends here, thinking that heaven somehow lies outside all that.

I view it differently. During our lives here on earth, I don't believe we're walking toward heaven—I believe heaven walks alongside us.

Heaven is *much* closer than we think.

Chapter 25
LEAVING ASHLAND CITY?

+

Although I had finished my obligation to the National Health Service Corps several years earlier, occasionally Karen and I questioned whether or not God still wanted us in Ashland City. Since our arrival, the quality of the health care in Cheatham County had improved dramatically. During my tenure, I'd watched as a clinic, then an emergency room, and finally a hospital was built. Since that time, they'd each expanded. The population was growing as more people moved to the outskirts of Nashville, and that increase attracted new physicians who started new medical practices. This made Karen and me ask, "Does Cheatham County still need us?"

In addition, we knew that our parents were getting older, and we wanted to spend more time with them and help them when they needed us. So every few years, the question of moving would bubble up.

Leaving Ashland City would mean leaving a community and many people we'd grown to love. Our kids were thriving and had lots of friends. Did we really want them to start over somewhere else? The answer was *yes*, if that's what God wanted for us. But the kids weren't the only ones who would miss their friends.

+ + +

Few things are better than having a friend who understands you and believes in you. Ashley, my second daughter, met hers in kindergarten when she and Emily became inseparable. As often happens, the parents of our kids' friends became our friends. We got to know Emily's parents through playdates, school performances, and birthday parties. Soon my son, David, began playing with Emily's little brother, Will. By the fourth grade, both boys were playing on the same basketball team.

During daily practices or games, Karen and Emily's mom, Mary Beth, became fast friends while watching their sons from the stands. They had a lot in common. Both women were from the Midwest, loved sports, and had husbands with high-profile jobs.

Well, Steven's job had a *little* higher profile than mine.

When I first met Steven Curtis Chapman, he was working hard to make it as a musician. As a singer/songwriter, he and his band had to be on the road often, playing and promoting his music at churches, conferences, and festivals. He worked hard and traveled harder. Over the years, he has become one of the most influential artists in Christian music. He's recorded over twenty albums that have sold over 10 million copies. He is the recipient of five Grammy Awards and fifty-seven Gospel Music Association Dove Awards— more than any other artist. But as his career took off, Steven wasn't at home as much as either he or Mary Beth would have liked.

Karen understood what it was like to have an absent husband. With all the hours I put into building my practice and spending nights in the ER, it was almost as if I were on the road too.

As our boys became more involved in basketball, Steven and I started traveling in a new way—attending father/son weekend basketball camps at the University of Alabama. We were two Southern boys married to Midwestern wives, each with lots of kids and not enough time at home. Just as our wives had bonded, Steven and I became friends. We spent hours with (and without) the boys, talking basketball and discussing how to be the men God called us to be.

As the Anderson and the Chapman families grew closer, we spent more time together, including birthdays, holidays, vacations, or even just a simple dinner to celebrate a big basketball win. With the other adults and kids paired up, my third daughter, Julia, and Steven's son, Caleb, began to hang out together. Over time, they became the best of friends. Somewhere along the way, they stopped watching their brothers play basketball and started watching each other. To no one's surprise, they eventually began dating—further binding the ties between our families.

I shared stories about my glimpses of heaven with few people. But inevitably at one of these "family" events, Karen or the kids would ask me to tell the Chapmans a story about something I'd experienced.

When I shared the details of my patients' appointments with heaven, Steven seemed to accept them as fact. This shouldn't have surprised me. I'd heard his music, and he explored some of the same themes. But after spending so many years trying to process the things I'd experienced with medical professionals who didn't seem to understand, it was nice to finally find a friend who did. Steven and I were cut from the same cloth. Though he wasn't a doctor who healed with medicine, he was a singer/songwriter who healed with music. Over time, our friendship and our families became very close.

That was one of the main reasons why the thought of leaving Ashland City was so difficult. Leaving the Chapmans would be like leaving family. Yet Karen and I were committed to following God's leading, wherever that might take us.

✦ ✦ ✦

"Doctor, I think you need to see this right now!" the nurse said.

I walked over to the EKG machine and was stunned by what I saw. My patient was having a heart attack!

Eunice was in her late sixties. She was diabetic and had high blood pressure. Complications from her disease had affected the circulation in her legs. For a long time, she had gotten around with the use of a cane, but now she had to rely on a walker or a wheel-chair. I'd admitted her to the hospital in Ashland City a few days earlier because her blood pressure was dangerously high. I thought if we had her in the hospital, we could get everything under control before sending her back home. While she was in, I had also ordered a routine EKG, which now revealed that her heart functioning was anything but routine.

"What's wrong?" Eunice asked. She tried to sit up to see what we were looking at, but the EKG's leads prevented her.

"Eunice, it appears you're having a heart attack," I said. "We need to send you to the hospital in Nashville so we can get a cardiologist to look at you."

We called an ambulance, and then we called the hospital in Nashville and advised them that she was on her way. They put me through to Dr. Wong, the cardiologist on call.

"As soon as she arrives, we'll see her in the cath lab," Dr. Wong said.

"Thanks," I said, and then added, "Take good care of her. She was one of my first patients when I started here."

"We always do," Dr. Wong said.

✦ ✦ ✦

Approximately five hours later, a nurse tracked me down. "Dr. Wong is holding on line three. He says it's about the patient you sent there today."

I walked to the phone, and I was pretty sure I knew what he was going to say: "We found a small blockage, but we cleared it." It was the same thing I'd heard countless times in the past when I sent patients to the cardiac cath lab or to angioplasty. I answered the phone, and Dr. Wong got right to the point.

"We took Eunice to the cath lab. Everything was going well, and just as you suspected, she was having a very large anterior myocardial infarction. She had a 99 percent blockage of the left anterior descending artery. We opened the vessel with the balloon and then . . ."

He paused. Everything he'd said up to that point made sense and frankly was what I expected to hear. But when he stopped mid-sentence, I wondered if something else was wrong.

"Go on," I said.

"We opened the vessel with the balloon and then, well, everything went south."

"What happened?"

"She died on the table."

"She died?"

"Flatlined. Right there on the table. I had a resident with me, and we worked on her for at least an hour. I was about to let her go, but my resident wanted to practice running a code, so I let him while I supervised."

It was hard to listen to the details of her death when I was still in shock that it had happened at all. I started to think about what I needed to tell her family.

"What was the time of death?"

"Well, see, that's the thing. An hour into the resident running the code, and two hours from the time she flatlined, her heart kicked in and started beating by itself."

"Are you saying she's alive?"

"I'm saying she was dead for two hours, and now she is alive."

"What kind of condition is she in?"

"I have her on a vent in the ICU, and she's in a coma. With that much time doing CPR, I'm really not sure how much functioning will come back."

"Wow. That's pretty unbelievable."

"You're telling me! She was dead on the table for nearly two hours. I would have stopped after the first hour. We weren't getting anything. The only reason I let the resident continue was because he needed the practice."

"Thanks for working with her and for continuing to take care of her. And please, thank your resident for me."

"Will do. I'll keep you posted."

It was an amazing story. Once again, I marveled at God's ability to break the laws of science for his higher purposes. I was acutely aware that Eunice's untimely death and subsequent return never should have happened. I also knew that CPR often caused irreparable damage.

She wasn't in the clear yet.

+ + +

Three days later, I was in Nashville having dinner with Karen when I received a call from the ICU where Eunice, still comatose, had been under observation.

"Dr. Anderson, you need to come in and see your patient," the ICU nurse said.

I explained she was technically Dr. Wong's patient, and since I didn't have formal privileges at that hospital, there was little I could do for her medically.

"I don't think she needs any medical help. She's asking to see you personally."

"She's *asking*? I thought she was in a coma."

"No, she awakened from her coma this morning, and we took her off life support at that time. She seems to be fine, both mentally and physically, but she keeps insisting that you come to see her. She says she has something important to tell you."

"I'll be right over."

Minutes later, Karen and I were at the hospital. Near the ICU, Karen found a bench while I approached the ICU doors.

A nurse stopped me. "Can I help you?"

"Yes, I'm Dr. Anderson—" I planned to tell her I didn't have privileges and that one of the nurses had called, but she interrupted me before I had a chance.

"Eunice has been asking for you," she said as her eyes lit up. "Follow me. She's waiting for you."

I walked into Eunice's room and was surprised at how good she looked—much better than I expected. Her skin was radiant, her eyes sparkled, and she looked almost girlish, something no one had probably said about her for more than forty years.

"Dr. Anderson!" she said, reaching for my hand.

"Hello, Eunice. How are you feeling?"

"Great, just great!" she said with much more enthusiasm than I would have expected from a woman who had been legally dead only seventy-two hours earlier. "Sit down. I have a story I have to tell you."

As soon as I was seated, she started speaking.

"The last thing I remember was lying on the table while they did something with my heart. Then suddenly there was a lot of commotion. People were yelling and handing medical equipment back and forth. I knew they were working on my shell. They said that I died on the table—that I was dead for two hours! But I don't remember it because I wasn't there on that table. I was somewhere else where I was more alive than I've ever been. Everything was peaceful there and calm, very different from here. It was the exact opposite of the craziness that was going on where my body lay on that table. A sensation of total peace enveloped me, and I felt as though I were floating.

"I didn't feel any more pain. Even before my heart attack, I always had pain, what with the arthritis and the neuropathy. But now, I no longer had that burning in my legs; in fact, they felt strong. For the first time in three years, I stood up and walked without a wheelchair or a walker!

"I walked down a path next to a stream. I could feel its icy spray blowing on me as I passed. I stopped to take a drink, and the water was as cold and fresh as an Alaskan stream, but the water was sweet—it tasted like honey.

"When I looked around, I saw an astounding array of colors, and the pigments seemed so concentrated! It was more colorful than anything I'd ever seen or imagined."

By this time, one of the ICU nurses had entered and was listening too. Eunice started talking faster.

"I walked around a bend in the path, and I saw an open field with the greenest grass—I've never seen that color of green before. Right in the middle of that meadow stood a horse-drawn carriage! My father *loved* horses. Seeing that beautiful animal with its gleaming coat reminded me of him. . . ."

Her voice trailed off for a minute, and then she picked up again.

"Suddenly, my view was blocked. A crowd of people stood in front of the carriage. I looked closer, and I saw my father, my sweet mother, and my dear brother! They died years ago. Then I recognized other people in the crowd who had passed away decades ago. But when I saw them, it was as if no time had passed at all. Our spirits were united with an understanding that defied words. In fact, I'm not even sure we used words to communicate.

"They all said they were doing great. They specifically asked me to tell you that what you're doing here in Cheatham County needs to continue. They wanted to encourage you."

Until that point, nothing she said had surprised me. Everything felt consistent with what I'd seen and experienced in my dream. Since the encouragement from some of the people in the crowd seemed so specific, I wondered if they were patients of mine who had crossed to the other side of the veil. It would make sense; both Eunice and I lived in the same community, and I'd likely taken care of some of her older friends.

"I sat down with them in the grassy meadow. They'd prepared a picnic lunch for me, and you know what, Dr. Anderson? There was no diabetic food there! I could eat whatever I wanted!"

I smiled at the nurse. I knew how much Eunice must have enjoyed that. She hated having to watch her sugar intake.

"Dr. Anderson, I've never felt that peaceful and content. It was like being snuggled in a velvet robe. I really wanted to stay there. But then, Jesus came and sat down beside me. He asked me if I could come back here for a while, so I could encourage others. He told me I wouldn't have to stay long, and I would be able to come back soon. He said he wanted me to come back here for two reasons. The first one was to encourage you. He wanted me to tell you that you are doing his will and that you should stay the course. I don't know what that means, but that's what he told me to tell you."

I teared up; a minute later, I was crying. I knew what that meant. God wanted us to stay in Ashland City.

"The second reason was to encourage my family and friends to believe that Jesus is real and that there truly is a heaven!"

"Eunice, I'm so jealous of your experience."

I'd never told her about my dream and wanted to now, but I could see that she'd suddenly grown very tired. Right up until she finished talking, she'd been excited. Her face was animated, and she gestured the whole time she spoke. But now, she reclined her head, closed her eyes, and started breathing deeply. She needed to rest; we would have other opportunities to compare notes.

"Get some sleep, Eunice," I whispered. "You need your strength, so we can get you out of here. God obviously has a job for you."

I held her hand until she fell asleep. Then I turned off the lights and went to find Karen. She was in the lobby reading a magazine. She must have sensed my coming because she looked up as I got closer.

"I can tell by the look on your face that this is a good one," she said, smiling.

I burst into tears as I told her everything Eunice had said. I felt so honored and humbled to have received such a blessing of encouragement. It reminded me of the day I'd walked out of the Tennessee wilderness (both literally and figuratively) after my conversion dream. I'd felt the same way then. I knew there were people who did more for God, who were better Christians than I was, or who desperately needed to hear his voice because of something they were going through.

"Why did he choose to send a message to me?" I asked Karen.

Her reply was simple. "You're his child."

✦ ✦ ✦

After Eunice left the hospital, I was able to tell her about my dream, and we marveled over the similarities between our experiences. Eunice's "short" time on this side of the veil turned out to be seven years, once again proving that God's timing is different from ours.

I knew that, with every passing day, she longed to go back; I knew, because I felt the same way too.

I saw Eunice once a month for those seven years, and she always said the same thing to me. "Keep doing what you're doing."

There was no question in the cardiologist's mind that Eunice had been dead for two hours. There was no question in my mind as to where she'd been. But most important, there was no question in Eunice's mind as to what she was supposed to do with her amazing story.

When I overheard her talking with nurses or even other patients, it didn't take long before her mind and spirit would find a way to lead the conversation back to the loving and peaceful place she'd visited—the place where, more than anything, she desired to return. She'd tell her story over and over. She must have told it at least once a day, maybe more, for seven years.

She often told me that she couldn't rest. "I want to bring as many people to heaven with me as possible!"

✦ ✦ ✦

It was clear to me that God had called us to Ashland City years ago, and this was still where he wanted us. The moving-away question never bubbled up again. Being a country doctor built my faith in ways I never could have imagined. Every day I saw God's presence and marveled at the work of his healing hands, especially when he used mine to participate in his miracles.

But just because God had confirmed his will for my life didn't mean that everything would now become easy for me. Sometimes as Christians, we believe that following God makes life simple and easy. Nothing could be further from the truth—often that's when life gets more difficult.

I was a young believer when the events surrounding the Alday murders tested my faith and caused me to turn away from God. But heaven reached down, and in that intersection between worlds, God stretched out his hand and brought me back to him. Since then,

I've had more brief encounters with heaven than I can count, and in more ways than I ever could have imagined. I fervently believe that God is real and God is good.

It's not an exaggeration to say that I daily see his hand move in my patients' lives. I continue to catch glimpses of heaven, to experience the warmth as a soul leaves the body, to feel heaven's breeze on my cheek, and to smell the sweet fragrance that wafts over into this world from the other side of a very thin veil.

But after practicing medicine for two decades, my faith journey wasn't over. There would be new tests to my faith, and these trials would cause me to reexamine the old questions all over again.

Would I respond differently this time?

Part 3:

DO I BELIEVE WHAT I'VE SEEN?

Chapter 26
TORN VEILS

✦

After deciding to stay in the Ashland City area, we did end up moving in 1994. When a farm with several acres of land came up for sale less than a mile from our subdivision in Kingston Springs, we bought it. The farm had a lake and an old barn, and we built a large farmhouse on the property. The kids loved the extra space, and throughout their high school years, we had room for all of them to have friends over. The spacious house was a blessing we felt God had given us to share with others. Karen even began dreaming about how, once the kids were gone, she might occasionally open our home to ministries that needed a quiet setting for retreats.

My parents had come to visit us many times over the years, including several extended stays when David had one of his surgeries to repair his cleft palate. Years before, Mom and Dad had started downsizing the number of animals they owned to make it easier for them to travel. After I went off college, they'd gotten rid of Tex the pony, giving him to a family who had young children. Over time, they'd reduced the animals dependent on them to zero. Since they enjoyed hanging out with the grandkids and being part of all their activities, they were able to visit us longer with fewer ties to their home.

When it came time for my parents to retire, it only made sense for them to sell their farm and move closer to us. First of all, my dad's health was starting to decline. He had a mass on his thyroid, and he and Mom wanted help navigating the medical system. Second, my siblings had moved away from Plantersville as well. My brother, Tim, lived in suburban Huntsville, not far from the Tennessee border, with his wife and their two kids. My sister, Cathy; her husband, Mike; and their kids, Jon and Jennifer, moved every two or three years because of Mike's job.

Because Karen and I lived centrally between my siblings and could monitor my parents' health, Mom and Dad decided to move to Kingston Springs. They bought a house within walking distance of our farm—in the subdivision that backed up to our property.

✦ ✦ ✦

While my sister, Cathy, and her family lived farthest away, they had always been an integral part of our lives. When I was in medical school in Birmingham, occasionally I would have dinner with Cathy and Mike, who lived in the area at the time. I knew they attended a local Baptist church, but we rarely discussed issues of faith; and of course, I never attended with them. After I had my dream, they sensed something was different about me, especially once I started dating Karen and attending church with her. But my faith was so new that we never really discussed it.

After Karen and I married, Cathy and Mike moved to Atlanta and had two kids. Jennifer was the oldest. She was a good student and, like my girls, was always involved in a ton of activities. Their son, Jon, was into Scouting and music, but he always seemed to be a bit of a loner. Mike worked as a technical educator for the nuclear power industry. So every two to three years, as one contract ended and another started, Mike and Cathy moved.

With the geographical distance between us expanding and our families growing, we didn't get to see one another as often as we would have liked. But we always made it a priority to gather at my parents' house in Troy, Alabama, for the holidays.

Mike was an only child, and his parents had moved to nearby

Dothan, so they often joined us too. With their Pennsylvania Dutch ancestry, they were a little more stoic and reserved than the rest of us ebullient Southerners. I'm sure we took a little getting used to. Despite our differences, I liked Mike and his family, and we got along well.

Once Mom and Dad moved to Kingston Springs, the holiday gatherings relocated to our house. By then, Cathy and Mike had moved to the Midwest. My brother, Tim, and his wife and two girls still lived in Alabama. So we became the central location.

Though their ages varied, the six girl cousins loved to hang out together. My son, David, and Jon had a harder time bonding. David loved sports while Jon preferred video games and reading. Karen and I always tried to reach out to Jon to make him feel welcome. Likewise, my parents did their best to make Jon, their oldest grandson, feel included.

✦ ✦ ✦

It was a sunny Tuesday in Ashland City, and the temperature was expected to be unusually high for April—around eighty-four degrees. That day in 2002 started out just like so many before it. After rounds that morning, I had a full load of patients in the office, but I hoped I'd also have time to catch up on some neglected paperwork. Karen had run out to do some errands and then planned to stop by the kids' school where she often volunteered. But our agendas that day were shattered by a single phone call.

"Reggie, I need you to sit down," Karen said, her voice trembling with emotion. Immediately I knew something terrible had happened. "Jon committed suicide a few hours ago."

"Oh, no!" I gasped. "How did you find out?"

"Cathy called your mom, and then your mom called me."

My stomach knotted, and I squeezed my eyes shut to hold back the tears. I could hear Karen sniffling. After a pause, she told me what had happened.

"Cathy fixed breakfast for Jon and Jennifer. When it was ready, she called the kids. Jennifer came, but Jon didn't. She called him again; still no reply. Cathy went upstairs to find him, but he wasn't in his bedroom or in the bathroom either. She looked everywhere in the house, but she couldn't find him. She thought perhaps he'd left for school earlier than usual. That's when she saw the box of donuts still on the table. Jon was supposed to have taken them to jazz band rehearsal that morning, and he'd forgotten them. So Cathy picked up the box and headed out the front door."

As Karen spoke, I pictured the scene. Cathy and Mike had recently moved to a new home, and though I hadn't seen it yet, I remembered her telling me that the door to the middle school, where Jon attended, was directly across the street from their front door.

"It was early, but she said she could see what appeared to be a person standing at the school door. As she got closer, she recognized Jon's coat. Something didn't seem right, and he wasn't moving. She started running, and when she got there . . ."

Karen was openly crying. I was too.

"Jon was dangling from a rope. He'd hung himself."

"She was the one to find him?"

"She screamed for help. A neighbor heard her cries and came running with a kitchen knife. Together, they cut him down, but it was too late. He'd already been dead for hours!"

As I listened to Karen's sobs, all I could think of was the mother's wail that I'd heard so many times before in my practice. I was sickened by the thought of Cathy having to find her son like that. It wasn't hard to imagine her guttural cries as she begged for help. Chills raced down my spine as I felt her fear and panic.

"How was Mom when you spoke to her?"

"She was really upset. I wanted to call you first before I headed over to check on her and your dad."

I told Karen I'd cancel my appointments and find someone to cover for me. "Get the Suburban packed, and we'll leave as soon as I get home."

✦ ✦ ✦

The last time I'd spoken directly with Jon and Jennifer was at Christmas. They'd recently moved three hours east, from Muscatine, Iowa, to their new home in Coal City, Illinois. They both missed friends from their old school, but by all accounts, the move had been a good one. True to her personality, Jennifer had jumped right into new activities and was making friends. Jon, on the other hand, seemed more pensive and distant than usual. Karen had even tried to talk with him one-on-one, hoping to connect with him. But he didn't have much to say. At the time, we chalked it up to normal eighth-grade behavior.

During the holidays, he had mentioned he was swimming competitively and playing trombone in his school band. He wasn't as enthusiastic about his activities as Jennifer, but that was typical of their personalities. He also talked about his new Boy Scout troop and an upcoming solo wilderness camping experience. He had mixed feelings about the trip, sounding both excited and a little fearful. At the time, it seemed like a normal reaction. I suspected that most boys his age would feel the same way.

Now I ached for Jon and thought about what he must have been experiencing emotionally in the hours and days leading up to the event. I racked my brain, trying to remember anything else. *Did I miss something? Was he depressed at Christmas? Was there anything I could have done to prevent this?* I felt responsible. I was a doctor. In hindsight, something had obviously been wrong, and I felt that I should have seen it.

Inside, every part of me hurt as I thought of what Cathy and Mike were going through. I had no idea what to say or do to take away their pain. We'd never really talked about where they were spiritually, but now it was my first thought. I remembered how the pain of the senseless Alday murders had made me turn against God. I'd had a lot of questions about who God was and how he could have allowed something so horrific to happen. But after seeing the Aldays so happy, I had no doubt God was real and God was good. Any remaining questions—such as why it had to happen like it did—seemed unimportant. Or at least, I could wait for answers until I was in heaven to stay.

But now, those *why* questions were once again rearing their ugly heads. *Why Jon? Why now? Why would God allow this? Why did Cathy have to be the one to find him?* I knew that Mike and Cathy had to be wondering the same thing.

✦ ✦ ✦

My parents, Karen, and I drove straight through without stopping, and when we arrived in Coal City, Cathy met us at her door. We cried as we clung to each other. Our pain melded together into one massive and shared open wound.

Over the next few hours, we learned that Jon had apparently snuck out of the house sometime after midnight. He left two suicide notes. One was near a burning candle, found next to the school door. It read in part, "The flame in front of my corpse represents the people who have been bullied. Keep my body there, so everyone knows that peer pressure and bullying is a big thing."

Cathy and Mike searched for answers as to how this could have happened to their brown-haired, smiling son. When rumors of Jon being bullied came to light, it seemed to be the answer to everyone's question as to why Jon took his own life. A second note was found in Jon's bedroom. In it, he requested that his body be cremated and spread in the Gulf of Mexico, where he and his dad had been on a fishing trip a few years earlier.

The services were held four days later at First United Methodist Church, and Jon's middle school band played. Band members had to quickly learn new music—funeral songs weren't a part of the planned repertoire for the year—but the grieving students did their best. Those on the stage and in the sanctuary couldn't help but notice the missing trombone player, who now lay before them. Instead of signing his school yearbook, his classmates took black Sharpies and inscribed their thoughts, memories, and prayers on Jon's polished white casket.

After the funeral, his body was cremated.

During the following days, Cathy and Mike came to believe that Jon had been depressed and contemplating suicide for a long time. They found a third note in his bedroom that had been written months earlier. In it he wrote, "I did this because my life isn't going my way. It seems like everything is going wrong in my life."

A second service was held in South Georgia, where half of his ashes were placed in an urn and buried in a family plot that was never meant to contain a fourteen-year-old's remains. The other half were spread in the Gulf of Mexico, just as he'd requested in his note.

+ + +

My dad felt responsible.

Once we were alone in Coal City, Karen told me that when she went down to my parents' house the day of Jon's suicide, Dad was mowing the lawn. That didn't surprise me. Dad wasn't good at expressing emotions. After getting such tragic news—in fact, anytime something bothered him—he liked to get busy and do something physical. Dad was also very practical; he'd want to make sure the lawn was mowed before we left for the funeral.

"He was crying," Karen said. That concerned me. I rarely saw my father cry. "He thinks Jon's death is *his* fault."

"Why would he think that? That doesn't even make sense."

"That's what I said, but he mentioned your great-grandfather."

After my great-grandfather had returned from combat in World War I, he was never the same. His head always seemed kind of messed up, and everyone knew he had problems. He eventually shot himself.

"But that was more than eighty years ago!"

"He also mentioned his nephew."

I hadn't thought about that cousin in a while. Growing up, I knew he'd felt the pressure of a high-achieving father, and he wasn't always sure he could live up to his expectations. My cousin struggled to get through college, and when he found out he wasn't going to graduate on time, he shot himself.

"He thinks the history of suicide on his side of the family is what caused Jon's death. Your mom and I both tried to reassure him that wasn't true, but Reggie, I don't remember ever seeing your dad look so sad."

"I'll talk to him," I told her.

As a physician, I was aware of studies that revealed a genetic predisposition to depression, and therefore, potentially to suicide—just as there is a genetic predisposition to heart disease or diabetes. But even with a family history of heart disease, there are things a patient can do to increase, or decrease, the likelihood that he or she will die from the disease or its complications. For example, smoking, a sedentary lifestyle, or the wrong kind of diet can influence the speed and severity of the progression of heart disease. Patients who exercise, eat a healthy diet, and don't smoke can dramatically reduce their risk of heart disease.

In the same way, even if someone has a predisposition toward depression, environmental factors could increase, or decrease, the likelihood that the depressed person would take his or her own life. A family history of depression, or even suicide, doesn't determine an individual's outcome—only his choices do.

Jon's death was a sad fact that we were powerless to change, but I was already starting to understand how such a tragedy could affect an entire family. Dad wasn't responsible for Jon's death any more than I was. Yet, both of us had come to the same conclusion from different directions. We knew that if we were responsible, we could do something to fix the problem. Plug the leak. If we could figure out how Jon got to that point, we could prevent it from happening again. I knew that Cathy and Mike had to be going through the same pointless exercises.

Jon was already dead, but the losses were just beginning to mount.

✦ ✦ ✦

Though Jon's suicide was the most personal one I'd ever grieved, it wasn't the first or, sadly, the last I'd see as either a physician or a friend. Everybody has a connection to suicide; either they know someone who took his or her own life, or they know someone who lost a loved one to suicide. Most of the suicides I saw were men who'd shot themselves. Women usually overdosed, and if caught in time, their stomachs could often be pumped to save them. While I worked on them, I'd feel God's presence in the ER, so I knew God had been with them even as they'd tried to take their own lives. But I later came across one case that proved to me that God wasn't just there—he was active.

George was not only mean; he was tough. He was in and out of the ER, often for lacerations received during his barroom brawls. Someone would bring him in and dump him on the ER floor—he was too intoxicated to know what had happened. But we did. The smell of alcohol and the sensation of evil permeated the room he was in. I knew one day he would die in a fight, and I just prayed I wouldn't be the one to pronounce him dead. When he crossed over, I didn't want to face the sulfuric stench or stare into the black abyss.

One night, George ended up in the ER again. It wasn't a friend who brought him in but an EMT. This time it was serious; he had a gunshot wound to the head. A note found on his body said it was self-inflicted. We stabilized him and called the trauma center in Nashville. I prayed for his soul as they loaded him up. He had a blown right temple, and his left side was flaccid. Word got out that he had been feeling desperate and didn't want to continue with his miserable life anymore. He was tired of fighting the pain.

In Nashville, the trauma team treated him and admitted him for observation. His family seemed relieved not to have him around.

But he survived.

A few weeks later, the rehab unit called me to review his discharge instructions and to set up an appointment for the following week. I was not looking forward to it. But as soon as his brother wheeled him in, I could see the difference. Though his face was distorted and his mouth was crooked from his wounds, George had a smile that lit up the room. I shook his hand, and he had a firm grip. By all accounts, his physical recovery had been remarkable. But his spiritual recovery was nothing short of a miracle.

"I felt something happen that night after I shot myself," he told me. "I knew it was the Lord."

I was stunned. This man had never said the name of God before, unless he was cursing. But he said that while he was in a coma, Jesus had visited him, and when he woke up, he was a changed man. He recovered enough to walk with a cane and had a new outlook on life. A few months ago, he said, "God's got me here for a reason," and then he told me how he's working with Alcoholics Anonymous and a mission group of homeless men. God had pulled him from the abyss, even after George had pulled the trigger.

I believe that suicide is never God's choice, but occasionally he allows the veil to be torn open from this side to admit a desperate soul into heaven earlier than he'd planned. Sometimes, like in George's case, he sends people back to get things right here, before they are allowed to enter. Either way, I believe God whispers in the ear of every despairing person who considers taking his or her own life, but depression may decrease the ability to hear that hope.

Despite what some denominations and religious traditions teach, as a doctor, I don't believe suicide is a sin that separates us from God; it is a cause of death that results from an illness. Much like heart disease or diabetes can be fatal, so can depression.

Friends and family members shouldn't fear that they'll never see their loved one again. If that person was going to heaven before deciding to commit suicide, that person is in heaven after committing suicide. God is love, and whom does he love more than the helpless and the hurting?

It gives me great hope to think about Jon being happy in heaven, especially after he was evidently so sad here.

✦ ✦ ✦

Unfortunately, when troubled souls cross over to the next world, they leave their pain in this one, and it spreads among those who loved them most.

I knew that Cathy had a special burden. She was the one who

found Jon, and for a while I am sure every thought of her precious son had to be tainted with the gruesome last images of his body hanging from the rope. But she leaned into her faith, and God held her up, giving her strength when she needed it most. Cathy used her pain to help others. She learned more about the causes of suicide and depression, and she met with others online who had also lost loved ones to the terrible disease.

Eventually, she took her knowledge and experience and began to speak locally to warn others about the hidden dangers of bullying. I knew it couldn't have been easy, and I was proud of how she turned her personal pain and grief into something that would help others.

But I was worried about Mike.

Men often have a harder time processing their emotions, and whenever we got together as a family, I could see the pain in Mike's eyes and the weight he carried on his slumped shoulders. He began to withdraw from people and from us, retreating to a back room or going on walks by himself. He was often distant, lost in his own thoughts, and disengaged from others. Mike also stopped going to church.

Several times I sat him down to try to judge the level of his depression. Suicide is contagious, and often one is followed by another in close proximity. I was truly concerned that Mike might blame himself and take on a guilt that would overwhelm him.

I recognized his pattern of withdrawal. It was similar to the way I'd reacted to the death of the Aldays. I couldn't imagine how much more intense the pain must have felt when the person senselessly lost was your only *son*.

I was scared for Mike, for his family, and for all of us. I truly believed the evil one was attempting to pull my brother-in-law into the depths of despair, and I wasn't sure if he would find a way out. We were all very concerned, and we prayed daily for God to protect him.

We also knew Cathy and Jennifer couldn't handle losing him, too.

Chapter 27
LIFTED VEILS

✦

SEPTEMBER 2006
ASHLAND CITY, TENNESSEE

It was the last week in September, but the weather was still balmy. I was busy seeing patients in my office when I received a phone call from EMS personnel. That in itself wasn't unusual. As one of the assistant coroners for the county, if anything abnormal happened in the field, EMS personnel were required to call me. By then, I'd been practicing medicine in Ashland City for more than twenty years. I thought I'd seen and heard it all. But I was wrong.

"I need to report a refusal to transport," the EMT said.

"Okay. Can you tell me what happened?"

"While driving around a curve, a nurse witnessed an older man fall out of a tree. She stopped, called 911, and waited with him until we got there. He was still on the ground when we arrived. He was sweating and had a few scratches on his arms, but we didn't see any obvious signs of broken bones. He refused treatment and transport."

There was always a patient or two who refused to be treated by ambulance personnel or to be transported to the ER. When this happened, I noted the details in a log, in case any questions came up at a later date. In this case, no injuries were visible, and the man's sweating was likely caused by the heat. There didn't appear to be anything to be concerned about.

"Okay, thanks. I'll note it in the log. What was the address?"

"That's the thing. We were called to your house. The man who fell was *your father.*"

My father? What was he doing in a tree? A dozen thoughts bombarded my mind. I knew Karen wasn't home. *But where is Mom? Why isn't she with him? What is going on?*

I realized the EMT was still on the phone. "Where is he now?"

"I'm not sure; he drove off with your mom."

✦ ✦ ✦

Dad loved to putter, and when he ran out of things to do at his house, he would walk up to our farm and find things to work on there. Recently, there had been a lot to do—we were getting the house and yard ready for a wedding.

Ashley was getting married!

My second daughter, Ashley, was my first daughter to fall in love and get engaged. She met Ciarán McCarthy while she was attending the American Musical and Dramatic Academy in New York City, where they were both studying musical theater. Ciarán was originally from Ireland, but he grew up in Canada. He was a fantastic soccer player and had hoped to play professionally, until an injury ended his career. His plan B was to go to teacher's college in Canada. Although he had the grades to get into the school he wanted to attend, they didn't accept him. That made him question God's calling for his life. Maybe God had another plan for him?

One day his father told him, "Get on with you, lad. You've always liked musical theater. Why don't you move to New York and follow your heart?" So Ciarán decided to do just that. Turns out that he not only followed his heart to New York City, but once there, he also met the love of his heart. When we visited Ashley at school, we suspected they were more than friends. Ciarán confirmed it the day he asked Karen and me for Ashley's hand in marriage. We said yes.

By then our whole family had fallen in love with Ciarán. He'd been a history major, so he and my oldest daughter, Kristen, often talked about history. My son, David, loved the fact that Ciarán was a good soccer player. And since he was a dancer, he also had something in common with Julia, our youngest daughter.

Ciarán wanted to surprise Ashley at the beach with the proposal and decided to ask her on an upcoming family trip. We were taking a vacation with the Chapman family, visiting Disney and then spending a few days at Vero Beach. But as Ciarán's excitement grew, he didn't think he could wait that long to ask her.

We were already at Disney when Mary Beth Chapman learned of the predicament and quickly set out to resolve it.

She arranged for the manager of Cinderella Castle to close the entrance slightly before midnight, allowing only Ashley and Ciarán in after closing. Karen and I, along with Mary Beth and Steven, were already perched in the stairwell and giddy with delight and anticipation. Just before midnight, as we stood in the shadows, we watched a nervous Ciarán enter with Ashley. She seemed confused and a bit bewildered by Ciarán's explanation as to why she was being dragged to Cinderella Castle at midnight.

Then Ciarán stopped midsentence. He dropped to one knee and proposed to her, saying he knew she was the one God had chosen to complete him.

The adults on the stairwell were all laughing and crying tears of joy. To me, it was another breeze of happiness bursting forth from heaven as I watched the first of my children become engaged. Ashley was fulfilling God's plan for her life. Overwhelmed by the blessing of my children and the thought that one day they'd also have children of their own, I couldn't hold back my tears.

The wedding of the Southern belle and the Irish immigrant was set for October 7, 2006.

✦ ✦ ✦

With less than a week before the big day, a lot of wedding preparations were taking place at the farm. The night before, Dad and I had been discussing the big white tent that would be delivered and set up on the tree-covered lawn. He'd mentioned how some of the tree limbs near the cleared area looked a little too low.

"We should cut those limbs back, so if kids are out there playing, they won't run into them and get hurt."

I hadn't paid much attention when he said it since there were still hundreds of small details that needed to be taken care of before the big day. But now, after hanging up the phone with the EMT, I realized, *That's what Dad was doing in the tree!*

I called my parents' house. Mom answered. "Where's Dad?" I asked.

"He's in the shower."

"I heard that he fell out of a tree."

"Oh, no. He was just cutting some limbs and fell off the ladder."

"He should probably be looked at."

"He says he's fine. He said that lady was nice to stop, but she never should have called the ambulance."

"Mom, that nice lady was a *nurse*. She thought the fall looked serious enough for him to be taken to the hospital. Listen, as soon as he gets out of the shower, you need to bring him to my office." Fortunately, my parents often asked for my advice. Occasionally, they even followed it.

Thirty minutes later, I heard them coming through the back door of my office. I took Dad into an examination room and closed the door. My first question was from a son to his dad: "Are you okay?"

"I'm fine. I don't know what happened. I was cutting a few of the lowest limbs, and next thing I know, I was on the ground."

My next questions were posed as a doctor to a patient. "Are you having any chest pains? Have you had any trouble breathing? Does anything hurt?" Something didn't seem right. I took his vitals and noticed that his blood pressure and pulse were a little high, but nothing too concerning. "We're going to do an EKG," I said. "I want to make sure everything is okay."

Once again, God had given me the sense that something was wrong, despite the fact that there was no medical evidence to indicate it. I was thankful that I followed God's prompting. The EKG revealed an acute inferior myocardial infarction. Dad was having a heart attack in my office!

"Dad, I don't want to alarm you, but you're having a heart attack. I need to make some calls, and then we're going to have to figure out what to do next."

I left the room to call Dr. Sykes, a cardiologist friend of mine. His son played basketball with my son, David, and so Dad knew him too. I filled him in on what I'd seen on the EKG, and I also told him how Dad had refused treatment earlier and might do it again.

Dr. Sykes said, "He needs to come to the cath lab. If he doesn't . . ." I understood exactly what he was saying and agreed. We had to send Dad to the hospital in Nashville so Dr. Sykes could treat him immediately.

The hard part would be convincing Dad to go.

✦ ✦ ✦

No son ever wants to think of his dad dying, and I was no different. Though I'd seen glimpses of heaven and knew what waited on the other side, I knew my experience wouldn't minimize the pain of loss for those of us who were left behind. I'd enjoyed having Dad and Mom closer to us, and I think they enjoyed being around the grandkids. But I knew one reason Dad had moved closer to us was because he wanted someone to take care of Mom if he died first.

A few weeks earlier, we'd been riding through the countryside. It reminded me of all the times we'd ridden together when I was little and Dad was an agriculture teacher visiting each of his students' farms.

"I'm glad we moved to Kingston Springs . . ." Dad said. I assumed he was thinking the same thing I was, until he finished his thought, ". . . because I know you'll take care of her. You'll be her protector when I'm no longer here."

At the time, I replied with something generic like, "Of course I will."

Thinking back on that moment, I had to wonder if Dad sensed

something I didn't. If so, I fully expected him to resist the treatment that could save his life. Dad knew where he was going when he left this world, and like me, he looked forward to seeing Jesus in heaven. He didn't want extraordinary measures used to keep him here. But I wasn't sure what he considered extraordinary. Did he believe clearing a blockage in his heart six days before his granddaughter's wedding was extraordinary?

✦   ✦   ✦

After hanging up with Dr. Sykes, I decided the best way to handle it was to tell Dad what was going to transpire and not give him an option. Then I'd deal with his protests. I took a deep breath and walked back into the examination room where he and Mom were waiting.

"I just got off the phone with Dr. Sykes, and we're sending you to Nashville to be looked at in the cath lab. And you know that ambulance you refused to get in? Well, it'll be the one taking you there."

He looked me straight in the eyes, and I met his stare. He knew I was serious.

To my surprise, he agreed.

"Okay. Will you bring your mom?" he asked.

I agreed, and Dad left for Nashville in an ambulance. We followed behind.

In the cath lab, Dr. Sykes found the blockage and put in a stent that afternoon. Dad was admitted to the hospital to be kept under observation for the next two days. He did fine and was released in time for Ashley's wedding.

On that beautiful night in October, when everyone celebrated the joining of Ciarán's and Ashley's hearts, I also celebrated the healing of Dad's.

✦   ✦   ✦

Ciarán wasn't to be the only Irishman in our family.

When my oldest daughter, Kristen, was in her final year of college at the University of Alabama, she went to Northern Ireland to volunteer in the youth group of a local church. As a theater major, she was put in charge of planning the skits. David Kernaghan, a local lad from Newcastle in Northern Ireland, was in charge of the music. They worked together and discovered they shared the same dream of serving God by serving others. When Kristen suddenly decided to move to Belfast to attend Bible college, there wasn't a doubt in our minds that, in addition to studying the Bible, she also planned to study whether or not David was the husband God had planned for her.

Nine months after Ashley married Ciarán on our emerald-green lawn, Kristen and David tied the knot on the Emerald Isle. Though I shared my firstborn's happiness in this magical land of castles, churches, and sheep, I also worried about the local tensions that so often placed it in the news. But once again, God showed me my worries were as ill-placed as my lecture on turning car hoods into sleds.

The day after the wedding, we were sitting in the airport praying that the political troubles of Ireland would lessen and that Northern Ireland would be a safe home for my daughter and her husband.

A few hours later, the British government announced they were pulling forty thousand troops out of Northern Ireland, signaling the end of thirty-eight years of continuous deployment there. It was a quiet milestone in the process of peace.

To me, it was another reminder of how big God is. Whether my children were in Belfast, Los Angeles, or Franklin, Tennessee, I had nothing to worry about. No matter where they were, he was in control.

✦ ✦ ✦

Over the years I'd noticed that as my patients got closer to the veil, everything became thinner and more transparent. When I was with them, I could see colors that were more vibrant, feel changes in temperature more acutely, and smell fragrances that seemed lighter than air. It was as if I was experiencing what they were experiencing. I was reminded of when I had looked into Ashley's and Kristen's eyes, lifted their wedding veils, and seen the joy in their faces. When we get close to the "real" veil, we can see through it in ways we can't from a distance, and certainly when it parts, we get an even better view of the joy that awaits us on the other side.

There were three special moments at Kristen's wedding that were echoes of Ashley's wedding, and I hoped to repeat them someday when our youngest daughter, Julia, got married.

The first was lifting my daughters' veils at the altar. When Christ died on the cross, the Temple veil was torn in two, removing the separation that had existed between man and God. Christian marriage is a metaphor for the union between Christ and his bride—the church. The lifting of the wedding veil is also a physical example of how husbands and wives are given full access to each other in marriage, just as removing the veil between this world and the next gives us full access to heaven.

The second moment was having Steven Curtis Chapman sing "Cinderella" for the father/daughter dance. It was a personal song that Steven wrote, inspired by his own daughters. In fact, during the past few years, the Chapmans had been busy expanding their family through adoption. In addition to Emily, Caleb, and Will, the Chapmans had added three little girls from China: Shaoey, Stevey Joy, and Maria. Not only did each of those girls join the Chapman family, they joined our family too.

The song "Cinderella" was inspired by the two youngest, Stevey Joy and Maria. One night, while quickly tucking the two girls into bed so he could get back to his studio, Steven thought about his oldest daughter, Emily, her upcoming wedding, and his regrets over not having tucked her in more often. That night, determined not to miss another moment with his daughters, he wrote the song "Cinderella." Hearing him sing it at my daughters' weddings was an especially poignant reminder that I'd missed some of those moments too.

The third special moment for me was when the DJ asked all the married couples to come to the dance floor to join in the "anniversary dance." While the music played, he'd instruct people to be seated based on how many years they'd been married.

"If you've been married for less than five years, please have a seat."

A few minutes later, he said, "If you've been married for less than ten years, please have a seat." This would continue until only a few couples were left standing.

Ashley's wedding was so soon after Dad's heart attack that it was especially poignant for me to see my dad and mom dancing together. As I watched them dance, I thanked God for allowing Dad to stay long enough to see Ashley get married. They were one of the last couples to leave the floor and they looked so happy.

But Cathy and Mike weren't. Mike stayed outside away from the other wedding guests. He obviously wasn't ready to celebrate. Cathy tried to make excuses, but they weren't necessary; we all knew he was suffering. Three months later at Christmas, we could still see the pain in his eyes.

The following July, Kristen got married. Mike and Cathy didn't attend the wedding because it took place in Ireland, but Mom and Dad did. Once again, I thanked God for the blessing of my parents. After more than fifty years of marriage, Dad and Mom were the last couple to leave the dance floor.

Chapter 28

WHY WOULD GOD
ALLOW THIS TO HAPPEN?

✦

After adopting their three youngest girls, God began to use the Chapman family in a special way to bring attention to orphans in China and around the world. The Chapmans were planning to build a care center for orphans in China, and they were already breaking through the political barriers to make adoption more accessible, so more children could be rescued. The Chapmans' work was changing lives, both for the orphans who dreamed of finding their forever families and for the couples who longed to adopt children. We were proud of what the Chapmans were doing on a global scale.

But closer to our home and our hearts, we fell in love with the newest additions to the Chapman family—Shaoey, Stevey Joy, and Maria. We often babysat the girls when something came up or when Mary Beth needed an extra set of hands. The girls allowed us to practice our grandparenting skills and taught us the latest in toy technology, keeping all of us young.

Shaoey was about three years older than Stevey Joy, who was just seven months older than Maria. The two youngest girls constantly played together and even wore matching clothes—except when it came time to play dress up. Stevey Joy preferred dance costumes, while Maria preferred to dress like a rock and roller. Though Maria was the youngest, she was also the loudest and sported the biggest personality. Her body might have been tiny, but her spirit and voice filled a room.

One day when I came home from the office, I heard squeals of delight and smelled the aroma of freshly baked chocolate chip cookies. I entered the kitchen to see Stevey Joy and Shaoey with chocolate smeared on their faces, sitting before a plate of half-eaten cookies. Karen stood near the counter with a naked little Chinese girl in the kitchen sink.

Maria giggled when she saw me.

"What's going on, girls?" I asked, thinking perhaps Maria had made a mess with her cookies. The older girls tried to respond, but their mouths were full, so I couldn't decipher a word they were saying.

Finally Karen spoke up. "We made cookies, and Shaoey and Stevey Joy wanted to test them out. But Maria wanted to 'help' with the dishes." Karen pointed to a tiny pile of pink and white clothes on the floor. "So she got ready and climbed into the sink to help!"

We'd often seen Maria "helping" with the dishes at home, and I knew she preferred to do it nude. Now I knew why. To her, it was fun! She poured water from one cup to another, took handfuls of soap bubbles and blew them into the air, and then splashed in the sink. In the process, poor Karen got soaked. She'd been baptized with liquid Dawn soap bubbles into Maria's church of fun. I'm not sure if the dishes ever got *washed*, but it was obvious that both Maria and Karen had to get *dried*.

The girls were like grandchildren to Karen and me, and little sisters to our kids. Through the years, our love for each of these dark-haired beauties only grew stronger.

✦   ✦   ✦

Mike's deep grief continued, and so did our concern for his safety. A couple of years after Jon's death, his work in Coal City ended, and he and Cathy were preparing to move to New York State for his next contract. This would be a critical move for them as he and Cathy would be leaving the friends who had stood by them through the initial shock and then supported them in their ongoing grief during the days and months after the tragedy.

The community of Coal City understood all they'd been through. Mike and Cathy didn't have to explain how they were feeling or pretend they were having a good day when they weren't. Moving to a new location meant starting over with new friends and having to repeat their story again and again. A question as simple as, "So how many kids do you have?" had the potential to trigger a lot of pain. Leaving their support system could plunge them further into grief. I worried that Mike's retreat inside himself would continue, and I wondered how much more he could take before he broke.

On the other hand, the move had the potential to bring positive change into their lives. If they stayed in Coal City, the reminder of Jon's death was literally right outside their front door. Every time they opened it, they saw the entryway of the school where Jon had hung himself. The school had placed a memorial on the site, so the memory of the tragedy was inescapable. I hoped that moving away from the constant reminders of Jon's death would help them remember his life and move on with theirs. Nothing would ever take away their loss, but maybe a new location could help them move forward.

For me, Jon's death and Mike's subsequent depression were painful reminders of the dark period I'd gone through after the Alday murders. Why would God allow things to get so bad that an eighth-grader felt he had no other recourse than to take his own life? Why did this have to happen to Jon? Why did it have to happen *at all*?

I believed that God was real and God was good, and though I don't think it was his perfect plan for Jon to die the way he did, I believed that God was big enough to use even the untimely death of a teenager for his glory. The problem was, I didn't understand how. With no ready answers, when the questions bubbled up, I just pushed them back down and tried to be strong for everyone else.

✦ ✦ ✦

Maria proudly sat before her Tinker Bell birthday cake, lit up with five flickering flames, and beamed while she waited for us to finish singing. No one actually knew when her real birthday was, but four years earlier, when she came home from China, May 13 was chosen. She now claimed it as her own. She waited patiently until the song finished, and then she blew out her candles and dug into the cake—with both hands.

Maria laughed as the cake squished between her fingers. She had a distinctive giggle, and her tiny laugh was contagious. She was excited about her birthday, and we were too. I couldn't wait for her to finish eating cake so she could open her presents.

Julia, our youngest daughter, was the one who had picked out Maria's gift. The girls had bonded not long after Julia and Caleb started going out, and their relationship had grown closer over the years. With rumors of a wedding in the future, the Chapman and Anderson baby girls knew they would be sisters one day. Together, they shared Cinderella dreams and wedding secrets the rest of us weren't privy to.

Maria ripped off the brightly colored happy birthday paper and squealed when she saw the butterfly packaging. She loved anything with wings, but especially butterflies and ladybugs.

"It's a butterfly cage and a net," Julia explained. "We can catch caterpillars, and you can keep them in the cage until they change into butterflies, and then we can let them go."

"Will you help me?" Maria asked. Julia agreed.

It was easy to see that Maria was intrigued with the idea of capturing a caterpillar and caring for it until it was transformed.

Maria may not have understood the metamorphosis involved with a caterpillar's turning into a butterfly, but she certainly understood change. She'd watched Emily go off to college, and now her big sister was getting married. Emily planned to have all three of her little sisters take part in the ceremony. She'd picked out sparkly silk dresses (from China, of course) with embroidered butterflies. Maria loved the thought of being in Emily's wedding and transforming herself into a wedding princess.

In addition, Caleb was set to graduate high school in a few days, and rumors swirled that he and Julia would soon be engaged. A lot of changes were coming to the Chapman household in the next year. I felt for Steven. I knew well the mixture of emotions that came with a daughter getting married. Knowing how happy Emily was made Steven happy too. And as fathers, we'd never want to stop one of our daughters from getting married to the man God had chosen for her. But in truth, when a daughter gets married, there is also a sense of loss. Before the big day, I reminded myself to help my friend prepare for those feelings.

✦ ✦ ✦

It was a week after Maria's birthday and a busy day for me in the office. Karen and I were leaving the next day to visit Kristen and David in Ireland, and I was trying to get things tied up, since we would be gone for more than a week. We planned to have dinner at the Chapman house later that night. They were hoping to finalize some of the details on Emily's wedding and wanted our input. We'd become de facto consultants because of our wedding experience, having walked two daughters down the aisle.

Earlier in the week I'd made Steven what I considered to be a very magnanimous offer. I would repay the kindness he'd shown at my daughters' weddings and sing "Cinderella" at Emily's. He still hadn't taken me up on it. *Maybe he will tonight?* As I went about my work, I chuckled at the thought and secretly wished I had the ability to sing publicly.

All day, I was swamped with patients and preparations for the ten days I would be gone. Time slipped away from me. When I finally checked the clock, it was almost five, and I still needed to finish some things before I could leave.

A few minutes later, my phone rang. It was Mary Beth. Part of my responsibility for the night was to help Steven understand how much weddings *really* cost. Mary Beth wanted me to remind him that it would be worth every penny. I picked up the phone and hoped to plead my case for being late, but I never got to it.

Even before the phone reached my ear, I could hear the sound of a mother's wail in the background. It was unmistakable.

And it belonged to Mary Beth.

The sound sent chills down my spine. I listened as she was apparently talking to someone else and then braced myself for whatever came next.

"Where's Karen?" she finally said into the phone. Her words were mixed with cries of anguish. "Something's happened to Maria . . ."

"What? What about Maria?"

"Will didn't see her . . . the car . . . tell me she'll be all right! Please, tell me! God, please let her be all right!"

Mary Beth wasn't speaking in complete sentences. She was talking to me and talking to God all at the same time. Something terrible was happening, but she couldn't focus long enough for it to make sense.

"There was so much blood . . . I tried to clear it out, so she could breathe . . . Steven did CPR . . . LifeFlight . . . they took Maria with them . . . please find Karen!"

"Where are you?" I was usually soft-spoken, but I raised my voice so Mary Beth could focus on my words.

"We're in the car. They're driving us to Vanderbilt Children's. Pray! Please pray for Maria! Just pray—" The line went dead.

I dropped everything I was doing, yelled some instructions to my staff, and headed to the parking lot. Once I got in the car, I called Karen and told her what little I knew.

"I'm on my way. I'll meet you there," she said.

Through a couple of quick phone calls, I learned that Will Chapman had just returned from an audition at school. The girls were playing in the yard, and when Maria saw him drive up, she ran toward him to beg him to lift her onto the monkey bars. But Will didn't see her. Though it was no fault of his own—he'd been driving slowly and safely—he was understandably distraught. Extremely distraught.

I had been silently praying since I first heard Mary Beth's voice on the phone, but alone in my truck, I began to pray out loud. I knew trauma codes weren't usually successful, and the last thing this family needed was false hope, if Maria wasn't going to live. "Oh, God. Please, if you're going to take her, take her quickly."

I headed east on I-40. "God, let me know what's going on. Please give me a sign, so I know what I am going to walk into when I get there."

I didn't even realize I had the radio on until that moment, but something caught my attention. I turned up the volume. It was a secular country station, but I heard Steven crooning the chorus from his song "Cinderella." I listened and remembered how Maria and Stevey Joy had been the inspiration for that song. He'd first sung it at Ashley's wedding, then at Kristen's. I knew the lyrics and listened as the final notes of the song played, "'Cause all too soon, the clock will strike midnight, and she'll be gone."[1]

That's when I knew.

Maria was gone.

Tears filled my eyes, and I lifted them heavenward as a way of thanking God for her life, for letting me spend as much time with her as I had, and for giving me the sign I'd asked for. The sky was blue and perfectly clear. Then, on the horizon, something caught my eye. Above and to the right, I noticed a solitary, soft pink cloud with a streak of silver sunlight reflecting through the center of it.

To me, it was a sign of Maria's soul passing through the veil.

As my tears continued to flow, I picked up the phone and called Vanderbilt Children's ER to confirm what I already knew.

"This is Dr. Reginald Anderson," I said. I tried to pull myself together and sound professional. "I understand you have Maria Sue Chapman on the way to your facility via helicopter." I explained I was a family friend and her family doctor, but I didn't have privileges at the hospital. I asked if they could update me.

---

[1] "Cinderella," words and music by Steven Curtis Chapman. Copyright @ 2007 Sparrow Song (BMI) (Admin. by EMI CMG Publishing) / Primary Wave Brian (Chapman Sp. Acct.) (BMI). All rights reserved. Used by permission.

There was a slight hesitation on the other end before a female voice responded. "How far out are you?"

"About twenty minutes."

"Please hurry. We'll meet with the family when they arrive, and we'd appreciate it if you were on hand."

As a seasoned ER doctor, I knew what that was code for—Maria was now on the other side.

My heart broke as I remembered that sweet little naked girl in my kitchen sink, the birthday girl blowing out her five candles, and the baby girl sitting on the floor, whispering with my baby girl, Julia. She'd never had time to catch a caterpillar and keep it in the cage Julia had selected for her. Now she was the one who was undergoing a metamorphosis, leaving her cocoon here on earth and spreading the wings she'd always longed to have.

Maria was flying with the angels.

✦ ✦ ✦

While friends and family prayed, hoping the Great Physician would break the laws of nature and bring our little girl back to us, the Chapmans were escorted into a back room and given the news. Then they asked us to come back with them to see Maria.

Standing by her bedside, I picked up Maria's tiny, delicate hand and held it in mine. She looked as if she were sleeping.

"She didn't suffer. She went to heaven immediately," I told Steven and Mary Beth.

The thought of Maria experiencing all that heaven had to offer brought me great joy. I wished I were there to explore it all with her. I smiled as I thought of her inhaling the fragrances, chasing butterflies through the green meadow, and seeing all the vividly colored wildflowers—Maria *loved* to draw flowers. I placed her hand back on the bed. The child who'd once been here was gone, and there was no point in holding on to her cocoon.

Unprompted by anyone, Shaoey and Stevey Joy began referring to the fragile body of their sister as her "shell." They knew that

Maria was in heaven. Their understanding could only have come from God. The unshakable faith of these precious children was contagious, and the rest of us stayed close to them, hoping their trust would spread to us.

Standing at her bedside, I remembered the soft glow I'd seen in the hospital room the first time I'd witnessed a patient die. I remembered how it had reminded me of Tinker Bell. Maria loved Tinker Bell. I thought of my blind patient who'd once seen the bright lights of the angels coming for her roommate. I imagined the joy Maria must have felt surrounded by the angels and their glorious lights. My thoughts brought me peace.

But I still had conflicting emotions.

✦ ✦ ✦

As a doctor, I've often seen the emotional and spiritual devastation parents experience when they lose a child. With Jon's suicide, I'd felt it on a personal level. Jon's death had also taught me the importance of watching those on the inner circle of grieving—like Mike and Cathy—but also those in the periphery who might feel responsible—like my dad.

Until now, I had watched all this from a distance. As much as Jon's death affected my immediate family and me, we didn't live in the same town with Jon. We saw him a few times a year, and we hadn't spent much time with him. Nor did we see Cathy and Mike on a daily basis. The best I could do was check in with phone calls and pay attention during holiday gatherings. But now, the Chapmans had been directly hit by the worse grief imaginable. And the carnage didn't stop there. The flying projectiles and flaming debris from the impact were still taking out other family members and friends who stood near them. Though it wouldn't always be so debilitating, we were all about to find out what it was like to live with grief twenty-four hours a day, seven days a week, for the rest of our lives.

Maria's death was about to take everything to a new level.

This pain was personal, and it hurt in the deepest way. Not only had we lost Maria, but Steven, my best friend, and Mary Beth, Karen's best friend, were grieving the loss of their daughter and were worried for their son Will.

What would losing Maria do to their family? What would it do to their faith? What would it do to their souls? These people, who were close enough for me to call family, had had something so unfathomable and unfair happen to them. In my own mind, that same ugly question came roaring back—the one I had asked about the Aldays' deaths and then tried to push down when it bubbled up again with Jon's death. It was the same question that parents and other loved ones asked me when I met them in the waiting room to deliver bad news.

Why did God allow this to happen?

It was the one question I still didn't have an answer for.

Chapter 29
A DIFFERENT KIND
OF GRIEF OBSERVED

+

Going home wasn't an option for the Chapmans. The media got wind of the tragedy, and reports from the Chapmans' neighbors said that news cameras were lining up outside their property that same night. In addition, the accident site still hadn't been cleaned up and the officials needed more time to finish their investigation. The Chapmans needed a private place for the next few days to grieve as humans, not celebrities. Our farmhouse was set back from the road, and behind it was a lake that was surrounded by woods. The grounds offered both private spaces to grieve and expansive spaces where people could gather in groups. So we took them home to live with us.

More family, and some of the Chapmans' closest friends, met us there. Soon the place was filled with grieving people. On the front and back porches, and in every large space inside the house, mourners held hands and prayed, allowing their tears to flow freely.

So much raw emotion filled the house and so many questions were being asked that I felt I could help best by keeping my feelings and questions to myself. So I stuffed my emotions deep down inside. After all, I was the physician and healer, guardian and protector. I needed to be the one who wouldn't break down, who everyone else could turn to when they needed someone strong. It was the least I could do for Steven and Mary Beth who, along with their children, were on the front lines of grief. In addition, I knew Karen and my kids were also dealing with their own pain while they tried to lend support to the Chapmans. The last thing any of them needed was for me to fall apart.

So I didn't.

✦   ✦   ✦

It was difficult to see Steven in so much pain while also trying to be strong for his wife and kids. Mere hours after the accident, Mary Beth was struggling with her profound grief, and she said she didn't want to go on living. She wanted to be with Maria. While I understood it was just the grief talking, I kept an eye on her to make sure she was okay. As her mother's screams for her daughter continued on and off throughout the night, I felt how desperately she wanted to be with her child.

We were all worried about Shaoey; she'd *witnessed* the accident. How does it affect an eight-year-old to watch her sister die and not be able to stop it? Then there was Stevey Joy, who was so close to Maria in both age and appearance that most people thought they were twins. The two had been inseparable since they'd become Chapman sisters. Not only had these two precious girls lost their little sister, but they were now watching everyone they loved fall apart.

The girls were too young to express their deepest feelings, but we made sure they had opportunities to talk if they wanted. We also included them in prayers and conversations that were appropriate for their ages. They were hugged by friends and family and held tightly by their mother. I kept my eye on them, and I was thankful when they finally fell asleep and found peace in their dreams.

Our biggest concern that night was Will.

Immediately after the accident, he'd tried to run away. His older brother, Caleb, tackled him and tore off his shirt—stained with Maria's blood—then wadded it up and threw it into a pond. Since then, others had tried to talk to Will, including friends and family members, some of whom had experienced similar tragedies.

It didn't matter. Will was inconsolable.

Though everyone knew it was an accident, Will felt responsible. He was devastated, not only because of his role in it but also because of his tremendous loss. Of the three older Chapman children, Will was the one who was closest to the girls. He was the one who *always* stopped to play with them. In fact, it was Maria's great love for Will and the knowledge that he would willingly play with her that made her run toward the car that afternoon.

But now the entire family was worried that Maria wouldn't be the only casualty of this accident. Was Will distraught enough to do something desperate to relieve his pain? Was it beyond the realm of possibility to think that he could take his own life?

Ever since Jon's unexpected death, I'd thought a lot about suicide and how quickly it could happen without anyone even being aware that someone was depressed. I'd also watched how Mike had changed after Jon's suicide, becoming more isolated and alone because of his grief. Now I had a house full of people experiencing horrible emotional pain, likely the worst they would ever endure.

Suicide was a very real threat if Will fell into despair and decided to end the pain. So even though Will wanted to be left alone, his big brother, Caleb, and my son, David, along with the other kids, wouldn't let that happen. They took turns sitting with him while he was awake and remained near him while he slept.

Will wasn't the only one we had to worry about. Mary Beth had a history of clinical depression. Would she sink so far into despair that she might never return? What if Steven got angry at God and turned his back on him, like I had so many years earlier? What would become of his Christian witness through his music? Or, for that matter, his livelihood if he couldn't sing? What if the kids turned against one another? Or, for some misguided reason, what if they felt responsible and caved under the weight of their grief?

We'd already lost Maria; I had to make sure we didn't lose anyone else.

✦ ✦ ✦

The first night was critical. The pain was so fresh that those experiencing it didn't have the coping mechanisms needed to deal with it. Dark thoughts seem to encroach at night and haunt us when we're tired. We were all susceptible to our minds wandering. If we could just make it through the darkness of that first night, when the morning light arrived, we could buy time to make it through another day.

I felt as if it were up to me to make sure everyone in my house remained safe. I didn't sleep much anyway, so I stayed awake keeping watch over those who needed their rest. I walked from room to room, assessing emotional states like I'd triage victims after a natural disaster. *She's doing okay, but I should keep my eye on him. This one looks like he's getting into trouble; has anyone talked to him? Why is she off by herself?* I tried to listen to those who looked especially burdened. "Are you okay? Do you want to talk?" I asked. As they spoke, I took their emotional temperature and assessed their status. I offered my shoulder to those who needed one to cry on and my hands to those who desperately needed something to hold.

The wounded were everywhere. People who'd come to pray with family members stayed for hours, and then fell asleep in corners or stretched out on the floor. The house reminded me of a field hospital in the middle of a battle zone.

I was terrified of what grief could do and how it could drag us all under. It had done that to me once before, and I'd vowed not to let it happen to anyone else. I could feel a sense of urgency to this battle. But I also knew I wasn't alone in my fight. Not long after we got to the house, we'd called Kristen and told her the sad news of Maria's death and that we wouldn't be leaving in the morning for Ireland. After crying with Karen and me on the phone, she promised to gather people to pray. Others in Europe and Asia were also praying for the Chapmans. I imagined that as Steven's fans heard the news, they added their voices in prayer too.

Why has this happened to such a good family who have given so much to the cause of Christianity? That thought echoed in my mind all night.

I truly couldn't imagine two better servants of God than Steven and Mary Beth. Every day through his music, Steven testified to millions about God's goodness and his love. In addition, he and Mary Beth were faithful examples of the character of our Lord; they lived it out by actively caring for the least of these through their public efforts to care for orphans.

As prayer warriors across the world got on their knees for this family, I knew others had to be asking the same questions. Prayer was our strongest weapon against despair, and we liberally wielded it on behalf of the Chapmans.

Throughout the night, I felt the sure and strong presence of God in the house. We were all so distraught; we didn't even have the strength to stand up. Yet somehow we were able to take care of the physical and emotional needs of everyone in the house. Food, blankets, or pillows just seemed to appear. No one was ever alone, even when they were praying. When we didn't think we could bear the pain a minute longer, it was as if God's angels surrounded us and miraculously held us up.

Earlier in the evening I had heard Steven say, "Satan will not defeat this family!" And he meant it.

Throughout the night, the Chapmans held strong. Everyone stood firm, refusing to give in to their worst thoughts or darkest fears. Instead, they clung to one another and to God.

✦ ✦ ✦

The next morning started slowly. It felt surreal. The carnage of the battle fought the night before was everywhere. It still looked like a war zone, but we had held the line. We were all still there. Yes, we were hurting, but we hadn't turned on one another in our grief; we'd turned toward God.

I also knew it was only the first of many battles.

Over the next few days, the farmhouse became a spiritual retreat and a respite for the grieving. The secluded lake had a solitary dock jutting from its bank. This was where individuals who wanted to be alone gravitated. Will spent hours there. Those of us who watched over him didn't disturb his time of grief, but we kept tabs on him from the back deck. He was never out of our sight. The dock became a sacred and holy place.

As news of the accident spread, people organized supply lines of food and water to keep the troops fed, sometimes even delivering random items that were exactly what we needed, when we needed them. One morning, we didn't have syrup for pancakes. Without knowledge of our need, our friend Terri dropped by with a big jug of maple syrup.

"I just thought y'all might need this," she said.

Bouquets started pouring in. They were a fitting tribute to a little girl who loved to draw flowers. Soon, our house looked like an indoor garden, and the smell of sweat and tears was overpowered by the fragrance of roses, lilacs, and lilies.

I was worried about Mary Beth, but she conquered tragedy by conquering the day set before her. She took charge of the logistics of picking out the casket and planning the funeral, while simultaneously making sure that each of her kids got exactly what he or she needed. Later, she would admit she didn't remember doing any of that, but during those initial few days, the busyness kept her going. Karen was right by Mary Beth's side, helping her when she needed it and holding her up when she couldn't stand on her own.

As a man, it was harder for me to know how to help Steven. He had obligations he'd committed to, and he wanted to honor those. Though his world was crumbling around him, he was still a public figure, and as abhorrent as the idea was, he had to keep his business going.

It didn't seem fair, and I cried out to God. *Steven makes music that proclaims your goodness, but how can he do that when you took his daughter away?* While I knew Maria was in a better place, I still didn't understand why it had to happen or why Will had to be involved. *Couldn't it have been an accident that didn't involve another Chapman child? Why would you allow this to go down the way it did?* It was hard for me to comfort Steven when I still had so many questions myself.

Steven's friends and I listened while he talked, cried, and prayed out loud. During one of those conversations, I shared with him the grief I'd experienced after the Alday Massacre and the loss of my cousins. Then I described how astounding it was to see them again happy and whole in heaven.

"I know my experience is different from yours, but I know what an unexpected and tragic loss feels like. And from experience, I know Maria's truly in a better place."

What I didn't tell him was that this had resurrected the questions I'd struggled with so many years earlier, as well as the ones I'd stuffed down after Jon's suicide. Once again, I wanted answers. *Why has this happened now?* Everything was going so well. Emily was getting married; Caleb was graduating from high school; and as the whole adoption thing caught fire, the Chapmans had big projects in the works for orphans in China. *Why did it happen to the Chapmans?* There were evil people in the world who deserved everything bad that could come their way. The Chapmans were good people who served God in everything they did.

While my time in heaven confirmed to me that God was real and he was good, Maria's death caused me to cry out to God. *Why can't we just go straight to heaven? Why do we have to suffer here first?*

However, I continued to be "the strong one." I didn't cry, I didn't talk about my questions, and I didn't tell anyone what I was thinking. I rose above my confusion and buried my feelings deep inside.

✦ ✦ ✦

The funeral was held a few days later, and more than two thousand people attended. Once again, the Chapmans surprised me with their strength. Though we were there to console them, they became the ones who comforted us.

Only a few days after the tragedy, Caleb stood in front of the crowd and spoke. "We prayed for healing for Maria, but God healed her in a way that we all didn't like. But he's going to heal my brother in a way that I think we're all going to like a lot." Coming from Caleb, these weren't platitudes. He understood the depths of what he was saying. He was the one who had torn off Will's bloodstained shirt and thrown it into the pond. He'd then held his brother and said, "It's not your fault; God allowed this to happen. He chose this for us." I marveled at the faith of a young man who could both acknowledge that God allowed tragedy to happen and, at the same time, credit God with the healing that followed.

Steven stood before the crowd and said, "We've got to look into eternity. . . . We're doing it today. This is the kind of thing we need to spend our time doing, just seeing and celebrating the glory of God where it shows up, in the pain and in the joy he gives us in this life."

I admired the faith it took to celebrate God in the suffering. I hadn't done that during the aftermath of the Alday murders; in fact, I wondered if I had *ever* celebrated the glory of God in my suffering.

✦ ✦ ✦

Over the next few weeks and months, I realized the reason the Chapmans saw God in their suffering was because they actively looked for him there.

The day after the accident, Steven and Caleb prayed for a sign that Maria was okay. Shortly afterward, when we went to the Chapmans' home briefly to pick up some items for Maria's memorial service, they found a drawing she'd started of a colorful flower with the word *SEE* printed on it. They didn't even know she could spell the word. But they knew it was a sign from her and from God confirming that she was okay.

In their pain, the Chapmans saw and thanked God for the things that he'd done in Maria's short life. A few months earlier, she'd been learning a new song by Audio Adrenaline that had raised questions.

"Does God have a big, big house?" Maria asked.

Steven and Mary Beth assured her that he did. They answered her questions and explained that heaven was forever and that asking Jesus into her heart meant that one day she'd go there. Then, in her own words, Maria asked Jesus to come live in her heart because she wanted to live with him in the big, big house. Though Maria was only four at the time, the memory of that moment will comfort Steven and Mary Beth for a lifetime. To me, the moment was proof that even the littlest Chapman had her eyes and ears turned toward God.

If I needed further proof of that, I got it just days after the accident when I attended Stevey Joy's dance concert. It was a bittersweet moment for the Chapman family, as Maria was supposed to have danced too. But now Stevey Joy was dancing alone. Karen and I took our seats near the Chapmans and chatted before the program began. Before the lights dimmed, I opened my program and saw the picture of Stevey Joy's dance class. It had been taken a week before the recital. While all the other girls looked straight into the camera, Maria looked up and to the right with an otherworldly appearance on her face. I recognized the look. I'd seen a similar look in my patients shortly before they passed through the veil.

It was the gaze of glory.

✦ ✦ ✦

From Steven all the way down to Maria, each one of the Chapmans had sought God in the midst of an unfathomable tragedy—or, in Maria's case, before that tragedy—and they had each found him there.

What will happen if I look for him too? I wondered.

One of my earliest questions was, *Why Will?* So I asked God for an answer. With time, he came to show me it could *only* have been Will. Caleb was much too sensitive. He would have crumbled under the burden of being the driver. Emily would have too. Will was stronger, and like his name, strong-*will*ed. Everything he did, he did full out. Knowing his personality, it was obvious he would be the best one to push through this pain and not believe the inevitable accusations that went through his head. In addition, he was the one closest to the girls in age and spirit. He was their buddy, the one who had so many good memories to chase away this bad one. Only Will could have survived such a direct arrow to the heart.

As I searched for God, I began to see his blessings in other areas. Had I not been preparing to go to Ireland, I wouldn't have already arranged for coverage for my practice and my patients. Because the trip was planned, so was the coverage. Had the accident happened even a day later, Karen and I would have been on a plane and of no help to the Chapmans.

Both Steven and Mary Beth had been home at the time of the accident—a rare miracle in itself—and Steven had been taking a phone call on the porch. He saw Will slowly driving in, leaving no doubt that it had been an accident. That assurance was a blessing to both Steven and Will.

Once I started to look for God in the tragedy, I could see him everywhere.

On my drive to the hospital, I'd asked God for a sign, and he gave me two. First, Steven's "Cinderella" on the radio, and then the pink cloud. When I was up all night checking on people and fighting to keep everyone safe, I'd felt angels surrounding me. I'd also felt them in the ER when we saw Maria's body.

I thought back to the Alday murders nearly thirty-five years earlier. If I'd looked for God then, instead of turning away, I realized I'd have seen him there, too.

Slowly, I understood that the Chapmans' grief wasn't different from mine because they doubted less, they had fewer questions, or their faith wasn't challenged—those things happened to them the same way they happened to me. What was different about the way the Chapman family navigated Maria's death was that instead of turning *away* from God in their grief as I had, they turned *toward* him.

Chapter 30
PURPOSE IN THE PAIN

✦

The first year following Maria's death was difficult for everyone, but we still found bright spots. The Chapmans' oldest daughter, Emily, got married in October as planned, and everyone pushed "pause" on their grief to celebrate her day. A few weeks later in November, Caleb and Julia officially announced their engagement. The Andersons and the Chapmans had been through so much together that we already felt like one family. Now it would be official.

Though Caleb and Julia were young, only nineteen and twenty respectively, their chronological ages didn't mean much to us. They'd been dating for three years and had already experienced a lifetime of emotions together. I saw the great spiritual maturity in Caleb that he used to care for his brother, and Karen and I were delighted to think he'd now spend a lifetime caring for our daughter. We gave them our blessing.

Julia wanted to get married at the lake behind our house. We already considered the place holy ground from the tears that filled those waters as Will and so many others had sat on the dock and wept for Maria. We agreed it was the perfect place to tie the knot that would now bind our families together. We also hoped that lifting another veil would bring us closure on the one that had parted too early.

The date was set for May 10, 2009, just eleven days before the one-year anniversary of Maria's death.

✦ ✦ ✦

During the rehearsal the night before the wedding, Julia and Caleb walked together into the lake and fully immersed themselves in a baptismal ceremony that left all of us in tears once again. But this time, we wept tears of happiness. I physically felt the warmth of God's presence surround us and smelled the fragrances of heaven—lilac and citrus. I knew he had blessed this place.

Weeks before the wedding, we cleared a road down to the dock where the lake lapped at the rocky hillside. A bulldozer flattened the area where the ceremony would be held. We wanted to make it easy for my parents and our other elderly guests to be driven to the lake without having to take the long and meandering staircase down from our house on the hill. Now my only concern was whether or not the dock would hold everyone in the wedding party.

Apparently, that shouldn't have been my only concern.

On the morning of the wedding, we woke to the sound of rain. That created a problem, as we didn't have a backup plan. We began to pray for skies to clear and then proceeded on the premise that they would.

One hour before the ceremony, God answered our prayers—the sun poked through the clouds, giving us just enough time to get some pre-wedding photos. Guests arrived and were seated. The music began, and Julia took my arm. As I escorted her down the stairs to the dock, I asked her the same question I'd asked her sisters as I'd walked them down the aisle. "Are you certain it's God's will for your life to marry this man?"

Without hesitation, and with resounding confidence, like her two sisters before her, Julia said, "Yes!"

As the music swelled, we arrived at our place on the dock. The pastor asked, "Who gives this woman in marriage?" and I wanted to shout, "God does!" But instead, I said my well-rehearsed line, "Her mother and I do." It would be the last time I uttered those words. As I had done for my first two daughters, I reached over and lifted my baby girl's veil to kiss her.

And I clearly heard a giggle.

I glanced down thinking it was Stevey Joy, but the little flower girl was preoccupied playing with her flowers. It was such a distinctive giggle, and I knew I'd heard it before. When I returned to my seat, I scanned the guests to see who'd made the joyful noise. When I couldn't see anyone, I made a mental note to ask about it later.

A few minutes later, it suddenly occurred to me where I'd heard that sound so many times before.

That was Maria's giggle.

Of course she was there with us! She and Julia had long conspired about Julia's wedding plans. From the other side of the veil, Maria was granting her giggly blessing on the union of our two families.

That night, Steven sang "Cinderella" while Julia and I danced. There wasn't a dry eye in the tent. The song had come to mean so much to all of us over the past year, especially as Steven rewrote the final lyric, changing it from " . . . then she'll be gone" to " . . . the dance goes on." Later that evening, my parents were once again one of the last couples to leave the dance floor during the anniversary dance.

Though it had been a year of sadness, these special moments were reminders that life can and would go on, and where there was sadness, joy could still be found.

✦   ✦   ✦

Though losing Maria was the hardest thing the Chapmans had ever faced, they continued to do the things they'd always done—this time with a greater sense of urgency. As difficult as it was, Steven, along with Caleb and Will, got back out on the road and started making music. They reminded me of my father who, after hearing of his grandson Jon's suicide, picked up his yard tools and went to work doing what needed to be done. For Steven and the boys, their God-given tools were guitars and drums. And with each note they played, they inspired hurting people everywhere.

Before Maria died, their plans had been to build an American orphanage in China. With her death, there was a huge outpouring of love and support. The Chapmans directed it all toward a project named after her. With the additional donations, the project expanded to a six-story orphanage called Maria's Big House of Hope.

Even after I observed how the Chapmans had turned to God in their grief, and then when I saw him in the tragedy myself, my questions didn't just disappear. I still wanted to know why. *Why did it have to happen? Why did we all have to go through such a tragedy? What did Maria's five years on earth mean?* Instead of the questions causing me to turn away from God, I was now looking to him for the answers. And I now had the patience to wait for them.

Finally, I was seeing the answers in Maria's Big House of Hope.

In late June 2009, we traveled with the Chapmans to Luoyang, China, to dedicate a brand-new, sixty-thousand-square-foot special-needs care center for orphans. The center was designed to care for newborns through four-year-olds with special medical needs that often prevented them from being adopted. If a child's medical condition could be repaired through surgery—for example, if a child had been born with a cleft palate—he or she would get the surgery needed to repair it in China with funding from Show Hope. After treatment, they would be cared for at Maria's Big House of Hope. Once healed, that child would then be put up for adoption. If any children couldn't be healed, they would be given the highest level of care so they could thrive at whatever level was possible. Children who were gravely ill would be humanely and lovingly cared for and prayed over in a hospice-type environment until they crossed over to receive complete healing on the other side.

When we arrived at Maria's Big House of Hope, we found approximately forty-five children receiving care from three nurses and seventy staff members. And the numbers have continued to grow. Not only were lives being saved and children being placed in forever families, but the center was also providing local jobs. The government of China has even modeled other state-run orphanages and care centers after Maria's Big House of Hope.

On July 2, 2009, Maria's Big House of Hope was officially dedicated. We attended ribbon-cutting ceremonies and other opening-day festivities. Steven performed, accompanied by Caleb and Will. I watched as the crowd clapped and swayed in time to the music. Officials from the Chinese government, the local province, and the community of Luoyang, along with the staff, the Chapmans, and the Andersons—everyone who attended was celebrating. Looking at the beaming smiles on my family's faces, as well as those of my extended Chapman family, I was reassured that though the past year had been excruciatingly painful and the wounds were still healing, everyone was going to be okay.

But standing among the people I loved, I wondered *if I would be.*

For the first time since Maria's death, I felt that I didn't have to be the strong one. I could let my guard down. The grief and sadness that I'd stuffed down inside me started to well up in a warm rush of emotion. While those around me grinned and cheered, I tried to hold back the tears I'd successfully restrained for a year. I felt terribly sad as the loss finally washed over me, and I ached for the little girl who was absent.

Maria should be here. She would love this.

✦ ✦ ✦

After Maria died, one of the earliest prayers that Steven prayed was, "We don't understand why. But we know that you are God, and we accept your providence in this. We know that there is a purpose. Just help us to find that purpose."

Later that night, I held one of the Chinese babies from the care center in my arms. He was very sick, and I knew he was about to take his last breath. Soon, my face was awash in tears. My sadness for this little boy mingled with the other losses I grieved—for Maria and my nephew, Jon. I cried for Cathy and for Mike, and for the grief they'd felt for so long. Then something in that sick baby's eyes reminded me to look for God, and I saw him.

I also saw hope.

Maria and Jon were in heaven, and soon the little guy in my arms would join them. The fact that a sick little boy had been so lovingly cared for and prayed for and was now dying in the arms of a Christian *in China,* was a miracle. He'd obviously been abandoned by his family. The fact that he'd been taken in by the staff of the health center and that someone now noticed his death was a blessing from God—too many babies weren't as fortunate. As I held the sweet boy in my arms and caressed his silky black hair, a thought occurred to me: *None of this would have happened if it weren't for Maria's death.*

Had the circumstances been different, Maria's death could have gone unnoticed. But the Chapmans' concern for orphans, combined with their fame and the tragic way Maria died, put the story of her death in headlines across the world. The love offerings that came in had built the place where I stood and where so many children could be cared for, now and in the future. What Satan meant for evil, God had used for good.

Maria's life was too short. But in her five years, she did more for the cause of orphan care in China than a hundred men could do in a hundred years. Because of her death, countless babies would be saved; many would find forever families; and even in a closed country like China, more people would hear the Good News.

✦ ✦ ✦

The trip to China helped me come to terms with a few things. Until the feelings of loss overwhelmed me at Maria's Big House of Hope, I hadn't really understood how much responsibility I'd felt for the healing of both my family and the Chapmans. It made sense. I was a doctor. I was trained to help others heal, and I felt that was the role God had called me to play in the tragedy. I chose to be the strong one.

But in China, I began to see that I didn't have to feel that way anymore. I needed to let the Chapman family go. I was no longer responsible for them. In the months after we returned, I discovered other areas in my life where I'd taken on the burden of responsibility, even when it wasn't mine to bear.

Like my father, I'd felt guilty for failing to recognize Jon's depression; I felt that, as a doctor, I should have seen something. Even though I quickly realized I wasn't to blame for Jon's death in any way, emotionally I couldn't let go of the guilt and the feeling that I was somehow responsible for making sure something like this never happened again. That was one of the reasons I was so worried about Mike. I wanted to keep watch over him to make sure he didn't succumb to depression like Jon had.

In addition, in a little more than three years, all three of my daughters had gotten married. But instead of feeling like my obligation to my family was decreasing, with each new son-in-law and each daughter moving away, I felt the weight of *more* responsibility. I should have known better. God had already shown me in Ireland that he would take care of my daughter. Even in the midst of great political turmoil that I could do nothing about, he was there watching and protecting my girls.

And truly, what was the worst that could happen to any of us? We'd be separated for a few short years, only to reunite for eternity in heaven. My patients had taught me that there was a time to disengage from this world and begin to look forward to the next, but instead, I continued trying to shoulder the impossible task of making sure everyone and everything around me was okay.

China showed me that both the Chapman and Anderson families were healing just fine. And God reminded me that sometimes there was a greater purpose to our pain and suffering. I began to see that it was time for me to let go.

When Karen suggested we take a trip to Italy, I readily agreed. Perhaps a vacation was exactly what I needed.

✦ ✦ ✦

While in Rome, we spent a day in Vatican City, and I was excited to visit St. Peter's Basilica. Over the years, I'd seen some pretty amazing cathedrals in Ireland and England, but staring nearly 450 feet up to the top of the dome of the basilica, I realized that the other cathedrals were poor imitations. St. Peter's Basilica was one of the largest churches in the world and one of the holiest sites in Catholicism.

A church has stood on this spot, thought to be the original gravesite of the apostle Peter, since the fourth century. The current structure was started in 1506 and took more than one hundred and twenty years to finish. That meant that no one who was there in the beginning saw it through to completion. I tried to imagine the faith it took to design and build a structure you'd never see completed.

As I walked through the church, I was similarly humbled by the stories of the martyrs who'd given their earthly bodies for the promotion of a God they had never seen in the flesh. Of course, the one exception to this was the man the church was named after. Peter was one of Jesus' disciples; in fact, Jesus had changed Peter's name from Simon to Peter, which meant "rock." Jesus said that Peter was the rock upon which the church would be built.

At the time, Peter had no idea what that meant. He was just one of twelve men who were following a very special rabbi. A rabbi whom Peter believed was the Messiah. But after Jesus' death on the cross and subsequent resurrection, Peter must have had a lot of doubts about whether or not the church would survive. Yes, there were marvelous miracles recorded in the book of Acts, but at the time, there were also a lot of obstacles facing the church. Political dissension was widespread, as were instances of Jesus' followers being driven underground or martyred for their belief that he was the Messiah. Some followers gave up and returned to their Jewish roots and religion. Others gave up and returned to no religion at all.

What kind of burden must Peter have felt for the church he was supposed to help build? Did he ever wonder if he'd done enough? Did he ever feel like a failure because he thought he hadn't?

Eventually, Peter was crucified. He felt so unworthy to die in the same manner as Jesus that it is said he asked to be crucified upside down. *What were his final thoughts?* I wondered. I'm sure he didn't think that, a few hundred years later, Christians would build a church over his grave, or a thousand years after that, they'd build a basilica and name it after him.

With the evidence Peter saw before him, how could he ever have envisioned how much the church would spread and grow or the impact it would have on the world now?

He couldn't.

He was just a simple fisherman who had been handed the keys to the Kingdom, and like the rest of us, he had days when he felt as if he'd gotten them jammed in the lock.

I walked down the stone stairs and stood before Peter's tomb, thinking about all the responsibility he'd been given and how he'd never seen how much Christianity had grown.

Standing before Peter's gravesite, I wept and I grieved. Most of all, I prayed. At first I wasn't sure why; then in a moment of enlightenment, I knew. God was asking me to hand him back the keys to my "kingdom." He had given them to me and asked me to take care of them for a time, but now it was time to give them back.

Lord, I can't carry this burden any longer. I looked on the grave of the man who was given the responsibility of being the guardian of Christ's church. Now Peter was gone, and only his bones remained; yet somehow the church had continued to thrive and grow. When Peter died, nothing fell apart. God had protected and guarded the church without Peter. Now there was this great cathedral built around his bones.

One day I would die too. Like Peter, I would no longer be able to guard and protect those I loved. God was asking me to give the responsibility that I had shouldered for so long back to him.

Lord, I'm like Peter; I'm a simple man from the country. I've guarded and protected those you've asked me to guard and protect. I've healed those you've gifted me to heal. But just as you released Peter from being the guardian of your church upon his death, release me now. I lay all my worries and my concerns at your altar, and I now give back to you what has always been yours—control. Please bless me, bless my family, and bless the Chapmans for your glory.

Instantly I felt God's presence, followed by a huge sense of release. A huge weight had been lifted from my shoulders. I can't say I never again worried about my daughters or had concern about how the Chapmans were doing. I did. But I no longer carried the burden of responsibility for them. In that moment, I also felt a release from my fear that something would happen to Mike and that Cathy and Jennifer would be left alone.

Something dramatic had changed for me.

I was still a strong shoulder to cry on, but now, I could cry too. Like Maria's butterflies, I had been set free.

Chapter 31
THE DREAM OF LIFE

✦

Mike and Cathy, along with their daughter, Jennifer, had been living in Oswego, New York, for months. It had been nine and a half years since their son's death. Emotionally, nothing had changed, either positively or negatively. Mike still seemed withdrawn and deeply sad. Though I no longer felt responsible for his well-being, I was still concerned about his level of grief.

Steven knew I was concerned. When he told me he'd be performing a concert near their home in New York, I invited Mike and Cathy to attend. They had met Steven and Mary Beth during previous visits to our house. They liked his music and, of course, were saddened by the news of Maria's death. I prayed that seeing the way Steven turned toward God in his grief would inspire them.

It had been hard for Steven to get back out on the road and to sing and write music again. But, in my opinion, his recent music had been some of his best. Perhaps because it was so profoundly heartfelt. Even in his deepest anguish, Steven continued to pursue the Lord and to take the name of Christ to the uttermost parts of the world. His music reflected his deep reliance on God. Recently, Steven also had begun to tell more of his story in his concerts. I hoped an evening of his music would be meaningful to my sister and brother-in-law and that they would be encouraged, knowing that Steven understood their pain.

✦ ✦ ✦

After the concert, Cathy called to tell me how much she had enjoyed it. "I've always loved Steven's music, and it was great to see him perform it live," she said. Her next words surprised me. "Mike and I also liked the church where the concert was held. We thought we might check it out sometime."

"That would be great!" I said, trying not to sound too eager. "I hope you like it."

I knew Cathy and Mike hadn't found a church home since they'd moved from Illinois—in fact, Mike hadn't been attending anywhere regularly since Jon's death. Listening to Steven's music and his testimony seemed to have broken through Mike's stoic exterior and awakened something inside him.

That night, Karen and I prayed for them. We prayed fervently that getting back into a church would help restore and grow their faith.

✦ ✦ ✦

Cathy had said that she and Mike would check out the church "sometime," and that turned out to be the following Sunday. The church happened to be holding a healing service, and while they were there, God healed something inside Mike's heart. They decided to come back the following Sunday, and then the one after that. For the first time since Jon's death, Cathy and Mike began attending church regularly.

God was beginning to repair the very large hole in Mike's heart, and Mike was finally willing to let him do it. Over the next few months, Mike's faith grew. The next time we were together, I could see that his eyes, which once looked dull and vacant, now burned with fire for the Lord. He became more vocal about his faith, and we often talked about all the things God was doing in his life.

With the renewed life in his eyes and the bounce in his step, his transformation could have come only from God. While growing closer to God didn't take away the pain that lingered in Mike's heart, it did make it easier for him to face each new day with hope. Mike was encouraged by the thought that Jon was whole and happy in heaven and that one day he'd see him again. I imagined the two of them side by side, their golden fishing poles dipping into a crystal-blue stream.

God reminds us that every day here on earth, we will struggle. He opens and closes doors in our lives, and sometimes, we're confused and bewildered by the things he allows to happen. Life is both precious and precarious. During the years when our pain was so fresh and raw, we still had questions about Jon's suicide. While we didn't have all the answers we desired, we had all that we needed. God is real, he is good, and he is our hope for the future.

Watching Steven and Mike survive the incredible pain they'd been through, I knew the answer to grief was to stay focused on God. But it was one thing for me to walk alongside loved ones who were grieving and encourage them to turn to God. It was quite another thing for me to step into my own grief, knowing how much pain awaited me there.

Soon, I would have to face my most personal grief yet, and I wasn't sure my faith was ready for such a challenge. Did I really believe God is who he says he is? Could I lean into him, or would I turn my back on him again? Most important, after everything God had shown me, did I believe heaven was real enough to act on it?

+ + +

It was late summer with hints of fall. Karen had gone out of town for the weekend, so on Sunday I took Mom and Dad to church and then out for lunch afterward. When the waitress took our order, Mom ordered what all Southern women order: a tiny plate of something that wouldn't have fed a bird. I ordered the day's special, and Dad, for some reason, ordered the biggest steak they had. After placing his order, he left the table to use the restroom. He was gone a long time, and when he came back, he looked pale.

"Are you okay?" I asked. For the past year, Dad had been struggling with myelodysplastic syndrome—sometimes called pre-leukemia. His bone marrow had stopped producing the white blood cells needed to fight off infection. Any sickness was cause for worry.

"I've been passing blood," he said.

"Like right now? In the restroom?"

"Since Friday."

"Didn't you think this was something you should mention to your son, who *happens to be a doctor*?"

"I didn't have any yesterday."

"Dad! You're eighty-two!"

"Well, I didn't want to bother you."

Just then, the server brought our food. Dad's steak plate was the last to be served. He picked up his fork and knife to take a bite, and I yanked the plate away from him. He looked like he could have bitten my hand.

"We need to go to the hospital and have this checked out, and you can't eat until we do."

Fortunately, Mom agreed. Mom and I quickly ate our meals, and as we were paying the check, Dad reached over to grab a bite of food left on Mom's plate. "Dad! When I said, 'You can't eat,' that meant Mom's food too!" I didn't know what was wrong, but I knew that if surgery or certain tests were required, the doctors would want to make sure he had an empty stomach.

He grumbled. "I should have told you *after* lunch."

We all stood up to leave, but Dad had to quickly sit back down again. We let him rest for a minute before he tried again, but he was so weak that I had to help him to the car.

At the hospital, doctors ran a few tests and determined there was probably some internal bleeding, though they couldn't identify where. He was given four units of blood. His blood count went back up, he felt better, and a few days later, he went home. We figured that would be the end of it.

✦ ✦ ✦

Two weeks later, Dad was out in our yard puttering around, and I joined him for some fishing on our lake. As the afternoon wore on, Dad started to look pale. "Are you feeling okay?" I asked when we finished.

"Not really."

"Well, let me walk you home."

On the way back to his house, I walked alongside him, and I noticed he wasn't doing well. He seemed tired and weak. I helped him into bed, and when he seemed comfortable, I left.

I told Karen about the incident when I got home.

"Your mom says he keeps getting weaker and is having a hard time getting up," Karen said. "Do you think we should order one of those lift chairs for him?"

I agreed, and a few days later the chair arrived.

We put it in his bedroom, where he liked to watch baseball on TV. "Let's see how you do getting in and out of this," I said. I put the chair in the standing position and helped him over to it. He seemed to favor one leg.

"My knee's giving me a little problem," he said.

Dad had surgery on his knee when he was a boy, and now he had arthritis in the joint. The orthopedic doctor had given him an injection so he'd feel better. Apparently, it wasn't helping. Despite all that, Dad was able to back up to the chair, sit down, and use the remote to lower it into a position where he was comfortable. Then, he successfully reversed the process to get up. It looked like the chair would do what he needed.

Once he was settled, we visited for a while; then I went back home. Two hours later, Mom called me. "Dad can't get up."

I took David and went down to my parents' house. Dad physically couldn't get out of his chair. Even though the chair basically raised him to a standing position, David and I had to lift him and put him in his bed.

He felt clammy and feverish. His heart rate was high, and his knee looked red. These were all signs of a raging infection—and for Dad, that could be deadly. This was serious, and something had to be done quickly. I looked at him lying in bed, burning up with a fever, and knew he was the one who held all the cards.

"Dad, you're not doing well. If you stay here, you will probably die within a day or two. Do you want to go to the hospital? We could treat you there." I knew he likely wouldn't want a lot of intervention; he'd had a DNR for a long time. "If nothing else, we could keep you comfortable."

"Whatever Margie says," he said, deferring to my mom.

There had been scares before, but suddenly the danger was real. Dad was dying, and I wasn't sure if I was ready to let him go. I wanted to make sure he understood what was at stake, so I tried again.

"Do you want to die at home? Mom can't take care of you. We'd have to have nurses come in 24/7 to help."

"Then let's go to the hospital," he said reluctantly.

As a doctor, there were measures I could take to treat him, but I wasn't sure if he would allow me to use them. I also wasn't sure if I wanted to. Both my dad and I knew he was going to heaven, and he looked forward to it. *Why would we prolong the inevitable?* But I already knew the answer. Although he would be better off in heaven, I would miss him terribly. I'd seen the intense grief that both Steven and Mike had experienced initially, as well as the longing they'd felt even years after their loved ones died. I wasn't ready for that. I reached my hand out and touched Dad's arm, intending to say something warm and comforting, but he spoke first.

"I said I'll go to the hospital, but can you move your hand? It's hurting my arm."

✦   ✦   ✦

At the hospital, doctors determined that he was immuno-compromised. He'd developed MRSA, a virulent staph infection that was extremely difficult to treat. Worse, as he fought the infection, his body had become septic, and the inflammation was causing irreparable harm to his organs. It didn't look good, and he was admitted to the ICU. Following Dad's instructions, his doctor wrote the order for his DNR into his chart—if anything happened, they wouldn't resuscitate him. The nurse started an IV with doctor-ordered antibiotics, and we were advised to call our extended family.

Breaking the bad news to my brother and sister wasn't easy, but I did it. Cathy still lived in New York. It took her a couple of hours to make arrangements to get to Nashville from Oswego, but she called me back and said she'd be there in two days. Tim still lived in Huntsville, and he planned to drive up the next day.

The medical choices before us were pretty simple—we could honor Dad's wishes and let nature take its course. After all, Dad was eighty-two and had lived a good life. Or we could keep him alive by any means necessary, including machines to help him breathe and tubes to help him eat. Dad had already decided that he didn't want the latter option; he was in a lot of pain. I didn't want him to suffer, so I understood why letting him go was a good option.

But I wanted to keep Dad alive at least long enough so he could say good-bye to Tim and Cathy. And selfishly, I just wasn't ready to let him go, to face the anguish of living without him.

I discussed the dilemma with Matthew Bueter, his doctor.

"We're not going to put him on life support," Dr. Bueter said. "It goes against everything your dad asked for. But there are a few things we can reasonably do to perk him up until your family arrives."

Dr. Bueter ordered several units of blood to replace what my dad was losing, which would increase his blood count. It was the same thing they'd done when Dad was in the hospital the prior week. Once again, it worked. After receiving the blood, Dad seemed reinvigorated. Over the next day and a half, he also began to respond to the antibiotics. His fever dropped; so did his heart rate. We knew he was feeling better when he started asking for food.

By then, the extended family had begun to arrive. Dad's younger brother, Clyde, who was suffering from Alzheimer's, and his twin sisters from Montgomery, Alabama, and Columbia, Tennessee, arrived. Other friends and family soon showed up as well.

Watching my dad rally and interact with his family gave me the assurance I needed that giving him the blood had been the right decision. Dad was able to say good-bye to each of them, and by the time their visits ended, everyone had closure.

When it was time for them to leave, Clyde shuffled toward the door before suddenly stopping and turning back. Looking at me in a moment of lucidity, he said, "Well, I guess it's up to me to carry on the family now."

I chuckled. "Yeah, Uncle Clyde, I'm right behind you."

Dad got stronger, and eventually it was decided he could be moved from Nashville to the hospital in Ashland City, where my office was located.

+ + +

The hospital has what's called a swing-bed unit. It's a rehab area for those who have been sick and need a few weeks of physical therapy before they can return home. That's where we put Dad. There were only two doctors on staff, and I was one of them. Since the other doctor was out of town, I was actually designated as Dad's attending physician. Unlike in Nashville, where I was able to consult with Dad's doctors when I wasn't sure what to do, here I *was* Dad's only doctor.

Dad was DNR, so almost everything we did was about physical therapy and attending to his pain. Typically, in that situation, I saw the patient only once a week, but with Dad I stopped by every day, every free moment I had. I wanted to make the most of the time he had left.

He was still on IV antibiotics, but after a few days, his blood count started drifting back down. I had a choice: I could order more units of blood and give him another transfusion as we'd already done twice, or I could just manage his pain. Dad and I both knew the downward cycle would continue. A transfusion every few days could perk him up, but then his blood count would start to drop again. Dad wasn't going to get better. He was going to die. Was the intervention worth a few more days? Continuing to prolong the inevitable wasn't what he wanted, unless there was a good reason. And he didn't think there was. Unless his bone marrow miraculously kicked in, it was simply a matter of time.

But the thought of letting him go and never being able to talk to him again made me ache inside. As long as he was here, even if it were only a few days or weeks more, I could still touch him and hold his hand. Once he was gone, I would never be able to do that again. I wasn't sure I could let him go. As his physician and his son, I had a lot of influence over the decisions he and Mom made, and I could make a case for aggressive intervention.

I thought about the hundreds of times I'd counseled patients in this very situation. While there were no right or wrong answers, when a death was inevitable, I had never really understood the point in dragging it out. But now I did. Everything changed for me when *I* was the one who faced the choice.

Regardless, I would need to make a decision by the next day.

Before I went home for the night, I stopped by Dad's room to pick up Mom and take her home with me. I entered the room and looked at the frail, weak man lying in the hospital bed. Pieces of my life with my father flashed before my eyes. I recalled those many drives we took in the truck throughout the countryside; the day he was outside straightening the antenna when I found out I had won Tex from the TV show; the Christmas he sacrificed his pride to buy me a bike on credit; the afternoon he stood in front of the lockers at my high school and told me about the Aldays; my graduations from college and medical school; his move to Kingston Springs; and the dances with my mom at the girls' weddings.

I reached out my hand and took his. "Dad, I don't think you're going to pull out of this one," I said, with tears stinging my eyes. As awesome as heaven is—and I'd seen much more of it than the average person—I wanted him to stay with me.

But he was ready to go.

"I know. I'm ready," he said simply. Then as he always did during times of great emotion, he picked up his tools. Only since he was lying in a hospital bed, he asked Mom to help.

"Make sure Reggie gets my tools for the garden. I want him to have the tiller and the hoe—"

I tried to hold back the sobs forming in the back of my throat. My dad had worked a garden for longer than I had memory; the thought of his giving up his gardening tools was a sign he truly was ready to go.

✦ ✦ ✦

I'd wrestled with what to do all day long. At home, I was sullen and withdrawn. Karen knew what was bothering me. While Dad and Mom could make any decision they wanted, she knew that whatever I recommended would have a great deal of influence on their decision. She also knew how much that responsibility weighed on me.

We prayed together before I fell asleep, and her final words to me were, "You're doing everything you're supposed to be doing. Don't worry." Unlike the previous nights when I had tossed and turned, I rolled over and immediately fell asleep.

I had the same sensation I'd had all those years ago while sleeping in the woods. I felt like I was falling, tumbling through the darkness, before suddenly landing in a very bright place.

✦ ✦ ✦

Once again, I was in a location that was more real than the world we live in. The colors were more vivid, and the scents of baked bread and freshly shaved cedar were more intoxicating than those I sniffed in my mother's kitchen or my father's workshop. I inhaled deeply and saw that I was standing in the narthex of a great cathedral—one that was even more magnificent than St. Peter's Basilica in Rome.

As I marveled at the surroundings, I wanted to go into the cathedral to see the splendor there, but I noticed a room adjacent to the narthex where some activity was taking place. I heard someone giving directions, almost as if he were teaching. The cadence and manner of speaking sounded familiar. I moved toward the voice, not exactly walking, not really floating, but more like thinking about heading toward it—and suddenly I was there.

I saw a man standing on the sixth of seven marble steps in an archway leading to a garden or garden room. The man seemed familiar; he was young, possibly in his thirties, and though his back was to me, I could tell he was directing or supervising workers who were constructing the doorway between the rooms. He seemed to be teaching them how best to sand and paint the great entryway they were working on. They seemed to be putting the finishing touches on the great orifice.

This was no ordinary passageway. The arch soared twenty feet above me at its apex. It had two solid-oak double doors, and they were partially opened, just enough that I could see the brilliant light inside. I walked up to the third step to get a clearer view of a glass greenhouse on the other side. A stream of crystal-blue water ran through the room past rocks jutting up from the ground and pooled at the entryway, giving a dazzling reflection of the greenhouse. Walkways from the door curved around the pool, inviting visitors to meander past the fish swimming in the gurgling water. I inhaled deeply. The fresh cedar and baked bread smells were there, but they were accompanied by deeper, richer, earthier odors—like the smell of fresh dirt after a spring rain.

"What's going on?" I asked.

The man turned toward me and smiled. I immediately recognized him. It was my father, James; only instead of looking like the weak and emaciated eighty-two-year-old who lay in a hospital bed, he looked like he was in his midthirties! He was happy, healthy, and whole.

"What do you think about this place, Reggie?" he asked. Once again, we didn't speak with audible words or hear with our ears. It was as if we connected on some deeper level. "It's almost finished.

I think I'll be very comfortable here. This place is even better than I imagined it would be!"

✦   ✦   ✦

I woke up and felt the peace and presence of God.

I knew what I was supposed to do.

Chapter 32

A PRESTO! ITALIAN FOR "SEE YOU SOON!"

✦

When I woke up, it took me a moment to realize where I was and where I'd just been. Then I caught the faintest whiff of freshly shaved cedar. The scent, which had been so fragrant and strong before I opened my eyes, now lingered on my sheets. Likewise, as I woke up, everything in my room seemed somehow dimmer and less sharp than the colors that had been so intense and powerful, so vivid and bright only an instant before. God had blessed me with yet another glimpse of heaven—in a dream that seemed more tangible, more authentic, and more real than anything here on earth—just like the one where I'd seen the Aldays!

I'd seen Dad on the steps of heaven, not at all looking like the emaciated man who lay dying in a bed in the Ashland City hospital. Dad looked amazing! Whole and complete. Much younger than his eighty-two years. It proved once again that time on earth isn't the same as God's time. Through the years, my experiences with my patients had taught me that we don't spend life walking toward eternity; we walk alongside it. Now, God had opened the veil and separated the present from the future, allowing me a foretaste of Dad's life in heaven.

I was so excited that I felt giddy.

Now I could truly let Dad go without regrets. I knew he would be happy and pain free. Most of all, I knew exactly where he was going and how to find him once I got there. He would be working in the garden room off the narthex, the room with the twenty-foot arch above the oak doors trimmed with freshly shaved cedar.

Karen rolled over and saw me smiling.

"Dad's going to be fine," I said. "He's going on a trip. We're going to be sad, and we're going to miss him. But *my dad* will be at home in the arms of *our Father*. That's something to celebrate!"

"What happened?" Karen asked.

"God gave me a glimpse of Dad in heaven, and he has this extraordinary room with everything that he loves waiting for him. Frankly, I'm a little jealous."

"Tell me about it," she said snuggling close to me. I wrapped my arm around her, and I told her about my dream, starting at the beginning and filling in details along the way.

"And there are plants in the garden, just waiting for Dad's care. There's a brook where he can go fishing, and there are construction workers to help him with his projects. In heaven he is completely healed; he's healthy and young again."

"Wait . . . there are construction guys in heaven?"

"I saw them." I thought about it for a minute and realized I'd never seen their faces. "But maybe they were angels."

With everyone healthy and whole, I realized God wouldn't have any need for doctors in heaven. "I guess I'll be a construction worker too; otherwise I'll be unemployed."

"Oh, Reggie," Karen said, chuckling, "you'd do anything once you were in heaven, as long as you could finally stay there."

She was right.

✦ ✦ ✦

Later that morning, I stopped by Dad's hospital room and told him and Mom about my dream. I explained that I didn't think there was much point in continuing to transfuse him any longer. His time was limited, and the transfusions only prolonged the inevitable.

He agreed. "I'm ready to go," he said.

As I expected, he continued to decline throughout the weekend. On Sunday morning, I could see he probably wouldn't make it through the day. Often, if a loved one says it is okay to go, that's the permission the patient needs to pass. I wanted to give my dad that permission. When no one else was around, I leaned over and whispered to him, "I love you, Dad. And it's okay to go when you're ready. I'll take care of Mom."

+ + +

The entire family gathered in Dad's hospital room that afternoon. Mom was there along with Karen; my sister, Cathy; and my brother, Tim. Three of my four kids were also there, as well as Ashley's husband, Ciarán. Kristen and David couldn't make it back from Ireland. The only person who hadn't yet arrived was Julia's husband, Caleb, who had performed at a concert the night before and was on his way back to town.

Mom was quiet. She didn't say much, and when she spoke, it was in a gentle voice. I could see on her face how thankful she was to have all her children and half of her grandchildren there to see Dad off. I reached for her hand and took it in mine.

"Dad's not dying," I said. "He's just getting ready to be born into another world." She patted my hand and looked at me with interest, so I continued. I explained the similarities between the final breaths of life—Cheyne-Stokes respiration—and a mother in labor. "They almost sound the same, a kind of rhythmic breathing followed by soft, moan-like breaths."

"What else?" she asked.

"When babies are born into this world, they do so kicking and screaming. But those like Dad, who know where they are going, leave this world and are peacefully born into the next."

"That's nice."

"Dad may be dying to the pain and suffering of this world, but he's being born into a much better one for eternity."

She smiled at the thought.

"Look around at these three kids you gave birth to. Right before we came through the birth canal, when the doctor saw the top of our heads, he said, 'The baby is crowning.'"

She nodded.

"What we're seeing with Dad is a crowning into heaven. When he enters the foyer, a crown will be placed on his head as he is birthed into eternity."

"I like the thought of that," she said.

I reminded her of all the things I'd witnessed in heaven—the smells, the colors—and how much more real and tangible everything seemed there compared to here. I told her about the joy on the faces of the Alday family and how, three nights earlier in my dream, Dad was young and healthy in heaven.

✦ ✦ ✦

Caleb arrived and greeted everyone, and then I joined him at Dad's bedside. When Dad stirred, I said, "Dad, Caleb is here now. Everybody is with you, and we love you."

"I love you too. All of you," he said, and then went back to sleep. We didn't know it at the time, but those would be his last words.

Dad had been lying quietly for less than an hour, and I knew he wouldn't be with us much longer. We'd been talking on and off, but it had been quiet for a few minutes when a voice spoke up and said, "Can we sing?"

Each of my kids is artistic, and several of them are also musical. In the room that day, we also had Ciarán, who works in musical theater, and Caleb, who plays guitar for his dad and has his own band. Any of them could have asked to sing, but it wasn't one of them who made the suggestion. It was a special request from my sister, Cathy, who like me couldn't carry a tune in a bucket.

"Can we sing a song?" she repeated. "For Dad?"

Someone started singing a hymn, and the rest of us joined in. We sang through all the classic hymns that we knew Dad liked. There were smiles as the kids harmonized when they knew the tune and improvised when they didn't know the words. The non-musical adults, like me, just did our best to follow along. Between songs, someone would pray or tell a story about Dad. It felt like a celebration. It was a party where Dad was the guest of honor, not the patient who was about to pass.

We all missed Kristen. Although circumstances prevented her from being there physically, she was with us in spirit. When someone suggested we sing, "In Christ Alone," I thought it was fitting—it was Kristen's favorite song, and she had it played at her wedding.

During the song, Dad's breathing became more erratic and more labored, and we all placed our hands on him to let him know we were there. Then, as we sang that song, on the afternoon of September 4, 2011, exactly thirty years to the day after his mother died, Dad took his last breath and was born into the next world.

I pulled out my stethoscope, put it to his chest, and listened as the last bit of life left him. I felt the warmth of his spirit drain away and a fresh breeze waft into the room. I'd explained this sensation to Karen and the kids many times before, so they'd heard me describe it, but they'd never felt it. This time, Mom, Karen, and my kids witnessed it too. When he took his final breath, they felt the warmth leave—the same sensation I'd talked about for years. Then we all watched as the pallor took over his shell.

His soul had left.

Dad was gone.

When Dad crossed over to the other side, it was as if his physical body withered. Karen noticed it too.

"That's not Dad," she said. "It's almost as if he aged right in front of us. The joy in his countenance and the glow he always had are gone."

I agreed. When I felt his spirit pass my cheek, it felt light and youthful. It was as if he had discarded his body, yet was now more whole than he'd ever been. It reminded me of when I'd seen Jimmy and Jerry in my dream. And I had this sense of Jesus standing with open arms, waiting to embrace my dad like he'd once embraced me.

We gathered our things, left the hospital, and headed back to our house. Only a few tears were shed that afternoon, and they were all tears of joy as we celebrated the birth of my dad into heaven.

✦ ✦ ✦

The funeral was held a few days later. Dad was buried in south Georgia near my mom's family and the farms where we had spent so many of our summers picking watermelons.

When we got back to Tennessee, it was hard to drop Mom off at her empty house, especially when I unloaded her bags and put them in her bedroom, knowing Dad would never be there again. I'd promised I'd be her protector, and yet I wasn't sure how to do that without becoming overwhelmed with the responsibility. I remembered the moment in Rome as I stood next to St. Peter's grave, when I'd given everything back to God.

But how do I do that now? How do I do that here, with Mom?

As I was getting the last few things out of the car, a neighbor I didn't know well drove up and said, "Can I help in any way?"

I'd met him a couple of times. He lived in the same neighborhood, a few streets down. He'd heard that Dad died and had been keeping an eye out for Mom to arrive home. We chatted briefly, and before he left, he gave me his number. "Give this to your mom. If there's anything she needs and you can't be there, you have her call me."

As he drove off, tears of thankfulness rolled down my cheeks. God had sent a kindhearted neighbor as a reminder that I didn't have to do it myself. God would always be with her.

And with me.

All I had to do was turn toward him.

✦ ✦ ✦

As a doctor, I've stood by countless patients as they took their last breaths and crossed over to the other side, but it is another experience entirely when the patient is your father. My dream helped me realize that, though I would miss him, Dad was truly going to *paradise*, and I would see him again soon.

In a way, death is like a trip to Italy.

When friends tell me they are taking a trip to Italy, I'm really excited for them. I've been there and know what they're about to see. I know how green and beautiful and fragrant the countryside can be. The art is astonishing, and in such abundance, that a local museum here dulls by comparison. I'm so eager for them to experience all these things and more!

Though I'm happy they're going to Italy, if I'm honest, I'll admit I have other feelings too. I'm a little sad; I'll miss talking to them while they're gone. The closer the people are to me—for example, family members or close friends—and the longer they'll be gone, the more that sadness becomes real. And I feel a twinge of jealousy. I know what an incredible journey it will be, and while they're off on this grand adventure, I'll be stuck here.

Even though I will miss the travelers and wish I were going, too, I would never try to make them miss their flight by holding them here. I truly want them to enjoy every moment they have in Italy and to experience all that the Italian paradise has to offer.

I know our separation won't last forever.

The same is true when loved ones leave this life and go to heaven. The good news is that I will be joining them soon! They simply have an earlier flight. That's because death isn't an exclusive trip—it's one we all will take; we just have staggered departure times.

I'm not sure when I am scheduled to leave. It might be months or maybe even years from now. But I know that Jesus already bought my ticket. His grace bought yours, too. He paid for them with his life. All we have to do is redeem them with our faith.

So as I stand in the airport terminal (or beside the hospital bed) and watch my friends and family who are fortunate to board earlier flights, I'm happy for them, and yet I know I'll also be sad not to be able to talk to them for a while. I'll also feel a little jealous that they're on an earlier flight. But when they leave, I won't say good-bye. Instead, I'll say, "*A presto!*" which is Italian for "See you soon!"

If you've had a loved one pass from this life ahead of you, I know it can be disheartening. But please don't turn your back, as I did so long ago, on the One who is offering you the ticket. *You can go too!* Your ticket has already been paid for; there's a seat waiting just for you. Simply reach out to the One who is offering it and receive it as a gift.

Once you arrive, we'll all be staying in the same heavenly accommodations. Friends and loved ones who left earlier will be waiting to greet you, and they'll be rapturously happy. But when they see you, I'm guessing that their joy will increase even more. Most important, the One who loves you most will be waiting with outstretched arms. At that moment, instead of arriving in Italy, you'll realize that you have arrived *home*.

While you wait for your time to depart, get to work doing the job God's given you to do here. Dad's hoe has a special place in my barn as a reminder that, even in my sadness of his passing to the *next* world, I need to follow Dad's example—pick up my tools and do what God has asked me to do for *this* world.

Though you may have a few more years to toil before your appointment to depart, be comforted with the thought that the unimaginable trip of a lifetime lies ahead for you. And for me. I may be traveling light, but once there, I plan to stay forever.

A presto!

Epilogue

✦

God has allowed me to see some inexplicable things. He has offered me glimpses of heaven that most people haven't been given, as well as the privilege of walking with many folks at the beginning and the end of their lives. As a result of all my experiences, I don't see death the way many others do.

I envision death as a joyful home going for those who know Christ. When an opportunity arises to escort someone home to Jesus, I want to be there! I don't dread my death, or anyone else's who belongs to him. Instead, those opportunities push me forward; they energize me and make me want to be a part of the miracle. Life has shown me that death is not the failure of medical science but the victory of the soul.

My desire to spend eternity with God is overwhelming, and each day I long for my final appointment, the moment I can go back and stay forever. I've never felt so warmed and comforted as when I was inside heaven, and I want everyone to experience those feelings.

Though I've had some very vivid experiences, I don't know what heaven will look or smell like on the day it becomes my home. I also don't know if it will look or smell the same for you. So many times God used the scents of lilacs and citrus to remind me of heaven; yet in the dream I had before my dad died, heaven smelled like freshly shaved cedar and hot bread from the oven. Will those smells be there just for me, or will everyone smell the same thing? I don't know. But I do know that whatever heaven looks or smells like to you, it will be more intense than anything you've ever experienced here on earth.

Not only are the colors and smells heightened, so are the feelings of love, joy, peace, and acceptance. Because I desire those things so much, I started looking for them on this side of the veil, and I believe that's why I found them—often with my patients.

When I tell other physicians, especially those who aren't believers, about the things I've seen, they try to compartmentalize them. It's as if they're saying, "That's fine, but it should stay in a religious box. You can take it out on Sunday. But your scientific training is the only thing that can be used in your medical practice Monday through Friday." They think it's nice that I've had these experiences, but they don't think my appointments with heaven should have any bearing on how I practice medicine. Even my medical school professors taught me not to believe something unless there was objective, scientific evidence behind it.

I understand this point of view, but ever since my dream, it seems that all my experiences—scientific and spiritual—are in the same space, jumbled up together. Everything is together in one box. When I practice medicine, I can't separate my faith from my training. To me, it all comes from the same source.

Though I've gotten early tastes of the afterlife, I don't believe it is because I am special. I think the scents of heaven, as well as the sights and sounds, are all around us if we pay attention to those who are closest to the veil—especially to the sick, the orphans, and the widows. The dream I had so many years ago on the Fourth of July stripped off my blinders and helped me to see God in places and ways I'd never expected to see him. If I hadn't been so angry and hurt, maybe I wouldn't have needed the dream to see heaven.

If you've kept your faith separate from your job, your relationships, or your hobbies, or if a hurt in your life has separated you from God, please don't wait for some future event that upends your boxes. Look around, and I think you'll see that it all belongs in God's box.

Heaven is closer and more real than anything we experience in this life. And ultimately, I think that's why I've seen these glimpses— I'm always on the lookout for them. I believe if you look closely, you can clearly experience them too.

A Final Note from Reggie

✦ ✦ ✦

I have come to view death not as an end but as a beginning of life in our forever home, where we will be united with many of our loved ones. Especially sweet will be our first face-to-face meeting with the one who loved us and came to find us—Jesus.

Though God has sometimes enabled me to peer beyond the veil separating this world from the next, my greatest insights into heaven come from a resource that is just as available to you as it is to me: Scripture.

If you long to know more about heaven, I encourage you to turn there. Let me direct you first to the Gospel of John, the book God used when he began revealing his truth to me.

> For God loved the world so much that he gave his one and only Son, so that everyone who believes in him will not perish but have eternal life. (John 3:16)

> Jesus told her, "I am the resurrection and the life. Anyone who believes in me will live, even after dying. Everyone who lives in me and believes in me will never ever die. Do you believe this, Martha?" (John 11:25-26)

When I returned to Birmingham after my Fourth of July camping trip, I began memorizing the book of Philippians with Karen.

As I worked through this letter, the apostle Paul's healing words seemed to strike a solid chord of grace within me. They were just what I needed.

> To me, living means living for Christ, and dying is even better. But if I live, I can do more fruitful work for Christ. So I really don't know which is better. I'm torn between two desires: I long to go and be with Christ, which would be far better for me. But for your sakes, it is better that I continue to live. (Philippians 1:21-24)

> We are citizens of heaven, where the Lord Jesus Christ lives. And we are eagerly waiting for him to return as our Savior. (Philippians 3:20)

The more I read Scripture, the more I wanted to know the God who was alive and who had found me when I was not looking for him. He made himself known to me in his timing and his way, since I had done nothing to deserve the renewed life he granted me.

I began my first formal Bible study in the book of Romans. What a gift it was to study one of the cornerstone books of the New Testament as a new person to the faith.

> What we suffer now is nothing compared to the glory he will reveal to us later. (Romans 8:18)

> I am convinced that nothing can ever separate us from God's love. Neither death nor life, neither angels nor demons, neither our fears for today nor our worries about tomorrow—not even the powers of hell can separate us from God's love. No power in the sky above or in the earth below—indeed, nothing in all creation will ever be able to separate us from the love of God that is revealed in Christ Jesus our Lord. (Romans 8:38-39)

I believe we are meant to share our stories to encourage others and to point them in our Lord's direction. I'm still amazed that God granted me the opportunity to tell my story, but I am so thankful he did.

As you think about the ways God has been at work in your life, I want to direct you to several other passages that I hope fill you with anticipation as you think about our heavenly home.

> Jesus replied, "I assure you, today you will be with me in paradise." (Luke 23:43)

> Stephen, full of the Holy Spirit, gazed steadily into heaven and saw the glory of God, and he saw Jesus standing in the place of honor at God's right hand. And he told them, "Look, I see the heavens opened and the Son of Man standing in the place of honor at God's right hand!"
>
> Then they put their hands over their ears and began shouting. They rushed at him and dragged him out of the city and began to stone him. His accusers took off their coats and laid them at the feet of a young man named Saul.
>
> As they stoned him, Stephen prayed, "Lord Jesus, receive my spirit." (Acts 7:55-59)

> Yes, we are fully confident, and we would rather be away from these earthly bodies, for then we will be at home with the Lord. (2 Corinthians 5:8)

> He raised us from the dead along with Christ and seated us with him in the heavenly realms because we are united with Christ Jesus. (Ephesians 2:6)

Finally, I leave you with the one passage that perhaps best reflects God's grace in my own life:

> Whenever someone turns to the Lord, the veil is taken away. For the Lord is the Spirit, and wherever the Spirit of the Lord is, there is freedom. So all of us who have had that veil removed can see and reflect the glory of the Lord. And the Lord—who is the Spirit—makes us more and more

like him as we are changed into his glorious image.
(2 Corinthians 3:16-18)

Freedom and peace are available to you, too, through Scripture. Read it attentively, listening for what God's Spirit is saying to you and asking him to make you mindful of the many ways he is at work in the lives around you. Then you will hear and see and know the reality of our Lord and Savior Jesus Christ, both here on earth and in our forever home—heaven.

Acknowledgments

✦ ✦ ✦

Soli Deo Gloria—Alpha

To Karen, my wife, my North Star, and my tether. Without you, this life—and therefore this book—could not have happened. Thank you for pointing me in the direction of our Lord and holding me accountable to his truth. I love you forever and a day.

To my children—Kristen, Ashley, Julia, and David—for the years of listening to our oral history, which has now become many of the stories framed in this work.

To Marjorie and James Anderson, Mom and Dad, for teaching me early and often the lessons of the life God had planned for me and for praying for your prodigal son until Jesus found me and brought me back into his family.

To Dot and Cotty Renken (Karen's parents), for raising such an amazing daughter, who loves the Lord first and loves me second.

To my Irish sons-in-law, David (northern) and Ciarán (southern), for showing me that God can change the world.

To Steven Curtis and Mary Beth Chapman, who have been ever so encouraging and helpful in guiding this book and delivering it to just the right people at just the right time—God's timing. Also thank y'all for giving me a great son-in-law, Caleb, and becoming family.

To Bobby and Terri Price and the "Von-Price" family singers, who inspired me to stop telling these stories and write them down. Thank you for sharing your life with us and standing on higher ground with us during the flood of 2010.

To the team of Creative Trust—Dan Raines, Kathryn Helmers, and Jeanie Kaserman—whose wisdom and guidance from start to finish have been amazing. Helping me find "my voice" on the written page has been nothing short of a miracle. The advice of finding the right cowriter was another moment of God's faithful nudging in his direction.

To Jennifer Schuchmann. Who knew that God would pair a Midwestern female cowriter with a Southern lyrical farm boy and keep each of our writing styles intact? From the beginning, neither of us was sure that our two very different styles of writing would blend, but God was—and he blessed us both through the process.

To the Tyndale Momentum team. I was humbled and honored that God would place this book with such a great family to continue to nurture and grow this work into what it is today. From the beginning, you have been spectacular. Only God knew before we met that Tyndale's *Living Bible* would be instrumental in bringing me back to him. For that, I am forever grateful.

To Jan Harris. In your call you said, "God will put this book with the publisher of his choosing, and the Momentum team would be honored if it was us." He did, and now I am the one who is honored. Thank you and the rest of the team: Yolanda Sidney, Sarah Atkinson, Nancy Clausen, Katie Fearnley, Dean Renninger, Brittany Buczynski, and so many others for being a part of his plan. You have taken us under your wing, protected us, and guarded us.

To Sharon Leavitt, who made our visit seem like a homecoming. You were always available to answer any of our questions and help navigate us through this new world.

To Kim Miller, my editor. If I may use a medical analogy, you have been that delivery room nurse who held the newborn baby first, placed it under the lights, and recorded the initial vital signs.

Your gentle, soothing words of encouragement will always be remembered. Thanks to you, the world will see my firstborn book all cleaned up and wrapped in a sweet-smelling blanket.

To my staff at the hospitals, ERs, clinics, and nursing homes who have stood side by side in the trenches helping the helpless and giving hope to the hopeless. I am forever grateful.

I would especially like to thank those patients who have allowed me to be part of their lives and hold their hand while God was holding their other one. It has been an honor and a privilege to stand with you and attend the veil of heaven.

Soli Deo Gloria—Omega

Dr. Reggie Anderson

About the Authors

+ + +

REGGIE ANDERSON, MD

Dr. Reggie Anderson was raised in the small, rural town of Plantersville, Alabama, and has come to embody the small-town wisdom and homespun morality that he grew up with. He graduated from the University of Alabama with a BS in chemistry and an English minor. While attending the University of Alabama Medical School, he met his wife, Karen. He completed his residency in family practice at the University of Tennessee in Jackson.

With more than twenty-five years of emergency room and family practice experience, Reggie has been exposed to nearly every kind of death possible, including murder, suicide, death from old age, and death shortly after birth. His positive outlook and view that the next life is more real than this one has allowed him to hold dying and grieving patients' hands, providing hope as he prepares them for the parting of the veil that separates this world from the next.

Reggie and Karen have raised four children, three daughters who are married and a son who is currently in nursing school. He and Karen reside on a farm in Kingston Springs, Tennessee, often opening their home as a refuge for those needing shelter following a natural disaster or other crisis.

Recently, Reggie was awarded The Frist Humanitarian Award by the Centennial Medical Center in Nashville. He was chosen from more than nine hundred doctors to be nominated for the national award.

Reggie is a member of the American Academy of Family Physicians and works at the Frist Clinic, where he continues to serve the poor and underprivileged in satellite offices in Ashland City and Kingston Springs, Tennessee. He also serves as chief of staff at TriStar Ashland City Medical Center, as well as the medical director of three nursing homes. Learn more about Reggie at www.appointmentswithheaven.com.

JENNIFER SCHUCHMANN

Whether writing or speaking, Jennifer loves the challenge of taking difficult concepts and finding ways to make them easy to understand, practical, and transformational. She excels at organizing masses of raw material into book form, while maintaining the voice and intent of the original communicator. She finds great joy in helping authors with compelling messages tell their stories to new audiences.

Recent books include: *Taylor's Gift* (Revell, 2013) by Todd and Tara Storch, about the story of a couple who donated their daughter's organs after a skiing accident and later met the recipients; *Spirit Rising* (Zondervan, 2012) by Jim Cymbala, an in-depth look at the Holy Spirit; and *By Faith, Not by Sight* (Thomas Nelson, 2012) by blind *American Idol* finalist, Scott MacIntyre. A selection of past books includes *One Call Away* (Thomas Nelson, 2011), a memoir of Brenda Warner, and *First Things First* (Tyndale, 2009), a *New York Times* bestseller by Kurt and Brenda Warner.

Jennifer is the host of *Right Now with Jennifer Schuchmann*, which airs weekly on the NRB Network, Sky Angel satellite, and DIRECTV. She holds an MBA from Emory University, with an emphasis in marketing and communications, and a bachelor's degree in psychology from the University of Memphis. She's been married to David for more than twenty years, and they have a son, Jordan. Learn more about Jennifer at WordsToThinkAbout.com, or follow her on Twitter @schuchmann.

Online Discussion *guide*

TAKE *your* TYNDALE READING
EXPERIENCE *to the* NEXT LEVEL

A FREE discussion guide for this book
is available at bookclubhub.net, perfect
for sparking conversations in your book
group or for digging deeper into the text
on your own.

www.bookclubhub.net

*You'll also find free discussion guides for
other Tyndale books, e-newsletters, e-mail
devotionals, virtual book tours, and more!*

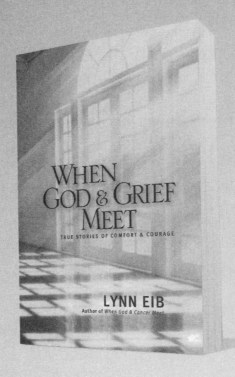